Art and Architecture

Art and Architecture
Strategies in Collaboration

Christian Bjone

Birkhäuser
Basel · Boston · Berlin

Design: Binocular, New York

Editor: Ria Stein, Berlin

Lithography: Licht + Tiefe, Berlin

Printing: Cuno, Calbe

Cover: James Turrell, installation *The Inner Way*, 1999, in an underground tunnel for the Munich Re Group Building, Munich, DMP Architekten, 1995. (Photograph: Florian Holzherr, Munich)

Frontispiece: Anselm Kiefer, sculpture *Falling Stars (Sternenfall)*, Grand Palais, Paris, 2007. (Photograph: Getty Images)

This book is also available in a German edition: ISBN 978-3-7643-9942-9

Library of Congress Control Number: 2009925663

Bibliographic information published by the German National Library: The German National Library lists this publication in the Deutsche Nationalbibliografie; detailed bibliographic data is available on the Internet at http://dnb.d-nb.de.

© 2009 Birkhäuser Verlag AG
Basel · Boston · Berlin
P.O.Box 133, CH-4010 Basel, Switzerland
Part of Springer Science+Business Media

Printed on acid-free paper produced from chlorine-free pulp. TCF ∞
Printed in Germany

ISBN 978-3-7643-9943-6

www.birkhauser.ch

9 8 7 6 5 4 3 2 1

Contents

1: Introduction

Ronald Bladen, *The X*, Corcoran Gallery of Art, Washington, DC, 1968.

Magdalena Jetelová, *Domestication of a Pyramid*, MAK, Vienna, 1992.

Here both sculptors challenge their architectural enclosure for dominance in these two installations located within the colonnaded courtyards of two Neoclassic museums. It is not just the juxtaposition of a modern object inside a nineteenth century framework, but the use of the artist's appropriation of the vocabulary of architecture that creates the visual dynamics between the art and the architecture.

The writing of history must implicitly assume a plurality of items existing together, a disjuncture of the present with itself. **Dipesh Chakrabarty**

There are many different models for the workings of a historian. One is the archeologist who digging deeper and deeper, layer after layer comes to the final understanding with the discovery of the primary source: the first city, the first house, the first tool. The other model, used here, is that of the coroner who derives from the fragments of destruction and failure, isolated bits of information: the struggle for survival, the extent of trauma and the time of death. It is never assumed that the entire body of knowledge will be reassembled but merely its outline.

These two directions could be summarized with the first case following the belief in the rock-hard truth of assembled neutral "facts" versus the second model where there is a personal and subjective interpretation of indeterminate "data."

The Ending

The traditional image of modern art in modern architecture frequently starts with the well-worn postcard figure of the autonomous and unintelligible abstract plaza sculpture at the entry of a gridded structure, continues to the vast and trivial office lobby mural, finally ends in the polite and tasteful decoration of the corporate board room. This static and compromised relationship reflects the confused and anxious alliance between the austere modern building and its acceptable embellishment in high art. But this pairing has been challenged in the last few years and several alternatives will be elaborated and explored in this book.

Seymour Lipton,
paired sculptures
Argonaut I and II, 1962,
at IBM Thomas Watson
Research Center,
Yorktown, New York,
Eero Saarinen, 1961.

Julian Opie, electronic
sculptures *Bruce
Walking*, 2004, and
Sara Walking, 2003,
at Tweed Courthouse,
New York, John Kellum
and Leopold Eidlitz,
1881.

Modern architecture has always held itself with the high ideal that it is the "Mother Art." But, that parental metaphor is also an example of undisguised Freudian control. It is a condescending view in which the architect is allowed to *smother art* and place it always within his or her power.

The majority of attempts in this confused union show that the assumed natural collaboration between artists and architects, both visual and cultural, is mostly nonexistent. The German nineteenth century ideal of the *gesamtkunstwerk*, that cumbersome ill-fitting crown of "total artistic unity," belonging only to Wagner's operas, is not for our time. We exist in a fragmented, not homogeneous, society and the production of culture is as equally divided. The pluralistic vocabulary of the contemporary arts does not allow for one simple consistent aesthetic effect.

This book explores a range of examples, starting in 1914, where artists and architects struggle to find a common territory in the public arena. It also limits its view to those attempts that were highly integrated schemes. Several of these projects do not involve a tasteful compromise or even a desire for physical beauty but a clear visual tension and frisson between the objects of interest.

In many cases the art employs the scale and formal language of architecture. Therefore the standards of architectural composition become the basis for the dialogue between participants. Indeed the chronological progress of the examples shows the eventual absorption of architectural compositional elements into the artist's vocabulary.

Like John Ruskin's *Seven Lamps of Architecture*[1] I have listed seven general compositional relationships that will be explored in the text:

1. Art as framed by Architecture
2. Art in contrast to Architecture
3. Art and Architecture with a common motif
4. Architecture appropriates form from Art
5. Art duplicating the scale of Architecture
6. Art singular in its temple
7. Art in conflict with Architecture

The last on the list describes the situation where art and architecture enter into a competition and conflict with a set of ideas, a sort of "suspended combat." It is not a

Martha Schwartz,
plaza design, 1990, for
HUD Headquarters,
Washington, DC,
Marcel Breuer, 1968.

dialectic debate resolved with a synthesis of the opposing points of view but remains a fully articulated argument that is unresolved, frozen in time.

The point of this book is to acknowledge the end of the illusion that modern artists and architects share a common visual language, a matching set of aesthetic beliefs and an agreed upon social objective.

ART AS FRAMED BY ARCHITECTURE In an instantaneous reflective response, architects, both modern and earlier, have always sketched in a pair of figures at the entry of any monumental staircase or plaza. Here the architect Eero Saarinen struggles with the vast scale of his IBM Research Center, desperately trying to mark an entrance of matching proportion. The

overextended arts and crafts rubble wall and the craggy Seymour Lipton sculptures fail so spectacularly that they become something else, emblems of microscopic 1950s sputniks set against the infinite curve of the universe.

The kinetic LED display of the walking manikins by the artist Julian Opie takes the symmetrical pairing of sculpture at the Tammany Hall civic building of Tweed Courthouse in New York City and plays a wonderfully strange mocking game of electronic mimicry with the nearby pedestrians.

ART IN CONTRAST TO ARCHITECTURE The Naum Gabo sculpture's articulated volume consisting of wires and rods makes a direct contrast to the granite clad cube of the Breuer's De Bijenkorf Department Store in Rotterdam. The blankness of

its façade allows the intricate weaving of the sculpture's assembly to be easily seen. The contrast can be reduced to an almost Neoclassic relationship between a rectangular masonry façade and a monumental symmetric abstract figure, placed as an entrance marker.

Whereas in the artist Martha Schwartz' renovation of the plaza of Marcel Breuer's HUD Headquarters in Washington, in 1990, the artwork is a repeated circular geometry of seating, planters and pavilions in direct and antagonistic contrast to the rectangular windows and angular columns of the 1968 Breuer building. The first example has the building accepting its role as a neutral backdrop to the art and the second has the art challenging the building for visual dominance.

View of the east
and south façade
of the De Bijenkorf
Department Store,
Rotterdam, Marcel
Breuer and Abraham
Elzas, 1953, with stain-
less steel sculpture
by Naum Gabo, 1956.

10

**ART AND ARCHITECTURE WITH A COMMON
MOTIF** The modern ideal of a *gesamtkunstwerk*, a "total work of art," can be seen in
the architect Walter Gropius' office in the
Bauhaus decorated in a multiple of subdivided
grids by furniture craftsmen, weavers and
metalworkers. All the artwork is united by
the visual limits of the motif of the square
and the rotated square becoming a cube.

   This work of art stands in stark contrast
to the installation by the German artist
Birgit Ramsauer on the Moscow subway
with a rectangle of fluorescent tape
limiting an inhabitable private space in a
public area. The artist has united the pile
of her belongings by the most absurd and
haunting gesture, creating the appearance
of a stage set for a Samuel Beckett play or
a contemporary variation on Leonardo da
Vinci's *Proportions of Man*.

**ARCHITECTURE APPROPRIATES FORM FROM
ART** Constantin Brâncuși's *Endless Column,*
on which he began to work in 1918, has
taunted architects for decades. Is it tribal
or technological? Is it one single element
or many separate modules? Is it finite or
infinite? For the architect Wallace Harrison
it became one of many art images (along
with works by the artists Richard Lippold and
Kenneth Snelson) to be appropriated for the
many design studies of this carillon tower for
the First Presbyterian Church in Stamford,
Connecticut, 1968.

Ibram Lassaw, wire
sculpture *Clouds
of Magellan* in Philip
Johnson's guest
house, 1956.

Antony Gormley, wire
sculpture *Clearing IV*,
White Cube Gallery,
London, 2005.

Jacques Lipchitz,
sculpture *Between
Heaven and Earth*, 1958,
at Roofless Church,
New Harmony, Indiana,
Philip Johnson, 1960.

Alfredo Ceschiatti, *Four
Evangelists*, 1988, at the
cathedral of Brasilia,
Oscar Niemeyer, 1970.

Rivane Neuenschwan-
der, installation *Rains
Rain (Chove chuva)*,
consisting of buckets,
steel cable, water and
ladder in the Museu
de Arte da Pampulha,
Belo Horizonte, Brazil,
2002, originally the
Pampulha Casino by
Oscar Niemeyer, 1942.

ART DUPLICATING THE SCALE OF ARCHITECTURE

In Philip Johnson's guest house the artist Ibram Lassaw's sculpture becomes a small focused articulation and elaboration of the wall's fabric pattern, traditionally framed by the arches at the ceiling.

The artist Antony Gormley's sculpture inverts this order and has his monumental wire sculpture dominate and establish the perceived volume of the gallery space, making shapes similar to the semi-circular vaults in the Johnson bedroom, having his artwork duplicate the scale of architecture.

ART SINGULAR IN ITS TEMPLE

Philip Johnson's Roofless Church was designed to specifically shelter the Jacques Lipchitz sculpture titled *Between Heaven and Earth*. In the sculpture's symbolism the flowing robes of the Virgin Mary make a curved, womb-like volume around the figure. The roof of the structure takes that same curved form, inverts it and mimics it as the next level of enclosure to the central figure. The sculptural symbol of the womb is encased in an architectural symbol of the body. Together the sculpture and pavilion stand enshrined within a tall rectangular brick wall defining the enclosed garden and this temple to art.

ART IN CONFLICT WITH ARCHITECTURE

The integration of monumental figurative sculpture in the government buildings at the capital city of Brasilia gave an unintended surrealistic representation by the fact that the human form was inflated beyond its normal scale so as not to be lost within the vast forecourts and plazas. The artworks have become compositional markers for finding the entrances to the buildings.

In contrast the installation by the artist Rivane Neuenschwander takes the approach of art mimicking and engaging in a critical stance to the building it resides in. For the lobby in architect Oscar Niemeyer's Pampulha Casino, 1942, the artist has arranged a grid of aluminum buckets, matching the diameter of the existing chrome columns, placing them both high and low. With the slow draining of the water from the top bucket to the lower one, a series of images (and sounds) are created whereby the buckets act as ghost columns dissolved within the constant dripping of the Brazilian rain forest, creating a contrasting image of culture and nature, building and forest.

In all fine art – that is, art which has as
an end the pleasure of the senses –
there are two qualities which must be
obtained: unity and grace. Unity is the
manifest connection of all the parts in
a whole; grace is the pleasing form of
the parts thus connected.
John Beverley Robinson
on composition

Collaboration may be said to be a
mode analogous to collage. The best
collaborations of the Dadaists and
Surrealists […] emphasize the theme
of abruptness, of textural changes,
and of the sense of rupture and
discontinuity.
David Shapiro

Definitions

The majority of the analysis in this book
is directed to the struggle of an artist and
architect working together to place art
in a building. To continue further in this
direction it is necessary to engage in the
slippery definitions of Composition[2] and
Collaboration.

At the very beginning of modern
architecture the word Composition belonged
to the academic Ecole des Beaux-Arts
imagery of symmetrically placed volumes
and formal historical rules. Modern
architecture was supposed to be about the
clear, scientific articulation of structure, of
program, of function, but most definitely not
about imposing a predetermined stylistic
sensibility or order. But when placing art in
a modern structure, architects fell back, in
many cases, on the simple framing devices

of a Neoclassical vocabulary and not on any
new compositional invention.

The use of the word, Composition, in
this text is an acknowledgement that this
concept was both denied and utilized for
the projects described. It will be applied
when art is placed in the formal organization
of spaces or masses of the building in
question.[3] Updating traditional forms such
as the Acroterion, Aedicule, Altar, Cenotaph,
Frieze, Gate, Monument, Medallion, Niche,
Panel, Pediment, Pendentive, Spandrel,
Spire, Stele, Screen, Terme, and Tympanum
was an unconscious response to the need of
locating art in a position that recognized the
hierarchy of its importance.

Collaboration will be used to cover all the
various degrees of engagement between the
artist and the architect. This activity would
range from the typical arrangement where

the art-worker is brought in during the design
of the building to the opposite extreme
of including an art piece anywhere near a
structure when either artist or architect are
no longer living.

The fact that either person may not have
physical contact with the other does not limit
the participation, commentary and conflict
one object may have for another. And with
that dialogue the objects hopefully merge
into a greater and complex whole.

Collaborationist:
a person who
works with an
enemy occupying
his territory.

The Beginning

UNESCO'S ART PROGRAM – THE SUM OF ALL THINGS

A perfect illustration of the range of connections and compromises between modern art and modern architecture would be the UNESCO Headquarters in Paris, 1957. Here at one spot are all the elements of the ideal cooperation between artists and architects: a socially progressive international institution, a specific program of intent, a roster of talented designers, a generous budget and a sympathetic audience. Yet the final products were so extremely disappointing that Lewis Mumford labeled them an "aesthetic void."[4]

The architects, Marcel Breuer and Bernard Zehrfuss with the engineer Pier Luigi Nervi, collaborated in the design of the building complex. It consists of three structures; a large office building, the Secretariat, curving to match the adjacent semicircle Place de Fontenoy, the angular Conference Hall flanking the open entry plaza and a smaller cube-like office structure, the Delegations Building, located at the rear of the site. Within the grounds are parking, an entry plaza, a garden and several specially commissioned artworks.

The dominant visual force of the buildings comes from their consistent use of exposed concrete structure: floors, beams, walls with select walls clad in travertine. The other image of the buildings is their contrasting geometries; the curving main office building has a curved entry canopy and curvilinear columns versus the Conference Hall with shallow angles for the walls in plan and the roof in section. Together they represent the post-war style titled "Brutalism," a label that could not have been complimentary even at its christening.[5]

The most successful of the artworks is Henry Moore's monumental reclining figure of carved travertine. The reason for this achievement is not the picturesque contrast between the carved figure and the building's linear façade, but the fact that this abstract artwork participates in the traditional function of figurative sculpture found in Neoclassic buildings: it is one step in an ornamental program that breaks down the scale of the large edifice to a series of components that can be related to the human figure.

Here at UNESCO this series begins with the eight-story (34 meters in height) façade which then visually steps down to the smaller angled, bent frame of the two-story Conference Hall (12 meters in height)

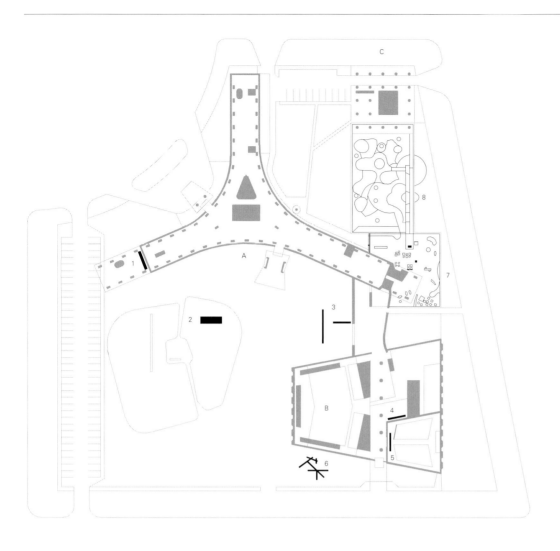

UNESCO Headquarters, Paris, Marcel Breuer and Bernard Zehrfuss with Pier Luigi Nervi, 1957.

Site plan:
A Secretariat
B Delegations Building
C Conference Hall

1 J. Arp, sculpture
2 H. Moore, sculpture
3 J. Miró, ceramic mural
4 P. Picasso, mural
5 R. Tamayo, mural
6 A. Calder, sculpture
7 I. Noguchi, Delegates Terrace
8 I. Noguchi, Japanese Garden

Entry court and pavilion of UNESCO Headquarters with Henry Moore sculpture.

Façade and sculptures,
Piazza Campidoglio,
Rome.

River god at the
Campidoglio, Rome.

and then steps down again to the curved hyperbolic parabloid entry canopy (6 meters in height) and then yet again to Moore's construct (2.75 meters in height with a 1 meter plinth) and finally to the visitor at the entry facing the entire assembly. The most successful and subtle gesture in the shape of the reclining figure is its legs twisting into an abstract rotated plane as a sympathetic mirror to the mathematically warped curve of the entry canopy.

A parallel pattern of arrangement can be seen in the Piazza del Campidoglio in Rome when revised under the plans of Michelangelo from 1535 to 1564. Here the great innovation was the architect's Neoclassic façade with two scales of columnar orders: one colossal and the other normal.[6] And within that range of new and renovated buildings Michelangelo arranged

the ancient sculptures of the bronze Marcus Aurelius equestrian statue and the two stone river gods (the Tiber and the Nile) like a modern collage. The antique river gods, so like Moore's reclining figure in Paris, give additional mass, weight and scale to the central building at the Piazza.

The visual composition starts with the panorama of the city from the top of the Capitoline Hill, brought down to earth by the bell tower of the Senator's Palace, then caged by the grid of the giant pilasters, and connected lower by the smaller portico columns, jumping across the piazza by the centrifugal oval paving pattern to the center figure of Aurelius and extending to the tip of his finger, pointing out to the city and completing the cycle back to its beginning. A political symbol of ancient Roman Imperial power and contemporary Papal power,

united with the city, a compelling visual trick that gestures to us across the centuries.

The contrast between UNESCO and the Campidoglio shows the obvious special differences of the two eras. The Modern one treats the assembly of buildings (and sculptures) as free-floating objects on a horizontal field whereas the Renaissance project aligns the collection of new and old buildings to define an enclosed public space related to the context of the city.

At UNESCO the Moore sculpture, more by chance then calculation, sympathetically connects all four elements of the building in its entry courtyard. Typically, modern art is brought into the vast impersonal modern office structure to humanize the environment. Unfortunately the art itself is usually overwhelmed and dehumanized by its surroundings. The isolated "statue on the

Jean Arp, sculpture at UNESCO Headquarters.

Pablo Picasso, *The Fall of Icarus* at UNESCO Headquarters.

lawn" is altered here with the Moore statue becoming one object that is visually equal to its neighboring structures.[7]

Most of the other artist contributions at UNESCO visually fail because the vocabulary of the artist does not engage with the building in any way besides simple contrast: the Jean (Hans) Arp asymmetric figurative bronze shape, pinned like pieces of jewelry on a lapel, is located at a wall near the library entrance. The interior mural by Pablo Picasso in the Conference Hall corridor and other murals in the same building seem unconnected to their place and purpose. The two exterior ceramic murals by Joan Miró are mounted on free-standing walls drifting away from the building.

Picasso's mural in the Conference Hall interior, *The Fall of Icarus*,[8] is perhaps the most disappointing of all the artwork in that

structure, not because of Picasso's stature but because it started, in its original studies, as one of the most promising of spatially engaging works. The assignment came when the artist was obsessed with numerous studies of Diego Velázquez's masterwork *Las Meninas* of 1656. The complicated multiple portrait by Velázquez has been described as "a mirror, a trap, interplay of reflections, and inversion of roles between the viewer and the viewed."[9] For Picasso, the older work fits perfectly into a series of his paintings he called "interior landscapes" *(paysages d'intérieur)*. For most of the winter of 1957 Picasso produced a large volume of studies and sketches of the theme of a distorted and reflected interior. The study for UNESCO of December 15, 1957 presents a complicated visual game with the artist's profile in the right foreground proceeding then to a large

canvas to extend farther back to a reclining model and finally the enclosing walls of the studio. What is a real person, a sculpture, a painted image, a shadow, a window or a mirror is intentionally confused and distorted. The evolution (or devolution) of the mural from the original amazing studies to the crushingly disappointing finality cannot be easily explained: a loss of nerve, a loss of time or a loss of interest? The original December study would have exerted a visually competing spatial illusion that would have recalled the angular beams and walls of Breuer's building and at the same time challenged the spatial order of that same system.

The ceramic mural by Miró is a perfect example of the visual disengagement between building and art, the introspection and isolation of contemporary art (and the artist) from the figure, social concerns and

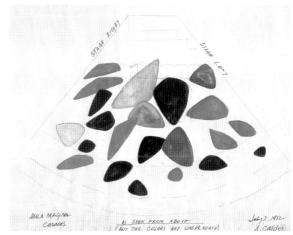

the world at large. Miró talks extensively about how this specific mural relates to this specific building, but the reality is that the work could be placed in front of any building, anywhere, with the same visual results.[10] Perhaps the basic flaw is that the artist is not concerned with the urban context but with an interior world. Its theme of nature seems inspired not by its final resting place but by its inception in the kilns of rural Spain. Like all of Miró's artwork it is in its own world, unconnected to the building complex physically and intellectually.

The Alexander Calder sculpture, located at the main entry against the blank wall of the Conference Hall, is another dislocated art piece. Nothing moors the object down to this location, neither reason nor impulse.

A more telling collaboration between artist and architect was Calder's interior sculpture of an auditorium ceiling by the use of painted wood acoustical panels (floating clouds) for the Aula Magna Theater of the Universidad Central de Venezuela in Caracas by architect Carlos Raúl Villanueva. The artwork merges with the vocabulary of the building and even connects to a straightforward functional reality, the reflection of sound waves through the volume. This scheme would be unthinkable at UNESCO because of the architect Breuer's need to articulate the repeated pattern of angled beams in the structure of the auditorium.

The three themes that have been described in UNESCO will return in many of the projects examined in this book. The first is the traditional placement of art as an appendage of the body of the building. The second is the blank incoherence between the ideas and vocabulary of the modern artists and the modern architects. The final effect is the rarest, being the aggressive engagement by all the visual arts for the same territory, battling not just for supremacy of the site but for the value of the ideas engaged.

Gallery White Walls Versus Kindergarten Blackboard

The traditional display of modern art in a visually "neutral" architect-designed setting has existed for years parallel with its exact opposite, the display of modern art within a "committed" artist-developed surrounding.[11] Before the art happenings of the 1960s and the site-specific art of the 1970s there were other similar voices. Perhaps it is the eternal human conflict of competitive control for territory (wall space) that is at the core of the impossibility of collaboration between the two worlds of artist and architect.

No architect better represents the cool, pure, austere, white box setting of contemporary art museums than Ludwig Mies van der Rohe. His precise collage perspectives of interiors articulated with cut out photographs of sculpture and paintings have established the universal model for the display of contemporary art. The rationality of the gridded spaces in these perspectives has been noted but never the surreal scale. The collage perspective for the Resor House, 1939, shows a Paul Klee painting, *Colorful Meal (Bunte Mahlzeit),* 1928, which is only 76 centimeters high to be projected the full height of the living room space. To know the piece is to understand that the world presented is a Surrealist dream of a miniature doll house.[12] In Mies' perspectives for Museum for a Small Town, 1942, the floating vertical figures, for all sculpture is reduced to be substitute columns,

and sliding horizontal textured planes, for all paintings are reduced to be substitute walls, become the chess pieces that are moved by the architect for the perfect compositional balance in the modern "Open Plan."[13]

But counter to those images/ ideas are the early environments by Kurt Schwitters in Germany, created continuously between 1920 and 1933: not only are these parallel with the International Style modernism of Mies but they engage in commenting on it and him as well. Schwitters' Merzbau (Merz building) constructions are site-specific installations before that word was invented.[14]

The first, in Hanover, Germany, is made by the incremental accumulations of discarded materials resulting in cave-like formations developing into miniature grottos, recesses, altars and chapels. Here symbols of the beauty and terror of the outside world are reduced to a small, safe, controlled vision. The various displayed works of art range from Schwitters' own bizarre *Murderers' Cave (Lustmordhöhle)* containing broken dolls covered in red lipstick to the calmness of the *Höch Grotto* holding two small photo-collages by fellow artist Hannah Höch. Colleagues and artists as Jean Arp, Naum Gabo, El Lissitzky, László Moholy-Nagy and Piet Mondrian were honored as heroes in tiny memorials. As the construction

continued, sections were walled off and entombed. And there in the corner shelf (or is it a mountain plateau?) is the worn-out stub of a pencil belonging to the architect Mies van der Rohe.[15] Another hero welcomed into this world, but one never to have visited.

But the story must turn one more time to complete itself, for Mies collected artwork himself. To everyone's surprise he did not purchase the sympathetic colored Cartesian planes of Mondrian but instead the tiny child-like drawings of Klee and the messy paper collages of Schwitters.[16] These purchases were made after the war, during the same time period that Mies' perspective collages were being made. For both men, Mies and Schwitters, these tiny pieces of glued photos and paper hold in their small perimeters each of their worlds reduced down to a size where, if only we could dream the dream of Alice in Wonderland, we could finally enter.

Portrait of Ludwig Mies van der Rohe in Chicago, 1953.

Lutz Bacher, installation, University Art Museum at Berkeley, California, 1993. This artwork shows a literal use of the gallery walls as a kindergarten blackboard.

I see you have removed the motifs
from your paintings, no recognizable
objects appear there anymore. You
reproduce the sweeping curve of a
chair, not the chair: The red of the sky,
not the burning house. **Bertolt Brecht**

Walter Gropius' Dream of Cultural Unity and the Artists of the Bauhaus

The Grinding of Gears between the Bachelor Machine and the Virgin Dynamo

The ideas and ideals that motivated and directed the choices of architects, artists and clients in the integration of artwork in modern structures were determined by a set of examples established directly after 1900. But for our purposes the working definition of "modern" excludes its decorative precursors. One of which is the Art Nouveau style which established a set of common curved motifs to be used in both architecture and the arts. The other is the Art Deco style with its disguised Beaux Arts compositions hiding under the mimicry of machines and geometry. The emphasis in this section will be on the early modernism of the artists around the Bauhaus, not only as an example of the struggle of cooperation in the arts but also because of its direct connection to design schools in the United States and their indoctrinated students who then became the commissioning architects of the next generation.

This chapter will propose that two main directions for the integration of the arts were present at that time and remain with us today. For this specific section those two separate attitudes will be presented in an extended metaphor of two symbolic figures labeled the "Virgin Dynamo" and its opposite, the "Bachelor Machine."[1]

The first term "Virgin Dynamo" recalls the American historian Henry Adams in his observations on the Palais de l'Electricité at the 1900 Exposition Universelle Internationale in Paris, that civilization has moved from the unified religious worship of

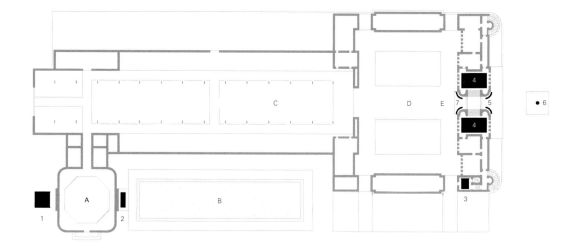

Marcel Duchamp, *The Bride Stripped Bare by Her Bachelors, Even (The Large Glass)*, 1915–1923, copy by Robert Hamilton (1966); Duchamp approved to show the artwork in the version before the glass was damaged.

Factory and Office Building, Werkbund Exhibition, Walter Gropius, Cologne, 1914.

Ground floor plan:
A Deutz Motor Pavilion
B Pool
C Machine Hall
D Courtyard
E Offices

1 Hydraulic steel press
2 H. Haller, sculpture
3 M. Kogan, relief sculpture
4 G. Kolbe and E. Hahs, mural
5 G. Marcks, relief sculpture
6 G. Kolbe, sculpture
7 R. Scheibe, relief sculpture

the Virgin Mary to the materialistic awe of the electric dynamo.[2] These two images: the Dynamo in the gallery and the Virginal "Fairy of Electricity" on the building's parapet, are together symbolic of the way of looking at art as part of a cultural unity.

Adams himself was obsessed with the motivations of historic civilizations and believed that you could divide societies into two types: one that represented a cohesive direction (Medieval Europe and the Age of Faith) and one that showed the conflict of change and expansion (the Industrial Revolution and the Age of Reason). Adams found himself trapped in the second but admiring the first.

The second category, the "Bachelor Machine," comes from the famous work of the twentieth century Dada artist Marcel Duchamp titled *The Bride Stripped Bare by Her Bachelors, Even (La mariée mise à nue par ses célibataires, même)*, 1915–1923. Duchamp presented a calm demeanor but conceived artwork that was corrosively destructive to the existing order of his time. His strange collection of "readymades," inverted urinals, bottle-drying racks and chocolate-grinding mills, introduced a strategy for dealing with contemporary culture and its industrial production in a critical manner. With an overt autoerotic symbolism and ambiguous authorship these "machines" mocked the pretension of high culture, material production and political power. Instead of forcing a cultural unity the "Bachelor Machine" enjoys the chaos of the era.

A set of interconnected examples in the development of each of these two sides can be seen in the beginning of modern architecture. In each case the examples are meant to emphasize a machine metaphor and a gendering of the machine. The constant imagery of the female form in the "Virgin Dynamo" implies its submissive stature, where the art (female) is contained within the control of the architect (male). And alternately, the "Bachelor Machine" shows an art that is an aggressive attack on its culture and enclosure.

The precedent for viewing the art world with these two divisions could be seen in an inverted reading of Heinrich Wölfflin's classic 1881 text *Renaissance and Baroque*. Wölfflin gives us a telescopic view of history

Factory and Office
Building, Werkbund
Exhibition, Deutz Motor
Pavilion with steel
stamp press.

Factory and Office
Building, Werkbund
Exhibition, with
sculpture by H. Haller.

Entry of Factory
and Office Building,
Werkbund Exhibition.

Temple of Poseidon,
Paestum, Italy, fifth
century BC.

AEG Turbine Hall,
Berlin, Peter Behrens,
1909.

through the long-distance enlargement of art details of these two worlds, one a climax of material power in the service of culture and the second as a spiritual power in a climax of cultural expression. But it is also possible to look through the other end of the historical telescope and see the examples as emblems of a much smaller claustrophobic world, where the first becomes an illustration of oppressive control and the second an example of mass hysteria.

The Virgin Dynamo in the Cathedral of Art

A direct example of the "Virgin Dynamo" is the immense and muscular hydraulic press displayed at the 1914 Werkbund Exhibition in Cologne, a display most similar to the one experienced by Adams (and near the date, 1918, when his writings on the Virgin and the Dynamo were posthumously published).[3] The architect for the machine exhibit structure was Walter Gropius with Adolf Meyer, a figure who was obsessed with the concept of the unification of the arts. What is so important about this machine is that it is placed as a symmetrically "equal" opposite the classical reclining female (and male) nude statues. Throughout this Gropius building there is a continual implied equality of art and technology.

The Nude (Virgin) and the Press (Dynamo) are a perfect example of the way Gropius, his teacher Peter Behrens and their organization, the Deutscher Werkbund, strove to force an integration of the new industrial age with modern architecture using an adapted Neoclassic vocabulary. Another similar example would be in Behrens' work where the image of the classical temple merges with his Berlin Turbine Hall, 1909, for the electrical company AEG.

But the more dramatic illustration of unified arts would be two buildings by Gropius built thirty years apart, one the Sommerfeld House in Berlin of 1920 and the second Harkness Commons at Harvard University of 1950. Though these two buildings and their art are separated by time,

Sommerfeld House,
Berlin, Walter Gropius,
1920.

Josef Albers, stained-
glass windows at
Sommerfeld House.

Second floor plan:
1 J. Albers, windows
2 J. Schmidt, carvings

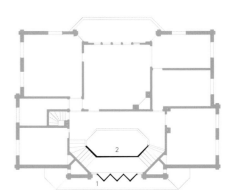

style and national culture, they both operate the same way in their attempt to integrate modern art into modern architecture, with the same priorities and the same limitations of success.

The Sommerfeld House was the first example of the collaborative work of artists and architects in the new Bauhaus recently formed in 1919 by Gropius through the combination of two art schools in Weimar, Germany. The Bauhaus was one of the most famous modern art schools and the Sommerfeld House is a perfect illustration of the originally stated objective of the school: the unification of art and industrial production. Gropius in the manifesto and program of the Bauhaus in 1919 states:

"The ultimate aim of all creative activity is the building. The decoration of buildings was one of the noblest functions of the fine arts, and the fine arts were indispensable to great architecture. Today they exist in complete isolation and can only be rescued from it by the conscious co-operation of all craftsmen. Architects, painters and sculptors must once again come to know and comprehend the composite character of a building, both as an entity and in terms of its various parts. Then their work will be filled with that true architectonic spirit which, as 'salon art,' it has lost."[4]

The Sommerfeld project was a private home for one of the school's patrons and it is best described as a log cabin with sloped

hip roof and extensive carved ornament. It does not appear very "modern," indeed it seems an exercise in eastern European folk vernacular.[5] But as Henry Adams longed for the class stability of the medieval world, the early Bauhaus was enamored with the idea of the medieval cathedral and its unification of art, architecture and culture. In the Bauhaus initial opening proclamation also the guilds are noted as inspiration.

The theme of the machine is seen in Joost Schmidt's carvings at the stair. Here is a set of five panels that contains within its geometric abstract cutouts small puppet-like figures and carved Masonic symbols. The symbolic narrative here is not the design or fabrication of the building but the

Sommerfeld House, carved wood ornament at stair by Joost Schmidt.

Marcel Duchamp, painting *Nude Descending a Staircase No. 2*, 1912.

manufacturing of the construction product (wood panels) at a saw mill owned by Sommerfeld. The "Virgin Dynamo" becomes the Virgin forest conquered by the production line. If we contrast the Joost Schmidt stair with Duchamp's *Nude Descending a Staircase (Nu descendant un escalier)* of 1912, we can see Duchamp's figure as a symbolic "Bachelor Machine" overwhelming the stair in a Cubist explosion of flying forms (called by a US newspaper "An explosion in a shingle factory") while the Schmidt carvings are the opposite with all the artwork tightly contained within the thick wooden frames designed by the architect. Both have the same "herringbone" angular motif to imply a movement across their surfaces.[6]

When examining other artwork in Gropius' building it is possible to see in the stained-glass windows of Josef Albers the same geometric motifs as in the Joost work and the same tight confinement by the massive architectural frames that hold up the glass panels. Albers cooperated again with Gropius after the war for the Harkness Commons at Harvard University.

To summarize the argument, at the Sommerfeld House each artist's work is outlined within a tradition that goes back to the niche for sculpture and the picture frame for painting. This forced attempt of unification is still seen today in the inter-action of artists and architects. However,

the Rabe House, built ten years later, shows an alternative strategy where the artwork bursts free of its confinement and establishes new ways for the arts to interact. The comparison between the two residences is also interesting because all the cooperating artists were part of the Bauhaus.

27

Rabe House, Zwenkau,
Adolf Rading, 1930.

Second floor plan:
1 O. Schlemmer, sculpture
2 O. Schlemmer, mural
3 O. Schlemmer, ceiling

Oskar Schlemmer, wire
figure *Homo with Back
View Figure on Its Hand*
at Rabe House, 1931
(replica 1968).

Oskar Schlemmer,
wall mural for Rabe
House.

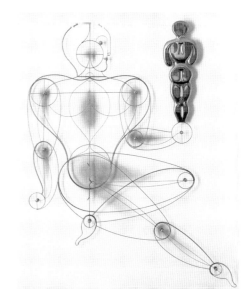

The Bachelor Machine
on the Marionette Stage

The Rabe House in Zwenkau near Leipzig
by architect Adolf Rading and artwork
by Oskar Schlemmer best illustrates the
ideas discussed concerning the "Bachelor
Machine." The decoration breaks out of the
traditional framing of art and establishes art
as a competing identity to the enclosure of
the building. Here at the Rabe House the
painted wall decoration continues across the
vertical and horizontal surfaces confusing the
exact line of the room's edges. Geometrically
shaped human figures, described in metal
bands, adorn the main two-story space in the
center of the house and present a tableau
distorting the space of the room.

The wire figures titled *Homo with
Back View Figure on Its Hand* are literally
machines in that the main figure has hinged
connectors at its joints. The figures and
decoration inhabit the house and engage its
elements in a way that distorts the scale and
spatial qualities of the interior.

The central figure appears to stand on
the stained wood door inverting the visual
function of the door as void, to be now
seen as a solid with the background of the
white wall creating the illusion of a void
of undetermined depth. The fact that each
of the three figures is in a vastly different
scale distorts the perceived location of
the wall in the transition from the large
(foreground) profile to the central (mid-range)

figure and finally to the smallest at the top
center (distant background). Followed by
the confusion as to whether the smallest
bachelor machine is a regularly scaled human
in the far distance or a doll-like sculpture in
the foreground.[7]

Although modest in scope the Rabe
interior prefigures many of the ideas of
contemporary performance art and site-
specific installation art. Schlemmer was
a teacher of sculpture and theater at the
Bauhaus during the Gropius leadership.
During that time he did work on wall murals
for the decoration of the school in Weimar
and Dessau, but both of those works show
less aggression in challenging their enclosure
than the Rabe House.[8]

Harkness Commons, Harvard University, Cambridge, Massachusetts, circa 1950, The Architects Collaborative (TAC) with the sculpture *World Tree* by Richard Lippold.

Gropius Brings Light and Culture to the Void

The update of the Virgin Dynamo could be seen in another Gropius building which this time translates the ideas of unity in the arts, shown in the early Bauhaus test in the Sommerfeld House, to the post-war United States and the Harkness Commons, 1950, at Harvard in Cambridge, Massachusetts. This project has various artists again participating in decorating the building: Richard Lippold (associated with the Bauhaus extension in Black Mountain College near Asheville, North Carolina, in 1944) at the entry sculpture, Herbert Bayer (student and teacher at the Bauhaus) at the main ramp mural and also at one of the dining room murals, Joan Miró and Jean Arp at the other dining

room murals, Josef Albers (an artist at the Sommerfeld project and a Bauhaus teacher) with a relief sculpture at the lounge and Anni Albers contributing textiles for the dormitory rooms. The map collage by György Kepes, located in an adjacent building, has been destroyed.

This unusually large collection of seven artists establishes this building as a model for much of the co-operative design in the United States for many years after in public structures such as schools, government and office buildings. The Harkness Commons is a direct link connecting the Werkbund to the Bauhaus, then to Harvard and on into our present time.

All the art pieces here work within the traditional frames provided by the architect

and have a common modernist machine image. The Lippold exterior stainless steel piece, titled *World Tree*, fits into a local tradition at Harvard, with figurative sculptures resting in the courtyards formed by the buildings (as seen in the statue of John Harvard in Harvard Yard). The Bayer, Miró and Arp murals are all placed in a traditional architectural framing provided by the high clerestory windows and the asymmetric surrounding columns.

The two artists directly from the Bauhaus, Albers and Bayer, fit their work tightly into the building composition. The Albers brick relief *America* and the Bayer tile mural both act as set-pieces around the diminutive main ramp up to the dining halls. The Albers ends the ground floor axis

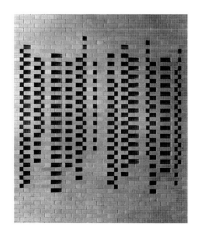

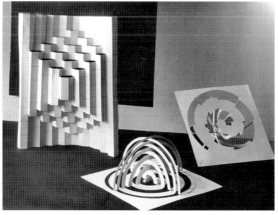

Josef Albers, wall relief *America* at fireplace of Harkness Commons, Harvard University.

Walter Tralar and Arieh Sharon, folded paper student work from Josef Albers foundation course at Bauhaus, Dessau, 1926.

Cover of *Architectural Forum: The Magazine of Building*, 1950, with the Harkness Commons ramp with the wall tile mural by Herbert Bayer.

of the ramp which is edged on one side by the Bayer mural. More interestingly, both of these works comment in an introspective manner on their mutual Bauhaus origins. The Albers piece takes the modular brick units of the fireplace wall and alters their pattern like a folded paper exercise in a beginning design course taught by Albers himself at the Bauhaus. The Bayer mural takes a grid of light and dark gray tile squares and injects a random sequence of colored alternatives just like the gridded color theory exercises taught by Paul Klee (Farbabstufungen = color shades) to art students in Germany.

The second Bayer mural *Verdure* can be seen as a surprisingly conservative abstraction of the view of the nearby tree tops from the same second floor faculty dining room. Bayer himself noted in an interview in the *Harvard Crimson* that the mural subject matter should be about "sprouting, glaucous verdure, an image of the idea of growing." The folded planes can be seen in his work of the same period with titles like *Foliage*, 1943. For all its graphic sophistication the mural is an abstracted landscape painting framed by the surrounding windows and columns like any usual landscape painting displayed in a frame.

The work by Joan Miró seems the most separated from the central theme and imagery of the other artists. The original canvas by Miró, titled *Barcelona*, has been replaced with a ceramic copy. The original is now at the Museum of Modern Art in New York City. The obvious theme is a bullfight with a Picador, Horse, Bull and Matador illustrated in that order (left to right). As Miró did in the art piece placed at the exterior entry court of the UNESCO complex he made little effort to coordinate with anything other than the required size. Both pieces were obviously dropped into their site from a distance (the Harvard piece was painted in Spain) and after the buildings were completed.

The last artist from this group to be discussed is Jean Arp. Here Arp has produced a set of cut wood reliefs of a bio-morphic quality that were placed along two wood paneled walls enclosing a smaller dining hall. The artwork's title, *Constellation*,

Joan Miró, mural
Barcelona, general
dining room of
Harkness Commons,
Harvard University.

Design study of
Herbert Bayer mural
Verdure, 1950.

Herbert Bayer, mural
Verdure in faculty
dining room of
Harkness Commons,
Harvard University.

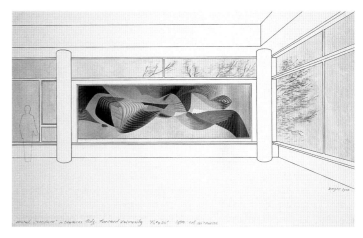

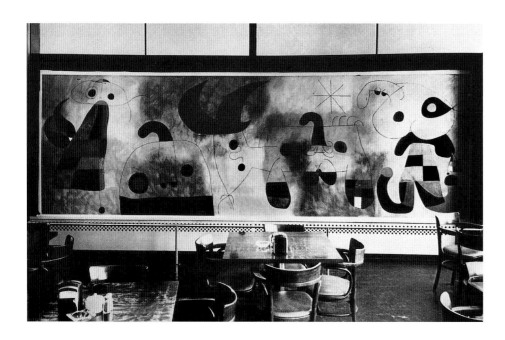

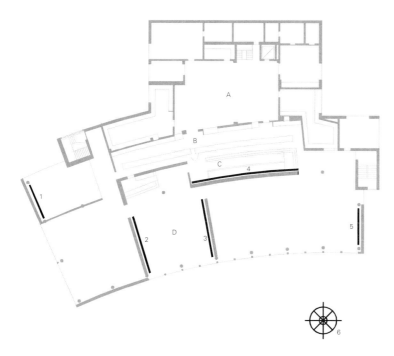

Harkness Commons,
Harvard University,
Cambridge, Massachusetts,
The Architects Collaborative
(TAC), 1950.

Jean Arp, wood relief
sculpture *Constellation*,
Harkness Commons,
Harvard University.

Second floor plan:
A Kitchen
B Servery
C Ramp
D Dining Hall

1 H. Bayer, mural
2 J. Arp, relief sculpture
3 J. Arp, relief sculpture
4 H. Bayer, tile mural
5 J. Miró, mural
6 R. Lippold, sculpture

Richard Lippold,
sculpture *World Tree*,
Harkness Commons,
Harvard University.

Marcel Duchamp,
Readymade *Bottle Rack*,
1914 (replica 1961).

 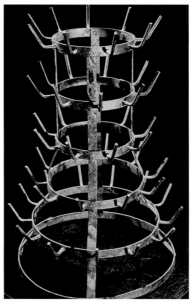

gives a clear image of the loose unattached collection of objects. Arp was the only artist recorded as working with Gropius on the artwork. It is written that he appeared at the architect's office with a collection of cut paper shapes and tossed them randomly on an elevation drawing of the wall.[9] Nothing was written about Gropius' reaction to this Dada-like action: amusement or embarrassment. Also nothing was written about the original scale of the proposed artwork in relation to the building. For Arp had previous experience with mural paintings and an installation of his work in a restaurant in Strasbourg in Alsace in 1928 which shows shapes similar to Harvard but with a different idea. In Strasbourg, the murals used a large and expansive scale that broke beyond their

enclosures distorting the shape of the room whereas at Harvard the shapes are all neatly contained (and aligned along a horizontal line) within their defined borders.

It is interesting to compare Lippold's *World Tree,* 1950, and Duchamp's Readymade *Bottle Rack (Porte-bouteilles)* from 1914. At first glance, it is possible to see some basic similarities: a vertical central form with radiating tubular arms at various heights. But besides the manufactured steel construction of both there is a major difference: the Lippold sculpture glories in its identity as an abstract high culture object unifying with the progressive technological image of the building while the Duchamp piece mocks these same sentiments. The Readymade is a

self-representing sculpture taunting an established order of representation, it is anti-art and anti-culture. The *Bottle Rack* presents us with the impossibility of making art as a spiritual escape from the realities of consumption. Duchamp's work offers an alternative critical path to an obviously forced and faltering visual unity of the Bauhaus artists.

In summary, the Harkness Commons was for its time an audacious assembly of modern art and architecture in America. It was an incredible testament to the vision and organizational skills of Gropius, his architectural office TAC and the administration at Harvard. But its artistic limitations are obvious. It also marks the climax of Gropius's career in America. The

Model of exterior entry elevation of Marshall Field & Co. Store, Houston, Johnson/Burgee Architects, 1977.

Claes Oldenburg, model of proposed sculpture for Marshall Field & Co. Store.

Marshall Field & Co. Store, exterior view.

academic designs he produced at Harvard were overshadowed by the much more important contemporary work of his German colleague Ludwig Mies van der Rohe at the Illinois Institute of Technology in Chicago. Gropius' reputation devolved from this peak moment to the low point in his assistance to the design of the Pan Am Building next to New York City's Grand Central Station, a project criticized for its gross scale, insensitive urbanism and crude detailing. Here, once more, he tried for an involvement of artists, commissioning both Lippold and Albers again for creating centerpieces in the main passages. Both gestures were insufficient to lift the massive boring block from its emotionally stagnate position.

THE FOX WHO BELIEVES HE IS A HEDGEHOG MEETS THE WOLF DISGUISED IN SHEEP'S CLOTHING The theme of the "Virgin Dynamo" versus the "Bachelor Machine" continues on to the 1970s and beyond as seen in the two contrasting designs[10] for the entry façade of the Marshall Field & Co. Store in Houston, Texas, 1977, by the architect Philip Johnson and the artist Claes Oldenburg.

The project is a huge curved entry façade for a retail store made of Austin shell stone panels developed with a series of rectangular niches. These recesses were specially designed for the 1960s Pop artist Claes Oldenburg, whose work Johnson had collected, and they relate to the tradition of sculpture contained in the pediment of a Greek temple. Johnson thought Oldenburg was a natural choice because he had in 1961 finished an entire installation of fake plaster food products in a real storefront called *The Store*. The architect proposed what is called an *architecture parlante*, a speaking architecture, which demonstrates its symbolic function in its outward shape: the equation being that this is a store; therefore the façade is a collection of merchandise.

Oldenburg's response was a classic Duchampian move of defacement. Instead of limiting himself to the niches provided he proposed to dominate the entire façade by a series of irregularly shaped cast aluminum sculptures taken from an enlarged paint splatter formation. Scatological to the extreme it appears as

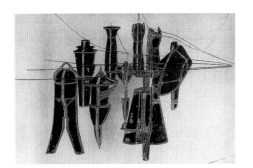

Marcel Duchamp, *Nine Malic Mold*s, 1914–1915.

Photo of Gropius (at bottom) and partners from The Architects Collaborative on top of *World Tree* sculpture by Richard Lippold.

a defiant graffiti insult to the monumental pretension of an over-scaled tiny door to a shopping center.

But on a second look the equation (or argument) becomes more complicated, for Oldenburg has subtly curved each huge glob of paint, making a small accommodating mimic of the curve of the building, thus starting a dialogue between objects. In the preliminary studies the artist used nail polish for the splatters, matching the cosmetic products sold immediately behind the façade, and the biomorphic shapes themselves connect to the vocabulary of the conservative modern murals by Jean Arp.

Johnson, who as a student of Gropius and a disciple of Mies, was the inheritor of the tradition of the forced unity of art as seen in the "Virgin Dynamo." But his chance to make the next move (how to incorporate the company logo) in this intellectual game, of insult or accommodation, was not possible as the project was canceled by the client. Even unbuilt and unfinished, it still remains one of the most intelligent and engaging of collaborations.[11]

The last contrast in this argument is a parallel set of photographs that illustrates Duchamp's *Nine Malic Molds (Neuf moules mâlic)* functioning as Bachelor Machines overlapping the machine imagery of the "Bride," and a souvenir snapshot of Walter Gropius and his five male business partners (avoiding the two female partners) perched on the artist Lippold's metal sculpture *World Tree* (Virgin Dynamo).

On one side is the dream of the symbolic machine as an abstracted cultural ideal, where art is dominated by the architect and on the other side is the gendered machine as the nightmare from our sexual subconscious unleashed and uncontrolled even by the artist.

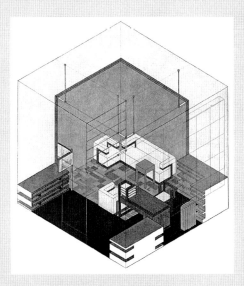

Herbert Bayer, axonometric of the Director's Office at the Bauhaus, Dessau, Walter Gropius, 1923. Various artists contributed to the design: wall carpet by Else Mögelin, floor carpet by Gertrud Arndt, light fixtures by László Moholy-Nagy.

I insist emphatically upon leaving to the art of building and to the architect the leading place in art and art training. It is not a question of giving one profession intellectual precedence over others, but a natural arrangement in keeping with their varying natures. A painter, a sculptor or an art worker builds up his work, personally with his own hands, whereas the work of the architect is dependent upon the collaboration of numerous assistants. Painting, sculpture and handiwork are all developed in organic relationship with the art of building.

It is the task of the architect of our generation to regain the lead in the arts which became lost to them during the change-over to the machine in our own era. They must once more develop the attributes of leadership by virtue of which there can be unity in the work as a whole, in spite of the multiplicity of collaborators. The object of the architect today is to become a comprehensive organizer who, starting out from the social conception of life, which are valid for the entire community, has to gather under one heal all the social, scientific, technical, economic and artistic problems of building, and, in conjunction with numerous artists, specialists and workers, to weld them systematically into a homogeneous whole.

Architecture, as mother of all arts, has to fulfill two different demands made by man: the purpose or object of the thing on the one hand, and its expression or its form on the other. The questions concerning the object or purpose of the thing are one of a super-individual nature. They represent the organic evolution as we see it in nature.

Today, we insist upon the form of a thing following the function of that thing, upon its creator's desire for expression following the same direction as the organic building – upon process in nature, and not running counter to that direction.

We insist upon harmony again being achieved between intellect and desire.

Walter Gropius

Gropius' building, the "Factory and Office," at the Cologne Werkbund Exposition of 1914 was published with very select photographs. The architectural historian Sigfried Giedion praised the office block and its all-glass corner staircases as an example of modern design far advanced for its time.[12] But this limited view ignored the many integrated figurative artworks built into the building's fabric. Giedion edited out all the relief sculpture, murals and reclining nude figures.[13] This is doubly surprising because the major purpose of the Werkbund was the unification of art and manufacturing design in Germany.

Certainly one of the most amazing art pieces of this exposition was the office lobby mural by the artist Georg Kolbe (assisted by E. Hahs). Kolbe is famous among architects for his evocative female nude sculpture, *The Morning (Der Morgen)*, chosen by Mies van der Rohe for the German Pavilion at Barcelona in 1929, a bronze construct turned into a flat collage by the scale-less single point perspective of its iconic photograph. But at the Cologne building Kolbe's mural, unlike his famous sculptures, is a strange stylistic combination of Jugendstil and Expressionism engaging the building in an unexpected manner. The theme of the mural is played out in a series of stylized nude figures, with their protractors and chisels, representing the Werkbund "Art Workers." They are as pretty as decorative wrapping on a confectioner's package. But with its wide brush strokes, thin glaze and incomplete covering of the stucco surfaces the painting does not imply a traditional wall mural but something more unusual. The interior walls appear not so much painted on as injected with the design, like a tattoo on human skin.

In 1908 the Viennese architect Adolf Loos had damned ornament in one of his most famous essays where he suggested that the image of a building's decoration was equal to the obscene tattoos on primitive tribesman.[14] Here Kolbe has completed the circle of Loos' argument: the ornament of the building is blurred into a tattoo-like wall covering. The mural stands on the fulcrum between two modern impulses: at one end it physically fades into the past of obsolete historicist ornament and on the other it remains as Loos' primitive obscenity embedded deeper within the skin of the structure, penetrating into the cultural subconscious: the figure buried within the field of abstraction but refusing to disappear.

Georg Kolbe (assisted by E. Hahs), mural in lobby of Office Building, Werkbund Exhibition, Walter Gropius, Cologne, 1914.

Mathieu Beauséjour, photograph *Document sur papier archive*, 2003.[15]

Café Aubette

Vilmos Huszár, *Mechanical Plastic Dream*, 1921 (original lost).

The Bachelor Machine Dances with Himself

Jean Arp's mural for the Harkness Commons at Harvard was one of a series of public murals and relief sculptures produced by this renowned artist. The list would include the relief designs for the City University at Caracas, Venezuela, 1956, and the United Nations Building in New York, 1957. But the first of these monumental works would be the decoration for the Café Aubette[16] in Strasbourg in 1927.

The modern decoration of this existing eighteenth century building was started by the new concessioners giving Arp and his wife Sophie Taeuber-Arp a commission for its interior re-design. Feeling overwhelmed by this large project the couple engaged Theo van Doesburg (modestly self-described as "painter, sculptor, architect, typog-rapher, poet, novelist, critic") to organize the decorative program.

There is an apocryphal story that when van Doesburg walked into the large upstairs hall of the Aubette he exclaimed "I'll break this architecture;" he then looked around further and stated "Yes, I'll break this space."[17] It is this bold opposition to the existing structure that makes van Doesburg's sculptural relief mural such a powerful statement.

Theo van Doesburg's life was changed by his early exposure in 1915 to the work of Piet Mondrian in Rotterdam. Van Doesburg worshipped Mondrian's art with its religious purity of gridded black lines and primary colored rectangles and attempted to convert the world to his new cause "The Style" ("De Stijl").

For his completed design of the *Cine-Dancing* he used Mondrian's grid of physical blocks of primary colors (including whites and grays) but sacrilegiously rotated and shifted from one surface to the next, asymmetric but balanced by the weight of the color combination. All of this was part of his intent to break the perceived edges of the room, to oppose the container in an articulated struggle. Along the wall of windows were placed large angled mirrors that further skewed the correct definition of the architectural space.

Instead of a smoky dark nightclub all was light, bright and reflected. The redefinition of the dance hall transformed it into an alternative entertainment: a stage for the Dada performance. A few years earlier the van Doesburgs were connected to the artists of the raucous and cacophonous "Dada" movement and in 1923 entertained their guests Kurt Schwitters, Tristan Tzara, Raoul Hausmann, Hans Richter and Jean Arp with nightly performances of sound poems, lectures and alcohol. The evening's opening image, projected on the wall, was a painting showing a stage set with the abstract marionettes of Vilmos Huszár, an artist and De Stijl member.[18] And there, in center stage under a bright light, is the bachelor machine dancing his mad dance to the music of Schönberg, with the background strangely like the interior found at the Café Aubette.

Historic photograph of the mural *Cine-Dancing* by Theo van Doesburg at the Café Aubette, Strasbourg, 1927.

3: Symmetric Identities

TWA Terminal, New
York, Eero Saarinen,
1962. The building in
construction.

Gateway Arch,
Jefferson National
Expansion Memorial,
St. Louis, Missouri,
Eero Saarinen,
1948–1964.

The enthusiasm for structural shapes runs very high in American architectural schools; shell construction, folded slab, hyperbolic paraboloids [...]. Probing deeper into the different possibilities of these structures, one finds that they are not necessarily just athematical [...]. Each direction is just as logical, but one looks better than another [...]. One has a feeling of flight in it, another has a feeling of earth-boundness in it and the whole thing really becomes much more a problem related to sculpture than to mathematics. **Eero Saarinen**

Saarinen the Elder and the Younger

Father to Son, Artist to Architect, Building to Sculpture

A major transition in the way architects viewed art as part of their building's composition is illustrated in the mirrored images of the work of the two Saarinens.[1] What the father saw as a correct, consistent and orderly artistic path the son turned inside out by making each of his own works follow a different style and direction. The comparison between them shows the transition from one architect's use of art as a partner in reaching a visually unified environment to another architect's literal appropriation of art as a source of form.

For Saarinen the elder (Eliel), art was part of an entire surrounding culture. Eliel Saarinen was trained first as a painter and then advanced to be one of Finland's leading architects and designers in the period

between 1896 and 1923. At the start of his career Eliel believed that design could become a political gesture supporting the independence of Finland, then part of the western edge of Imperial Russia.[2] Rather than simply making a beautiful object, Eliel wished to create a total artistic environment, the *gesamtkunstwerk*. An entire movement, called National Romanticism, was the main aesthetic project for a number of artists and architects at the turn of the century. The various styles as shown in the English Arts and Crafts movement, the American Prairie School, the Catalan Modernista and the German Jugendstil are other localized examples of this approach. Though the artistic disciplines may have shared the same motifs, each maintained its separate and traditional identity: sculpture as the free-standing carved figure, painting as the

Such harmonization would not be
possible if it were not for the fact that,
in years of working together, the two
designers have become perfectly
attuned to each other. As both designers
are strongly individual, one cannot be
the subjective partner. The collaboration
is possible only because father and
son are in intellectual and spiritual
accord. **Albert Christ-Janer**

decorative wall surface, architecture
as the dominant enclosure and container.

For Saarinen the younger (Eero),
those classic divisions of the arts were
unnecessary, and in his time it would be
possible for the designer to use the formal
vocabulary of any of the arts. His buildings
borrowed directly any effect from the
current work of artists he knew, and
eventually his structures evolved to become
pure sculpture themselves. Eero, who came
to America at the age of thirteen, developed
in a different culture than his father's; he
was part of the explosion of wealth and
power in the post-war United States. At
that time there was a new confidence in
the achievements of American artists, as
seen in the drama of American Abstract
Expressionist painters seizing the mantle of
the avant-garde from Europe. For modern

architects/artists the hyper-competitive
American commercial culture required that
they move from the communal political
priorities of Europe (their real or symbolic
fathers) and produce a unique identifiable
style, in order to market themselves. Eero's
office was known for producing endless
alternatives of each scheme. The stated
purpose was to find the form that matches
the requirements of the program, but the
unstated reason was the desire for the
identity of the "new." With these forces
a building's form no longer derived from
functional or socially progressive needs
but reached more aggressive and irrational
shapes. Eero's work distorted and contorted
the logic of structure to become the
abstract expression of corporate branding,
media spectacle and advertisement for
the designer.[3]

Finding the Country Within a Poem

To elaborate first on the work of Saarinen the Elder, one can see that at the turn of the century, he struggled with the integration of sculpture in the buildings designed in his native Finland, while attempting to follow a simple metaphorical narrative. The Finnish National Romantic movement searched deep into the native culture to find a language they needed to assert their uniqueness. Buildings were inspired by vernacular barns, construction was achieved using native stones,[4] traditional crafts and weaving were resurrected and decorative motifs were derived from peasant handicrafts.

Yet not all of Eliel's projects were a successful integration between the vocabulary of a medieval peasant culture and a sophisticated twentieth century artist. The most famous example of this would be the 1900 Exposition Universelle Internationale building in Paris representing the then Grand Duchy of Russia: Finland. For all the acclaim of the building as a political gesture it is obvious this was as false a fantasy as its painted wood façade that simulated native Finnish granite. The asymmetric massing of the building is inspired by the work of the nearly contemporary American architect, Henry H. Richardson, rather than by any treasured archaic lodge.[5] Saarinen's main innovation was the exotic curved pinnacles wrapped by circles, a fertility symbol of both today and yesterday. The art on the interior walls was traditional without any transformation for the new era. The murals by Akseli Gallen-Kallela, based on the main folk epic of Finland, the *Kalevala* (the Tale of Heroes), are charming faux-primitive children's book illustrations. No wonder that this polite statement of political nostalgia was ignored by the Czar. What was Lenin doing at the time of this aesthetic revolutionary statement?[6]

What soon appears in later buildings by Eliel Saarinen is a much more innovative struggle with the integration of sculpture into architecture resolving to a deeper symbolism. I am referring to the repeated use of partially carved figures in the ornamentation of his buildings: Gargoyles and Grotesques emerge from balustrades, Stone Giants and Angelic Sprites are born out the stone piers of a façade.[7] The sculptural vision in these examples is of a symbolic force coming out of the past, liberated from its earthly bounds, a sculpture that is always being born and emerging from its monumental block. Although this technique was extensively used in the Art

Sculpture at proposed
Finnish Parliament
House, Eliel Saarinen,
1908 (unbuilt).

Pohjola Insurance
Company Headquarters
staircase, Helsinki,
Herman Gesellius and
Eliel Saarinen, 1901.

Emil Wikström sculptures at the entry of the Helsinki Railway Station, Eliel Saarinen, 1914.

Deco period[8] at this early time it was an effective transformative force that changed the building into an emotive political symbol. Freud used a specific term for the release of the internal pressure of vital needs: "Ananke" (the Greek word for necessity).[9] The psychoanalytic usage of this term covers a wide range of necessities and compulsions associated with human life but can also be used to label this condition of stone and wood.

An example of architecture as a political declaration through the use of Ananke sculpture would be the Pohjola Insurance Company Headquarters in Helsinki finished in 1901. Here Eliel and his partners again referenced the ancient epic poem of Finland, the *Kalevala*, first published by Lönnrot in

1849. The company's own name Pohjola (North) is an important theme in the *Kalevala*. The Pohjola Insurance Company's façade and its main stair is a collection of fantasy Ananke sculpture. Some have commented that "the staircase ornamentation represents the dangers and accidents that the insurance might provide relief for, the creatures are drawn directly out of the epic poem with names such as [...] Boil, Itch, Cancer and Plague."[10] These crude, playful and insulting characters are innovative in the synthesis of examples of vernacular carving, folklore narratives, client marketing and building design.

The same phenomenon can be seen in the double-paired massive stone colossi at Saarinen's Helsinki Railway Station entry,

1904–1919. Here an Ananke sculpture carved by artist Emil Wikström (who made a name for himself in his design of his own home, styled in the "native" Finnish manner) presents a more somber image of the national identity emerging out of the 1917 separation from Russia and the violent conflict within Finland during that civil war.

Cranbrook Academy
of Art, Museum and
Library, Bloomfield
Hills, Michigan, Eliel
Saarinen, 1942.

Site plan:
A Museum
B Peristyle
C Library
D Pool
E Studio Building
F Milles House
G Saarinen House
H Arts and Crafts
  Building

1 J. Mantynen,
  sculpture
2 C. Milles, Orpheus
  Fountain
3 Chinese lion dog
  sculpture (fifth
  century)
4 C. Milles, sculpture
  Europa and the Bull
5 C. Milles, Triton Pool
6 Eero Saarinen,
  ceramic relief
  sculpture
7 W. Aaltonen,
  sculpture
8 C. Milles, sculpture
  Running Deer
9 C. Milles, sculpture
  Sunglitter
10 C. Milles, sculpture
  Orpheus

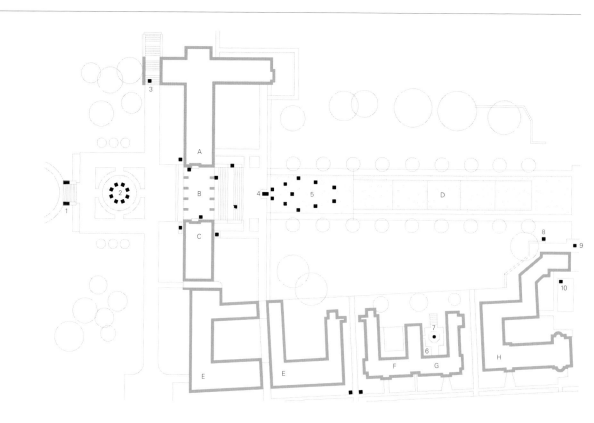

Helsinki to Chicago and Windsor to Detroit

When Eliel won second place in the Chicago Tribune Tower Competition of 1922 and brought his family to the United States, the idea of the integration of sculpture into the physical existence and moral fabric of the building was all but abandoned. The times had changed and explicit architectural ornament had been replaced by the austere modernism of the International Style. Now for Eliel the association of art was no longer an expansive political vision but instead one of a smaller world of the elite. In 1924 he was asked to participate in the development of a new educational community called Cranbrook by the Detroit Newspaper Publisher George S. Booth, who would become the main patron of Eliel's American career. Mr. Booth's vision of the

schools at Cranbrook was inspired by his dream of an idealized Anglo-Saxon private school. It eventually grew to include an artist colony that would be a place for the creation of quality art products (weaving, pottery and silversmithing were included at the beginning) and the education of young artists. Sculptures, murals, gardens, fountains and ornamental gates at the Cranbrook schools are meant to create a scenographic image of an idealized Eton, updated with a Scandinavian artistic sensitivity and better American plumbing.

For Eliel in America, art was no longer tied physically into the mass of his buildings, but he still tried to weave art into the fabric of the setting. Throughout the grounds of various schools at Bloomfield Hills and the Cranbrook Art Museum he scattered dozens of bronze statues by the resident Swedish artist Carl

Milles. Although the exact placement of the works was probably determined by Saarinen, Booth and Milles collectively, the arrangement still illustrated Eliel's new aesthetic. At the Art Museum entry the placement of eight elongated figures duplicating Milles' Orpheus Fountain in Stockholm set up a traditional image of the imperial forecourt fountain found in any European palace. From that point a single axis continued through the loggia of the museum to the long pool at the garden side with a duplicate set of Milles' Triton pieces. But then the simple axial arrangement fell apart and was replaced with a random, chaotic organization establishing the new order. This aleatoric sensibility is that of the Dyser (see page 58) or gambler: the desire to arrange an art asymmetrically in a way that still maintains loose visual ties to the building, landscape and other artwork.

Carl Milles, sculptures
at Orpheus Fountain in
Stockholm, 1935–1940.

Millesgården,
Stockholm, Carl Milles
and Evert Milles,
1906–1955.

Site plan with sculp-
tures by C. Milles:
1 *Dancer Girls*
2 *Jonah and the Whale*
3 *Orpheus*
4 Sculpture on
  C. Milles' grave
5 *Europa and the Bull*
6 Triton
7 *Sunglitter*

Time Will Tell If the Work is Good

Although there were other participating
artists at Cranbrook the majority of the public
artwork is by the sculptor Carl Milles. (The
line "Framtíd Må Visa om Verket Var Godt"
(Time Will Tell If the Work is Good) was
carved in stone at one of his statues.)[11]

Carl Milles was born on Midsummer's
Eve in 1875 and educated at Paris, in the
style of Rodin. He achieved renown for
his public sculpture in Sweden during the
1920s, and in 1931 moved to America at
the request of Booth and Saarinen. His later
work in America is extremely traditional and
characterized by his mannerist elongated
nudes and sets of aquatic sea creatures
suitable for his large public fountains. The
works are naked without being erotic,
stylized without being abstract, floating on
water or high on top of columns detached

from gravity and reality. For all appearances
they are expressionless and unemotive, like
a fable; to kiss the delicate child-like face
of bronze would both release its spirit from
sleep and condemn us into a trance erasing
the modern world.

Milles seemed to ignore all the work
of his contemporaries – Brâncuşi, Lipchitz,
Giacometti, Gonzalez, Moore and Picasso –
in a retreat from the ideals of abstraction.
A telling anecdote has Milles lecturing to
his students in a darkened room articulating
his points with a flashlight picking up details
from his collection of ancient Greek statues,
a dream-like image of a darkened world
closed in on itself.

Eliel Saarinen used the works of
Carl Milles at Cranbrook in a classic
"counterpoint" to the buildings of the
school. Milles' rounded shapes contrasted

with Eliel's flat walls, the sculpture's green
bronze patina opposed the yellow Mankato
limestone, standing as vertical accent
points (substitutes for Eliel's beloved towers
and chimneys) in the long low horizontal
courtyards. Eliel used art as a sign, beauty
as a marker, bronze figures as the ideal sole
inhabitants in an imaginary world.

Eero Saarinen, sculpture of vertical female nude, note artist standing in background, 1929.

Max Pollack, etching *Freud at his Desk*, 1914.

In his first description of the anal character Freud has said that certain neurotics present three particularly pronounced character-traits, namely, a love of orderliness which often develops into pedantry, a parsimony which easily turns to miserliness, and an obstinacy which may become an angry defiance. **Karl Abraham**

The Transfiguration of the Body of Architecture into the Spirit of Art

In talking about Eliel's son Eero, one must start with Eero's own education. Eero Saarinen had been drawing and designing in his father's studio in Finland since he was a child. Later, as a young man in America he produced designs for furniture, ornaments and sculpture for his father's buildings.[12] His formal art education extended to a year (1928–1929) at the open atelier studios in Paris of the Académie de Grande Chaumière.[13] Here his sculptures followed a surprisingly conservative direction: he focused on precise realist figurative portraits with an emphasis on craft ignoring any ideas from contemporary Parisian abstract artists. The first figures were almost totemic, simple and slightly archaic.

But Eero's artistic aspirations continued beyond his short lived formal art education. His office was famous for his "hands on" carving of large scale building models (larger than any of his sculptures), which he made not for client presentation but to better understand the exterior form, interior space and intersection of materials.

The first example of Eero's transference[14] of his love of sculpture to his building projects can be seen in the earliest of his major works: the General Motors Technical Center in Warren, Michigan, 1948–1956, a vast complex of long, low modern offices and laboratories grouped around an equally vast reflecting pool. The project had a number of participating artists: Alexander Calder designed a fountain for the pool,[15] Harry Bertoia fabricated a decorative metal screen for the cafeteria and the Russian born sculptor Antoine Pevsner produced a characteristic bronze sculpture, titled *Flight of the Bird*, of warped surfaces (delineated by a continuous series of articulated white lines) for the Design Building entrance.

The Pevsner piece was dramatically mimicked by a nearby lobby stair designed by Eero's office.[16] Located in the nearby Research Administration Building this spiral stair consisted of granite treads that radiated out from an open center, with both edges of the steps supported by vertical stainless steel rods. The central supporting rods started from a small circle in the floor and were then organized in an asymmetric angled manner that developed a surrounding form within the stair itself. The entire assembly of the floating metal tube handrails, the flying wedges of the steps and the asymmetric cage of the

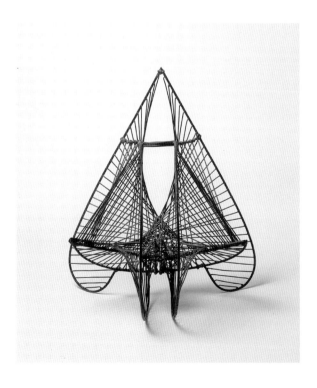

Antoine Pevsner, sculpture *Flight of the Bird*, in front of the Design Building at the General Motors Technical Center, Warren, Michigan, Eero Saarinen, 1956.

Spiral stair in the Research Administration Building at the General Motors Technical Center.

Antoine Pevsner, Constructivist sculpture *Maquette for the Construction of the World*, 1946.

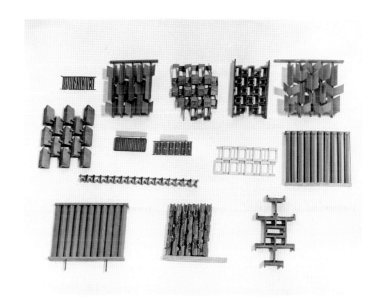

central supporting rods made an obvious Constructivist sculpture. It didn't matter which came first, the staircase design or the Pevsner piece. The assembly of the stair was directly related to the whole body of work by Pevsner and the Russian Constructivists.

Another example of Eero's interest in sculpture reflected in building design was the parallel development of the façade of Eero's US Chancellery in London with the series of decorative metal screens designed by his friend, the artist Harry Bertoia.

The Chancellery was built at the time (1955–1960) that American architects were adding to the simple glass boxes of the Miesian solution that dominated the 1950s. The desperate attempts to "humanize the box" without losing the established image of the modern object led to a fashionable solution of wrapping the building with all kinds of decorative metal screens, that acted both as a functional sun protection and an illicit nonfunctional decoration.

Eero studied endless alternatives of decorative grids for the London building. The rejected options were preserved in a photo that documents solution after solution. The final choice was developed as a series of load-bearing stone rectangular boxes that alternated in a grid that recessed one set and advanced the other from the front plane of the building. The arrangement mimics a similar composition that Bertoia created for many of his early metal screen sculptures.

The rectangular welded metal screens appeared in a number of Bertoia's commissions: the Manufacturers Hanover Trust Bank in New York for the architects Skidmore, Owings & Merrill, 1954, and in two projects for Saarinen: the previously mentioned General Motors Cafeteria screen, 1956, and another for the Dulles International Airport, 1962, in Washington, DC. In each case Bertoia created a playful effect by shifting two separate layers in an alternating rectangular pattern. The results gave an illusion of depth and an implied kinetic impulse by activating a simple repetitive grid format.

Harry Bertoia was born in Naples and immigrated as a child with his family to Canada and then to the Detroit area. He landed, by great luck, within a few miles from Cranbrook. A scholarship student, he met many of his future patrons, including Florence Shu (Knoll furniture) and Eero Saarinen, there in the open ateliers at Cranbrook. Bertoia crossed the typical boundaries in his art: his grid sculpture

Eero Saarinen and
Costantino Nivola at
model of Ezra Stiles and
Samuel Morse Colleges,
Yale University, New
Haven, Connecticut, circa
1960.

Harry Bertoia, sculpture
screen for Manufacturers
Hanover Trust Bank, New
York, Skidmore, Owings
& Merrill, 1954.

became Knoll furniture, his modular block prints were the basis for his rectangular wall sculptures, his vertical rod sculptures were developed into musical instruments.

The model study fragments from Eero's office show the transition from the idea of using a literal metal screen in front of the actual windows of the Chancellery to the development of the Portland stone façade into the "Bertoia" screen. The fusion of the artist's signature stylistic effect with the architect's façade is initially disguised by the fact that the building is composed of stone, not metal, and the two layers are collapsed into an alternating shallow recess. This mimicry went unnoticed at the time of the building's completion because of the distracting argument of how the façade pattern was an abstraction of the surrounding Georgian façades.[17]

One of the most obvious examples of this transfiguration of the body of a building into the spirit of sculpture was in the matching of the shapes and textures between the sculpture of Costantino Nivola and Saarinen's dormitory buildings for the Ezra Stiles and Samuel Morse Colleges at Yale University, 1962. The blending of the broken angular stone/concrete façades and the irregular angular cast concrete relief sculptures was so perfect that one could not find the artwork. It had melted into the wall and consequently the building, in a reciprocal exchange, had become a monumental version of the same sculptures.[18]

The documentary photograph of Nivola and Saarinen playing with the huge model of the colleges shows various other solutions they had considered. The location of both built and proposed art illustrates the way the

relief sculptures became a substitute for the articulated language of traditional masonry architecture. It is possible to see in the center of the photo Nivola's work crowning the top of the piers for the cafeteria in an explicit Palladian image. In other locations Nivola's angled concrete pieces are placed over doorways acting as a visual substitute for a keystone in a masonry arch. Elsewhere they are placed at the edges of walls where they duplicate the same articulation as quoins in a Neoclassically designed façade.

The photograph also shows, behind the designers, on the walls of the studio, the long continuous roll of Nivola's sketches. On that roll the sculptor's drawings of his proposed artwork shows an evolution of the studies from small items to large sculptures of human scale. The human figure returns in this project, not just for the sculptor but also

Entry lawn at the
Ezra Stiles and Samuel
Morse Colleges, Yale
University.

Ezra Stiles and Samuel Morse
Colleges, Yale University, New
Haven, Connecticut, Eero
Saarinen, 1962.

Site plan:
A Stiles College courtyard
B Master residence
C Dormitories
D Dining hall
E Morse College courtyard
F Entry lawn
G Retail building
H Existing building
I Central passage

1 C. Nivola, sculpture
2 C. Nivola, fountain
3 C. Nivola, fountain (unbuilt)
4 S. Johnson, sculpture
5 C. Oldenburg, sculpture

To paint a picture is art,
to hang it is architecture.
Eliel Saarinen

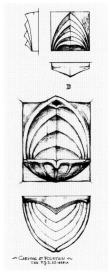

for the architect. The texture of the granite stones mottling the surface of the building's concrete walls matches the small pellets of clay molded by Eero as the young student in Paris when he created the mottled surface of his portrait busts.

The memory of the figure and the body remains until finally Eero creates a building that is a pure sculpture: the Trans World Airlines Terminal at JFK Airport (previously known as Idlewild) in New York.[19] The design problem came at a time when American architects were fascinated by thin concrete shell constructions as a means of spanning large distances to create an elegant warped surface. In this design Eero takes an idea of structural clarity and transforms it to its inverse: confusion, illogically placing a skylight opening where there should be major stress connections, sculpting the ground piers into massive arbitrary shapes, producing a hulking symbolic and willful form instead of a light floating, scientifically objective shape.

The TWA Terminal qualifies as an *architecture parlante*, a speaking building that communicates its function by its symbolic shape. The argument was that if the function of an airport structure is for the facilitation of flight movement it therefore should have a shape that recalls something of that action: a curved section of an airplane wing or the body of a bird. The TWA Terminal is the confused end of Eero's short career as an architect, for he tragically died in 1961 at the age of fifty-one. But it also stands as an audacious peak of his long career as a frustrated sculptor.

The Hall of Mirrors

The contrasting mirrored portrait of these two, the artist/architect and the architect/artist, Eliel and Eero, can be summarized in the opposition of two terms. One that stands for the Father is the *"Zeitgeist,"* figuratively translated as the "spirit of the age," it is meant to be the obvious, hard, definitive, singular direction of a culture, the one answer. It describes the historical definition of each time period as distinct and qualified, marching step by step into progress and the future. For the Son this is inverted so that the organizing idea could only be the *"Fiebertraum,"* literally translated as "fever dream" – it is both vision and illusion, which shows us another world, in which any answer is correct and suspect, tangible and elusive, shifting between physical and psychological. It is an image of a culture in flux, unstable and undefined. It is the hall of mirrors that we stand in today.

Two Doorways as Entries into Darker Places

The Art Museum at Cranbrook, 1938–1942, was the last major commission that Eliel Saarinen built at that school and it marks the transition in his architectural office from father to son. With the theme of this transition of power and the story of each architect's life it is possible to propose a "pathography" that explains two symbolic works of decorative art in the context of their buildings.

One of the psychologically most potent images of an assumed sublimated internal rivalry between father and son is the ornamented bronze door at the Cranbrook Art Museum. Here an abstraction of the architect's monogram, ES for Eliel Saarinen, was dramatically woven into the ornament of the door.[20] The development of this hieroglyphic symbol is extended to become an asymmetric decorative pattern on the ceiling of the loggia and down to the adjacent library door. Therefore the scribed lines in the exterior ornament are in reality all slightly altered signature symbols, as if the author/architect was constantly rewriting his signature, unconsciously obsessed in the labeling of this object in order to maintain authorship. The frustration is that both father and son have the same initials: ES. No matter how many times the ideogram is written it remains ambiguous. The name of this phobia, the fear of losing power to a son, can be called the Laius complex.[21] Laius, in the Sophocles drama, was the king and father of Oedipus and was warned by an oracle that his son would eventually kill him and conquer his kingdom.

Another door at Cranbrook leads to more observations on the theme of the unconscious conflict between father and son. At the kitchen door to the Eliel Saarinen home in Cranbrook is a small ceramic plaque by Eero mounted on the brick wall. At this back door to the family home (second best door for the second place architect) is the art piece which depicts a wresting conflict, in the mode of a Neoclassic drama, between two men, one standing and one seated.

The paired male wresting motif was repeated by Eero in his youth: in his grade school soap carvings, in his high school year book[22] illustrations and in his mosaic tile designs of athletes for a fireplace surround. The theme is obviously about the father/son conflict, but the intricate design is of more interest. There, in the shallow space described by the relief carving, the limbs of the two figures are graphically overlapped and intertwined. It is at this point that an analysis by Freud on a drawing by Leonardo da Vinci, *Madonna and Child with St. Anne*, is a useful comparison.[23] For Freud, the unrealistic weaving of the legs of the two women, Mary and her mother St. Anne, represents the confusion of identity of these two characters. In Freud's interpretation this is the key to understanding Da Vinci's emotional conflict. For here is the illustration of the two most important women in his life, his birth mother that he never knew and his adopting parent. But the women merge and dissolve to become one character at one moment and then transform into two in eternal conflict. At the Saarinen plaque there is a similar overlapping of the legs of the two characters, illustrating the ambition of the son wresting with the fame of the father.

The memories of most who knew them noted the respect and love between father and son, between Eliel and Eero, between the old world and the new. Yet, in the recesses of darker places another voice speaks out.

Kitchen entry at Saarinen House, Bloomfield Hills, Michigan, 1928–1930.

Ceramic relief sculpture of wrestlers by Eero Saarinen, 1928.

Drawing of wrestlers by Eero Saarinen, published in *The Baldwinian*.

Leonardo da Vinci (1452–1519), unfinished sketch *The Madonna and Child with St. Anne*.

Eliel Saarinen, bronze
entrance door at Cranbrook
Art Museum, 1942.

Cranbrook Art Museum
loggia and museum
entrance, 1942.

Monogram of Eliel Saarinen,
circa 1940.

Gambling on Controlled Chaos

The term "Dyser" is used here to describe the previously unnamed phenomenon of a scattered but controlled placement of art in a landscape. It derives from the Old English word for a dice thrower (also known as the "player," "shooter" and "joueur aux dés").[24] The random results of tossing dice across a velvet table relates directly to the Dyser's apparently disorganized arrangement of art pieces placed before us. The observed effect is asymmetric, random and chaotic, but like the game of chance, no matter how disorganized the system, it is still ordered by the arbitrary rules of play. For this phenomenon, that some label as "scatter art," there is always a tenuous order, a compositional friction, a story line that binds the scattered elements. In this metaphor the dice are loaded with the inevitable contradiction that the results are always a surprise.

The most obvious example of such a random arrangement is the artists's studio. Here the focused object of interest is floating within the creative debris of its inception. The sculptor Brâncuşi elaborately staged his work to create an arrangement with a dream-like visual density of comparable shapes and forms. He photographed them to freeze the constantly changing order for that one moment.[25] Brâncuşi, in this sense, was a Dyser, allowing chance, dirt, confusion, accidents, misalignments, whim and luck to enter into his choices.

It is possible to see this effect in a smaller scale. The mark of a Dyser can be found in the arrangement of the small antiquity collection of Sigmund Freud on his study desk in Vienna. The objects filled with symbolism, memories and metaphor crowd each other like a curious silent audience watching the Doctor writing his observations. They are a miniature landscape, an archeological excavation, a gaggle of ghosts and the precious playthings of a child. For the Dyser Freud these were a comfort and reference in the long journey to understanding.[26]

And of course the artist Carl Milles was a Dyser, but only at his Stockholm home studio "Millesgården" and not in his major public works. The contents of his studio were constantly assembled and disassembled. In the studio garden a stair directing you to slide past sculptures ends in a separate axis and then picks up with a grouping of others, which in turn frame the vista of yet another set down the path. The Dyser Milles is part narcissistic collector, insane architect, eccentric bricoleur, controlling parent and withdrawn intellectual orphan.

Because all the previous examples are private by nature, the Dyser could be considered pathological or indulgent. But there are the Saarinens who in two cases display themselves as Dysers par excellence. For Eliel this is the Cranbrook Art Museum and for Eero, the dormitory buildings of Ezra Stiles and Samuel Morse Colleges at Yale University. The Carl Milles sculpture at Cranbrook and the Costantino Nivola sculptures at Yale are pieces in a puzzle that rearrange the perception of interest and focus. They form small symmetric clusters and make tenuous visual connections across a courtyard to yet another set of pieces.

They fade from the foreground and scatter along our peripheral vision. The purpose is quite obviously a nostalgic recall of a culture that produced a total aesthetic vision, which of course ours is not. That is why the compositions of the Dyser Saarinen never climax in one great single unity between art and architecture, but always fray and fall away. The architect may control the loaded dice but history always has a surprise.

Freud's desk in Vienna with his arrangement of antique totem figures, 1938.

Millesgården in Stockholm.

Ezra Stiles and Samuel
Morse Colleges, Yale
University, New Haven,
Connecticut, Eero Saarinen,
1962.

Brâncuşi studio, Paris,
circa 1925.

4: Minotaur in the Labyrinth and Christ on the Cross

Fine art is not art in the true sense of the term until it is also thus free, and its highest function is only then satisfied when it has established itself in a sphere which it shares with religion and philosophy, becoming thereby merely one mode and form through which the Divine, the profoundest interest of mankind and spiritual truths of widest range, are brought home to consciousness and expressed. **G.W. F. Hegel**

Modern Artists and Architects in Post-War French Church Design

There existed in France, after the Second World War, a brief moment of public enthusiasm for a new artistic expression, a "Synthesis of the Arts," to represent the optimistic beginning of the new Republic where Marxists, Gaullists, capitalists, workers, intellectuals and the clergy could be united in peacetime as they were in the Resistance during the war. The community of French architects and artists were consumed by the fever of the ideal of the unified arts. In the late 1940s the editor of the magazine *L'Architecture d'aujourd'hui*, André Bloc, organized the "Association pour une synthèse des arts plastiques" for the unification of artists with architects and publicized another organization UAM, "Union des artistes modernes" that proposed the same idea. But before that, as a foundation to the movement, a few

key people in the Dominican Order of the Roman Catholic Church led an institutional change. They were given editorial control of the publication titled *L'Art sacré (Religious Art)* in 1937 whose battle cry of "Great men for great works," forcefully advocated the idea of using modern art in the world of their Church.

One of those men was Father Marie-Alain Couturier, who was originally trained as an artist and worked extensively in stained glass. Couturier, as an artistic advisor (called a "plasticien" for master in the plastic arts), was able to convince both sceptical church elders and avant-garde artists, on the importance of including modern art and modern architecture in the vocabulary of the Catholic Church. He was responsible for, or participated in, the three major works of the Sacred Art Movement: The Church

of Our Lady of Total Grace (Notre-Dame de Toute-Grâce) near the town of Assy by the architect Maurice Novarina in 1950, the Convent Chapel of the Rosary (Chapelle du Rosaire) in the Mediterranean town of Vence by the artist Henri Matisse in 1951 and the pilgrimage chapel titled Our Lady of the Heights at the village of Ronchamp (Notre-Dame-du-Haut) by the architect Le Corbusier in 1955.[1] The movement was short lived, for Couturier died in 1955 and the magazine L'Art sacré was shut down soon after. As an experiment, it was seen as an amazing success for the artists and a total failure for some at the Vatican. In 1952 as a response to the art in these churches an edict was formally announced from the Sacred Congregation of the Holy Office condemning the "corrupt and errant forms of sacred art" which "have found their way into our churches."[2]

These three churches, the objects of this analysis, are all linked by the same religion but are severely different in their respective interpretations of the unity of art and architecture: each has its own "Synthesis of the Arts."

The first building completed, Our Lady of Total Grace by the architect Novarina, is a nostalgic vernacular structure meant to establish a "neutral" environment for the traditional placement of unorthodox modern icons. The architectural design of the building is intentionally conservative in order to offset the politically disruptive effects of the radical art inside.

The second building, the Convent Chapel by the artist Matisse also produces a total work of art, but this time the hand of the artist excludes the architects: Brother Louis-Bertrand Rayssiguier, Auguste Perret and Louis Milon de Peillon. Matisse quite frankly admitted that he did not care about the space of the building; he was only interested in its "decoration."

The third and last building, the pilgrimage chapel at Ronchamp by Le Corbusier, is the climax of the career of a great architect. A striking, innovative set of alien shapes makes this church an exercise in pure sculpture, an object that is a total work of art unified by the architect's single hand. The arts of sculpture, painting and architecture are unified by the elimination of any competing artistic voices.

The limitations of the three methods are obvious: for the first the failure is in the

Beauty alone opens the
heart to the inexpressible.
Marcel Billot

clashing cacophony of too many voices,
each artist with a different style, a different
material and a different saint. For the
second and third designs to be successful
would require an individual with the talent
and ego of a Michelangelo. Even then the
achievement would be an atypical aberration
of the system which cannot be duplicated in
any meaningful way.

The theme of this chapter is about these
three modes of conflict and cooperation, one
with the architect as participant with fellow
artists, another with the architect as only
a technical support to the artist, and finally
with the architect as the complete artist.
How the designers and clergy engaged
in this crisis, was labeled at the time, the
"quarrel of the sacred arts" (querelle de l'art
sacré).

The Church of Our Lady of Total Grace

The Church of Our Lady of Total Grace at
the Plateau d'Assy would be considered the
first church in France which answers the
challenge of the Sacred Art Movement: "That
to keep Christian art alive, every generation
must appeal to the masters of living art."[3]

It functioned originally as a chapel to
the nearby tuberculosis sanatoria, where
the ill could pray to the saints who were
believed to have curing powers. The transient
nature of the parishioners explains how this
experiment with modern art met with no
initial resistance. It also explains the unusual
iconography of the stained-glass windows
by the various artists: Georges Rouault,
Jean Bazaine, Paul Berçot, Paul Bony and
Marie-Alain Couturier, which show a wide
collection of saints associated with the

sick: Saint Therese of Lisieux (who died of
tuberculosis), Saint Peter, Saint Louis (who
died of the plague), Saint Veronica (healed by
touching the hem of the garment of Christ) ,
Saint Joan of Arc (who helped the wounded),
Saint Vincent of Paul (who founded hospitals
for convicts), our Lady of the Seven Sorrows
and Saint Francis of Assisi (who helped a
leper).

The church was started in 1937 by the
architect Maurice Novarina and Canon
Devémy, with Couturier as collaborator. In
1939 an un-commissioned stained-glass
window designed by the artist Rouault,
Christ Mocked (Christ aux outrages), was
purchased for a built wall of the church and
became the first "miracle of Assy" when it
fit perfectly in the already finished opening.
Later Pierre Bonnard did the painting of Saint

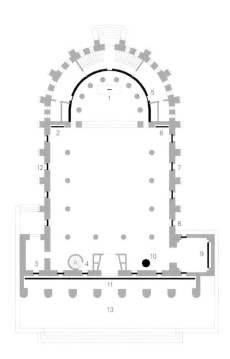

Preliminary sketch of the mosaic mural by Fernand Léger, *The Virgin of the Litanies*, 1946.

Entry portico of Our Lady of Total Grace with mosaic mural by Fernand Léger, *The Virgin of the Litanies*, 1949.

Our Lady of Total Grace, Plateau d'Assy, Maurice Novarina, 1950.

Ground floor plan:
1 G. Richier, crucifix
2 H. Matisse, tile mural
3 G. Rouault, window, *Saint Veronica*
4 G. Rouault, window *Christ Mocked*
5 J. Lurçat, tapestry *The Apocalypse*
6 P. Bonnard, painting
7 Various artists, window
8 M. Chagall, window
9 M. Chagall, baptistery mural *Crossing of the Red Sea*
10 J. Lipchitz, sculpture
11 F. Léger, tile mural
12 P. Berçot, window *Saint Francis of Assisi*
13 G. Braque, bronze plaque (original location)

Francis of Sales in 1943–1946. Artist Fernand Léger started the design for the mosaic on the façade in 1946. Georges Braque and Jacques Lipchitz worked on sculpture for the church in 1947 and then the rest of the artists followed: Henri Matisse submitted a tile mural of Saint Dominic, Marc Chagall produced a mosaic for the baptistery, Germaine Richier a bronze crucifixion for the altar, Jean Lurçat a vast tapestry above the altar, Jean Bazaine and others more stained-glass windows.

Quite obviously the building was completed first and the artists were fitted in at some later date. This makes the project not about collaboration but about becoming a laboratory for Couturier in experimenting with various artists and fitting them into the traditions and iconography of the Church.

Our Lady of Total Grace was finished with the artwork installed and consecrated on August 4, 1950.

Couturier's objective was to give complete freedom to the artists, but the problems of the artworks and the interior were immediately noted as "masterpieces pitted against each other in a space ill prepared to accommodate any one of them."[4] In the selection of artists there was no attempt to unify the materials used, the range of colors, the scale of the works, the themes of the images or even a consistent representation of religious symbols. The space between the individual artworks rarely allows clarity of the individual works themselves nor supports a dramatic juxtaposition.

In many cases it appears as if the artwork is a recent addition to an ancient structure:

this is true for the smooth Matisse tile mural at the end of the rough hewn granite arcade. Elsewhere, one finds the opposite and it seems as if a piece of historic artwork has been placed in a contemporary building: the medieval looking tapestry of Lurçat located in the curved apse of the church with its Art Deco ornamented woodwork. The most interesting and successful set pieces are the monumental exterior mosaic by Léger, *The Virgin of the Litanies (Litanies de la vièrge)*, and the five brooding stained-glass windows by Rouault.

The church by Novarina seems simplistic but its variation on the "vernacular" Swiss chalet image was seen by the architect as a way of expressing a contextual modesty. Couturier did not write about modern architecture in his publication *L'Art sacré*,

Henri Matisse, ceramic tile mural *Saint Dominic*, 1949, at Our Lady of Total Grace, with relocated relief sculpture by Georges Braque at lower center.

Interior of Our Lady of Total Grace with tapestry by Jean Lurçat, *The Apocalypse*, 1945, at the center and tile mural by Henri Matisse, *Saint Dominic*, 1949, at the left and mural painting by Pierre Bonnard, *Saint Francis of Sales*, 1943–1946, at the right; in the center at the altar is Germaine Richier's sculpture of *Christ on the Cross*, 1949.

but he did write about the "modesty of the past" embodied in the austere geometric Romanesque monasteries. Novarina's design for the church in Assy could have come out of the pages of the magazine with its ashlar stone construction, massive shed roof and simple geometric volume.

Its innovation, in working with the traditional Latin cross plan, is in the unusual juxtaposition of the massive stone colonnade placed parallel to the huge gable roof. This assembly emphasizes the massive mountain-like weight of the roof and gives a serial screening device that visually shatters the continuity of the mosaic behind. There have been many negative comments concerning the piers hiding the mosaic, but the resulting partial views through the columns correspond with the fragmented

floating images that are part of Léger's most famous series of paintings which he called *Objets dans l'espace*.

These paintings combined a series of common objects (keys, pipes, ropes) and recognizable human figures (the Mona Lisa, dancers, athletes) and abstract color fields in a reinterpretation of Cubist compositions. Here at Assy the face of the Virgin is centered and surrounded with blocks of bright colors such as red, blue, yellow, green and various symbolic motifs: the Tower of Ivory, Vessel of Honor, Morning Star, Ark of the Covenant, House of God and Gate of Heaven, all drifting across the surface of the wall in a multicolored puzzle-like pattern.

A comparison of the Léger mural in Assy, finished in 1949, with the ones the artist created for his own memorial museum, the

Musée national Fernand Léger, Biot, France, finished in 1960, shows how successful the Assy composition is. At the museum, the mural is part of a modern rectangular composition with the façade squared off and broken into discrete functional zones with windows of a corresponding size and shape. At Assy the mural and colonnade are locked in space with their imagery moving back and forth from the traditional figurative to the modern and from the recessed plane to the foreground. The combination and balance required in this aesthetic experiment reaches its best with the visitor's first image of the building.

The other successful translation of modern art into a modern ecclesiastical icon is Rouault's small stained-glass windows. It has been noted that Rouault's paintings,

Façade of the Musée
national Fernand Léger
at Biot, France, 1960.
Architect of preliminary
design: Paul Nelson,
architect of record:
André Svetchine.

Many are outside who believe
themselves to be within,
and many are within who believe
themselves to be without.
St. Augustine

with their broad brushstrokes surrounding figures, resemble church windows with the lead tracery already drawn. As a young man Rouault was trained in stained-glass restoration and that plus the influence of the German Expressionist movement had a bearing on the way he articulates his themes of sorrow and pain through line-work. The feeling of these windows is not the joyful bright yellows, pinks and reds of a medieval Gothic cathedral with its themes of redemption and salvation but the much darker, mordant and broken images of a suffering Christ. In Rouault's window at Assy, *Christ Mocked*, the composition and pose of the figure make it seem as heavy as the massive stone walls that surround it. The other stained-glass artists at the church, Jean Bazaine, Paul Berçot and Marie-Alain

Couturier, employ a decorative Cubism that simply did not match the seriousness and figurative power of Rouault's work.

Among all the different artists Léger and Rouault resemble each other in their partial fragmentation of the figure. Léger with his Cubist broken-field mosaic of whole but drifting objects matches Rouault with his isolated figures floating in chunks of glass and thick black outlines. Even the face of Saint Veronica by Rouault is similar to the face of Mary by Léger. The visual sympathy between these two artists could have guided the other participants to a more visually unified effect.

Unfortunately most of the other artists were dramatically unsuccessful. The crucifix by Germaine Richier is the most innovative religious work in the church but also the

most loudly rejected. It shapes a crudely textured drooping figure in the traditional pose of Christ on the cross, but without the cross. The figure seems suspended only by the force of will. Its general simplification is matched by the cross designed by Matisse in his convent chapel, but the Richier has some additional qualities. The sculpture's aggressive abstractness and texture gives a surprisingly emotive content which charges it with great power. Unfortunately its unique quality was not appreciated and the Bishop of Annecy personally removed the work from the altar to a more peripheral area.[5] This sculpture (called "an infamous profanation") and its relocation was the beginning of the attack on the modern art program (labelled "the Protestant plot against figurative art")[6] of the short lived Sacred Art Movement.

Georges Rouault, stained-glass window *Christ Mocked*, 1939, executed by Paul Bony, at Our Lady of Total Grace.

Paul Berçot, stained-glass window *Saint Francis of Assisi*, 1947, at Our Lady of Total Grace.

Stained-glass windows. I don't understand why the stained-glass window, which awoke and fell asleep in accordance with the passing of the day, was ever forsaken […] Art preferred its own light. But the stained-glass window – quickened to life by the morning and obliterated by the night – has brought creation into a church to make it one with the faithful. The stained-glass window finally yielded to painting when it welcomed the innovation of shadow – and died from it.

André Malraux

The distinction between "religious art" and "sacred art" is very important to the arguments presented here. The former is a general term used to cover any art with a spiritual direction, but the latter applies to art that is connected to the celebration of the liturgy in the Catholic Church. As such it must follow definitions and rules as determined by the hierarchy of the Church. For sacred art the emotive and visual qualities of the modern artistic styles were always subservient to the exacting qualifications of propriety.

That this building at Assy with its modern artwork was achieved at all is a triumph, for the innovation was not just artistic but political as it allowed atheists (Bonnard and Matisse), Marxists (Léger and Lurçat) and Jews (Chagall and Lipchitz) to participate and express their personal view of spirituality within the walls of the church. The building is a utopian ideal representing a France that could have existed, embodying the good will and unity born from the shared deprivations of the war. But the inherent conflicts of modern religious art appealing to a select few "connoisseurs" and sacred art required to satisfy the many "faithful" was the quarrel that Couturier's artists and architects could never resolve.

He is the artist, and it is only for himself that
he is able to make the terrific effort in order
to emerge from the darkness.
Le Corbusier

Interior of Our Lady
of the Heights.

Pilgrimage chapel Our
Lady of the Heights,
Ronchamp, France,
Le Corbusier, 1955.

Ground foor plan:
1 Enamel metal door
2 Painted and tinted
   glass windows
3 Crucifix and
   tabernacle
4 Historic sculpture
   Virgin with Child,
   seventeenth century

Exterior of Our Lady
of the Heights.

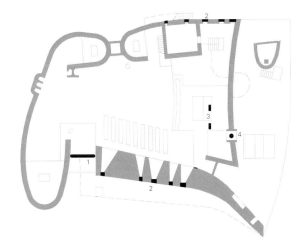

The Pilgrimage Chapel Our Lady of the Heights

The chapel of Ronchamp is undoubtedly one of the great buildings of the modern era; it was designed by the Swiss/Parisian architect Le Corbusier (the artist pseudonym for Charles-Edouard Jeanneret) who is considered the master architect of the twentieth century. However, it contradicts the basic principles of modern architecture as defined by Le Corbusier himself.

The chapel has been analyzed extensively from a number of different viewpoints: for its illustration of the architect's personal mythology and symbolism,[7] in its distortion of his theoretical spatial types,[8] in metaphors for the ancient and primitive[9] and as a rejection of the machine aesthetic in a "crisis of rationalism."[10] To investigate the composition of the art and the building

this study will not treat the church as a part of Le Corbusier's architectural work, instead it will look at it as the climax of his alternative career as an artist. The interaction between art and architecture in this case is based on two ideas, the first being the free interchange of abstract principles between the art forms[11] and the second the use of painting as a testing ground for experiments in architectural form.[12]

Le Corbusier once said that he efficiently organized his day by painting in his studio in the morning, working in his office on architecture later in the day and writing poetry, when he could do neither of the first two, while traveling in an airplane.

He started his formal artistic career linked with the painter Amédée Ozenfant and their self-proclaimed style of Purism announced to the world in 1918. This simplified and

"purified" the decorative direction of the relatively new style of Cubism created by Pablo Picasso and Georges Braque. Two elements of the Purist work overlapped and influenced the world of architecture. The first was that the artists should limit themselves to painting only still life arrangements with a carefully selected set of common manufactured objects (glasses, bottles, carafes, guitars, books, pipes, etc.) which they called *Les objets-types*, and the second was the spatial implications of flattening the objects by showing them in both plan and elevation, as if they had been unfolded at the top by an imaginary hinge, while creating depth in the canvas by making multiple parallel shallow layers of these same elements into a "Cubist Space."

How do those elements resurface in Le Corbusier's architecture? The first idea was

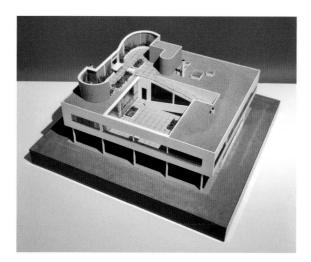

Model of Villa Savoye, Poissy, France, Le Corbusier, 1929.

Painting by Amédée Ozenfant *Still Life. Dishes*, 1920.

Le Corbusier at his painting studio, circa 1955.

that the selection of the objects *(objet-types)* for the paintings was directly connected to elements *(element-types)* in the "new" modern architecture. The mass-produced unadorned tableware had the same simple geometric shapes and mechanical finishes of the metal spiral stairs, glass skylights and slender cylindrical columns (labeled *pilotis*) that were used in making modern buildings.

In the second idea, the clarification of Cubist space by Purism was applied by Le Corbusier to the plan organization of his early modern houses. The essay titled "Transparency"by Colin Rowe and Robert Slutzky describes the appropriation of an ideal in painting to a working principle in architecture. Later Bernard Hoesli produced two diagrams that illustrated the essay in the book of the same title. Here the Villa Stein at Garches, 1927, by Le Corbusier is

shown abstractly in an axonometric drawing as being organized as a series of frontal rectangular planes, which loosely layer the space that the occupant walks through. This is then compared to a painting by Le Corbusier, *Still Life,* 1920, which is dissected in a similar way to show the same layers of Cubist space.[13]

A simpler analogy can be made between the composition of one of the Purist paintings by Amédée Ozenfant and the reuse of similar forms in Le Corbusier's modern house, the Villa Savoye from 1929. This free-standing suburban house is a one-story rectangular volume raised off the ground by a series of thin cylindrical columns which resembles, in another scale, a traditional table supported by thin furniture legs and providing a surface for the rooftop collection of curved shapes

and angled forms. The building's roof is the tabletop holding the material for a Purist still life as seen in a similar painted example by Ozenfant titled *Still Life. Dishes* of 1920. The canvas acts both as the table of the painting, on which various objects are displayed, and as the roof of the villa; the neck of the guitar can be seen as the central ramp, the bottle necks appear like exhaust chimneys, the multiple curving profiles of the guitar and carafe add up to the curved rooftop windscreen, while the flattened-out drinking glasses act as the large glass skylights.

But sometime after the economic depression, in the 1930s, Le Corbusier became disenchanted with his imaginary technological utopia and became interested in other ideas about form. The smooth machine finish was replaced by rough natural textures, the grid became dominated

I am only known as an architect,
people will not recognize me as a
painter, and yet it is by way of my
painting that I came to architecture.
Le Corbusier

In reality, the key to my artistic
creativity is found in the work
I began as a painter in 1918
and which I pursued regularly
every day. Le Corbusier

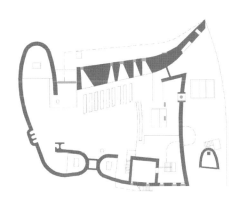

by the human figure and a new set of
objects became important *objets à réaction
poétique*: stones, shells, bones, ropes and,
most importantly, the female nude. Although
there is no label for this new polemical style
(Pantheism replacing Purism) it does follow
the lead of other contemporary painters as
Fernand Léger and Pablo Picasso.

The new shapes in the paintings became
the vocabulary tested out again and again
in the plan developments for his buildings.
We can compare the multiple curves in
plan (mirrored for ease in analysis) of the
chapel at Ronchamp, consecrated on June
25, 1955, with a post-Purist painting by Le
Corbusier titled *Icône*, 1950,[14] and see a
range of similarities. The head of the figure in
Icône corresponds to the main curved light
apse volume in the church. The church's large
curved west wall from the combined head/

apse to the paired half cylinders opposite
is matched by the asymmetric blue curved
block at the left of the painting (representing
the back of the chair for the seated figure).
The paired forms making a building entry are
parallel in shape to the interlocking heads
in the center of the canvas. The model in
the painting lounges in an odalisque pose
and her body spreads out to the right as a
curved block much like the main volume of
the church extends out to the west curved
façade.[15]

This is not to say that the drawing *Icône*
is the basis of the building's plan (although
drawn at the same time as the building
was developing) or that the chapel is subtly
reminiscent of a woman's form (although not
inappropriate for a chapel dedicated to the
Virgin Mary, Queen of Heaven) but that Le
Corbusier's artistic work was the basis for

the experiments with and compromise of
drawing forms and their later interaction and
manipulation in architectural plans. The unity
or synthesis of arts was in the most basic
similarity of all art forms, the drawing of a
line in space.

The pilgrimage chapel at Ronchamp is
obviously the result of a singular vision in
which all the elements: the entrance door
mural, the recessed painted windows,
the curved side chapels, the startling
monumental exterior form and the mystical
interior space are all united. But for a religion
with a shared and specific iconography the
building's forms and symbolism are highly
personal and strangely opaque.

One of the central tenets of Christianity
is that the suffering of Christ, the son of God,
and his death is a sacrifice to atone for the
sins of mankind. There is a parallel myth of

Detail of enamel metal entry door of Our Lady of the Heights, Ronchamp, France, Le Corbusier, 1955. In his design for the metal entry door Le Corbusier noted his admiration and inspiration by the French medieval altarpiece of Boulbon, originally located in the Chapel of Saint-Marcellin and moved to the Louvre in 1904. The asymmetric placement of figures in the generally symmetric painting can be seen as describing various hidden geometric lines (golden ratio) and figures (pentagons). And the isolation of religious icons matches nicely the vocabulary of isolated Cubist objects in Le Corbusier's design.

Altarpiece of Boulbon: *Christ Bleeding*, circa 1450.

A work of art is a game. One sees the rules for one's own game. Then it is necessary that these rules are seen by those who wish to play as well.
Le Corbusier

the modern avant-garde artist as a prophet-like figure who stoically struggles against society for a greater truth through his work only to be rejected in his own time.[16] Le Corbusier identified with this struggling artist image and used several autobiographical avatars to place himself within his symbolic paintings, the Crow, the Donkey, the modular shadow figure and the Minotaur.

The Minotaur is the mythological creature with the head of a bull and the body of a man who was feared and isolated in a labyrinth by the people at Crete. It is a symbol used by Picasso to represent himself and evoke animal eroticism, but also to show his isolation. Le Corbusier's *Taureaux* series of paintings on the Bull/Man are in their own way a coded message by the artist and a variation of the same theme of sin and

sacrifice that we can see in the story of Christ, the anointed. This example shows one of many personal allegories that need to be penetrated to lead out of the labyrinth of symbols.

We may never completely understand the entire symbolic meaning of the building at Ronchamp, but we can still be moved in its presence and experience the sensations of inward mediation and outward aspiration through the architecture, an achievement that can match those of the greatest medieval cathedrals.

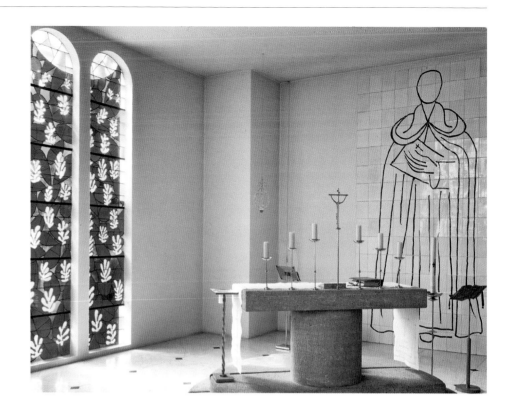

[The drawing] has got to be done
blind, with my whole heart.
Henri Matisse

The Convent Chapel of the Rosary

The Convent Chapel of the Rosary is a
building beloved and praised by numerous
writers, but the adulation connected to the
last major work of the great artist Henri
Matisse prevented most from seeing it
critically.[17] The sad reality is that the building
is an indulgence of an old man, eighty-two
at the completion, who was far removed
from the physical skill and ability to produce
a work of art and architecture that is a
coherent statement let alone a great work.
Like Picasso, who in his later years was
trapped in his fame, there was no critical
voice that could engage the artist concerning
the ideas or composition of his work.
For Matisse that voice could have been
the ignored associate architect Auguste
Perret[18] – but it wasn't.

Matisse is certainly one of the giants of
modern painting. His contribution has been
summed up as "the synthesis of line and
color."[19] From his start as part of the group
of painters labeled the *Fauves* (wild beasts)
in 1910 to his studies in colored paper cutouts in the 1940s he has been an innovator
with paintings of calculated theatricality and
complicated color schemes.

The history of the chapel begins with
a young nurse, Monique Bourgeois, who
helped Matisse through his recovery from an
intestinal cancer operation; she would later
become a model for the artist and after they
parted she went on to take religious vows
and become a Dominican nun. The twist
in the story is that in 1946, the now Sister
Jacques-Marie was stationed in a convent
near the artist's studio in Vence in the South

of France. The re-acquaintance of the two
friends, along with some of the first floor
plans by the monk Brother Louis-Bertrand
Rayssiguier, engaged Matisse into the four-
year process to design and decorate a new
chapel for the convent.

The chapel was consecrated on June 25,
1951, and is a simple one-story structure
with its exterior dominated by its blue
tile gable roof, white washed walls and
arabesque metal bell tower. The interior
consists of a single volume in an L-shaped
plan 6 meters across, with 5-meter-high
flat ceilings; the L-plan allows for a break
in the room that creates a special transept-
like area of pews for the nuns. The artist
has decorated the room in three areas: the
stained-glass windows, the painted ceramic
tile murals and the priest's vestments.

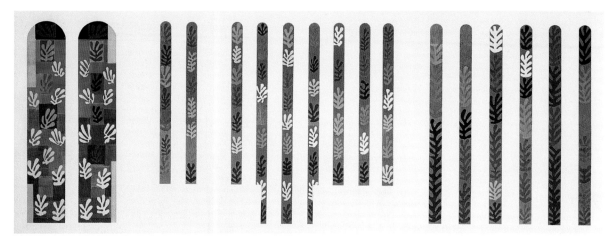

Henri Matisse, colored paper study with philodendron leaves for chancel stained-glass windows, 1949.

Henri Matisse, study for the Stations of the Cross, 1949.

What interests me is to give space and light to a place that is characterless in itself.
Henri Matisse

The effect of the interior has been mystically described by the Dominican Father Couturier: "It is idle to hope that words or pictures could evoke the atmosphere created there silently, by the whiteness of the walls, the pure colors, the noble proportions."[20]

Matisse produced numerous design studies and models with incredible energy for a man with his age and poor health, but the mere fact that the project was completed does not mean it is a total success. The failures of the chapel are first in the articulation of the space of the room, second in the graphic composition of the murals and third in the iconographic images.

As the project developed, Couturier was engaged and later, by Matisse's choice, the famous architect Auguste Perret. Perret came from a family of contractors and was an innovator in concrete construction and designed one of the first modern churches in France, Notre-Dame du Raincy in 1922. Unfortunately Matisse's way of collaboration with Perret was to eliminate elements that did not suit the artist. Matisse eliminated the architect's proposed vaulted ceiling, he eliminated the architect's proposed stone façade, he eliminated the architect's proposed louver sunscreen. As the design progressed the building became smoother, simpler and less articulated. For the interior the restricted palette of materials, glass, ceramics, marble and plaster, establishes that all surfaces are smooth, hard and glossy. The building became a blank canvas with space only for the artist.

The three wall murals are of Saint Dominic, the Virgin and Child, and the Stations of the Cross. All are simple black line drawings on a layout of square white glazed ceramic tiles set flush to the wall. They were produced after numerous studies and the final images were quickly made in a single setting by Matisse drawing on the assembled blank tiles with a charcoal stick extended on a long bamboo pole. The disconcerting reality is the extremely crude draftsmanship that seems even more surprising when contrasted with the simple but elegant penultimate studies. According to Matisse this development resulted from his decision on how he wanted to compose the room. The large thick black-line drawings were intentionally reduced to the simplest possible elements and non-colors so as to allow the smaller colored glass windows on the opposite walls to dominate the room. The idea is similar to the graphic design of the book *Jazz* that was done by Matisse;

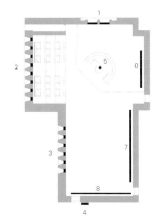

Ground floor plan:
1 Chancel window
2 Nun's window
3 Window *Tree of Life*
4 Stoup
5 Crucifix
6 Tile mural *Saint
   Dominic*
7 Tile mural *Virgin and
   Child*
8 Tile mural Stations
   of the Cross

I should be very comfortable saying my
prayers in your studio, indeed more
comfortable than in many churches.
Brother Louis-Bertrand Rayssiguier

there on one page is the arabesque black-line writing and on the opposite page the colored paper cutouts. The obvious problem is that the simplified images made by Matisse present religious icons without faces, an extreme contradiction. This fact along with others gives a feeling of incompleteness in all three of the murals, as if we were in the artist's studio waiting for the process to continue.[21]

The stained-glass windows utilize another technique that Matisse had developed when his health no longer allowed him to hold a paint brush steady. He cut pre-colored sheets of paper with scissors in a motion with his wrist and arms. Those paper cutouts *(gouaches découpées)* were moved around a background sheet until the composition was deemed correct. The chapel windows were designed as tall thin arched openings filled with color forms based on the paper cutout studies. The theme of the work is the *Tree of Life (L'Arbre de vie)* showing shapes of simplified leaves and cactus flowers in three basic colors: blue, green and a background of yellow. The windows were extremely innovative for their time, but looking at them now it seems that the subject is almost pantheistic and totally unrelated to the iconography of anything else in the room.

Matisse noted some of these problems,[22] but there is always the counterargument that the artist had never intended to make a great unification of art and architecture but merely a calm and attractive place for an introspective moment during the celebration of the mass: "I want those who will come into my chapel to feel purified and relieved of their burdens."[23]

But it is also possible to see that Matisse may have been proposing something more symbolic. The photos of the artist's large studio in the Hotel Regina show the full size mock-ups of the chapel artwork as one part of a continuous decoration of the studio itself. This would explain the discordant flat ceilings of the chapel, for they are the same as his studio. It would also clarify the strange location of the door interrupting the chapel's south mural, for it comes directly from the studio layout. The botanical motif for the chapel windows can be seen as further studies of Matisse's own large philodendrons. The chapel and studio were further tied together when the artist's favorite chair was reproduced for the Priest's chair at the altar. That same altar's unusual rotated position comes directly from the 45-degree-angled table used by Matisse in

Interior of the Convent Chapel of the Rosary showing the *Tree of Life* stained-glass windows and convent pews.

Man becomes aware of the sacred because it manifests itself [...] as something wholly different from the profane [...] a reality that does not belong to our world, in objects that are an integral part of our natural "profane" world.
Mircea Eliade

Dieu c'est moi.
Henri Matisse

Portrait of Matisse with pole, 1949, working on the mural for the Convent Chapel of the Rosary.

Germaine Richier, sculpture *Christ on the Cross*, 1949, Our Lady of Total Grace.

Le Corbusier, sculpture *Christ on the Cross*, 1955, Our Lady of the Heights.

Henri Matisse, sculpture *Christ on the Cross*, 1950, Convent Chapel of the Rosary.

his study. The clean open image of the chapel matches the way Matisse had organized his own studio, now that he had given up easel painting. And most dramatically, the great struggle of Matisse to return back to life and work after his operation occurred in another studio with Monique, certainly in its own way the story of a resurrection.

That the Convent Chapel of the Rosary can be seen as the construct of the artist's studio would not necessarily be sacrilegious. For Matisse the "Studio" was the center of the world of worship that he knew best; full of the great struggle for creation, beauty and eternal life.

Conclusion

In summary, the range of experimentation in these three chapels could be seen as the impossible task of uniting the arts in transforming the profane modern object to serve the eternal sacred experience. The reality that most of the artists were nonreligious does not limit the importance of what was produced. Rarely has the entire range of cooperation and composition between modern artist and modern architect been tested so thoroughly. The very fact that these examples are considered as failures by many in the Roman Catholic Church only makes their relevance to this study, of the artistic struggle in public art, more important.

Our Lady of the Angels in Twenty-First Century Los Angeles

As a representative of the most recent work in the Roman Catholic Church the Cathedral of Our Lady of the Angels in Los Angeles, California,[24] is an example done with taste, intelligence and a generous budget. The project illustrates the realities of what is currently acceptable for art to display in a church and what is not; although the final product is amazing in its scale and refinement it has not gone without the inevitable criticism.

The church in its art program, defined by Father Richard Vosko, a liturgical design consultant, selected artists to present a multicultural image for the diverse ethnicity of the city congregation. The selection process completely avoided any comment on abstraction in the arts. All the artists selected had a background in realist artworks that was rigorously reviewed during stages of production. As gently noted by Vosko: "It is seldom an advantage to give the artist a completely 'free hand' in creating something for a worship environment."[25] It is only within a narrow range of image, iconography and materials that the artists were able to maneuver for approval. In my opinion out of the total of eleven artists working on the project only two reached a level of interest and integration with the building while still producing acceptable "devotional art."

The Cathedral building is a symmetric plan containing a central worship space with side aisles, niches and chapels giving an easily familiar pattern to negotiate. In contrast with that conservative organization the architect, Rafael Moneo, has placed the main entry, stairs and windows in asymmetric locations, thereby producing a more contemporary massing and exterior image. The building is a container for the artworks and is itself an example of innovative efforts within a conservative range of options.

The most prominent works of art, in scale and cost, are the bronze entry gates and raised figure of the Virgin Mary by the sculptor Robert Graham. The Los Angeles artist is renowned for his hyperrealist sculptured nudes that display a distinct distortion by enlarging the figure's head, hands and genitals slightly out of proportion to the whole body.[26] How the highly sexually charged work of this artist is adjusted to be usable in the cathedral and integrated into the building proceeds from two points: 1. The figure is clothed with the modest innovation of eliminating traditional sleeves and headdress. 2. The entry is off-center from the axis of the nave and slipped from the main mass of the structure allowing it to command a smaller building volume.

On the interior of the church, the twenty-five tapestries depicting the *Communion of Saints* by the artist John Nava were woven with a photographic realism, a nubby texture and a sympathetic color pallet that makes the works meld into the nave's concrete walls. They exist as a set of substitute stained-glass windows:

Exterior of cathedral Our Lady of the Angels.

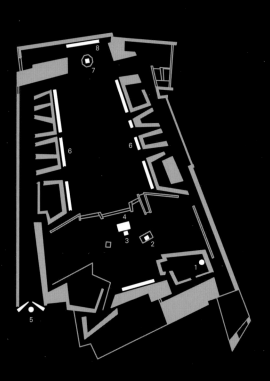

Cathedral of Our Lady of the Angels, Los Angeles, Rafael Moneo, 2002.

Ground floor plan:
1 M. DeMoss, tabernacle
2 J. Tortorelli, bishop's chair
3 S. Toparovsky, sculpture *Red Crucifix*
4 M. Snowden, altar
5 R. Graham, sculptures
6 J. Nava, tapestry *Communion of Saints*
7 R. Vosko, baptismal font
8 J. Nava, tapestry, *Baptism of the Lord*

Interior of cathedral with tapestries by John Nava.

John Nava, detail of tapestry *Communion of Saints*.

Robert Graham, sculpture *Virgin Mary* and the main bronze doors entry to the Los Angeles Cathedral.

recognizable images of 135 saints and "blessed ones" instructive to a congregation with non-English speaking immigrant members. The value of the work is the transformation of photographs of contemporary adults (some developed as watercolor) to scanned images for the production in computerized looms. The mythology of the icon figure is dislocated by the obvious "from-the-street" faces and the disjunction of having a tapestry where a window should be. The range of innovative technology, images and placement is made acceptable by the direct educational symbol of each saint as a realistic figure (all walking towards the altar), duplicating the historic function of medieval liturgical arts.

The art pieces in Our Lady of the Angels struggle to free themselves from the definition of sacred art. To find an artist who has produced innovative and provocative art with the iconographic narrative and symbols of the church it is necessary to go to the artist Robert Gober and his infamous *Untitled* installation work displayed at the Geffen Contemporary Gallery at MOCA (The Museum of Contemporary Art) in Los Angeles in 1997.

The large scale mixed media assembly by Robert Gober is an alternative vision of the realistic iconography of the Church in a mystical environment by the artist. Each piece of the imaginary chapel has been hand-built from scratch in an obsessive devotion. In the center of the window-less room is what appears to be a standard mass-produced plaster statue of the Virgin Mary seen in every Catholic church in America with a 1.8-meter-long metal culvert pipe running perpendicular to her abdomen and creating a 30-centimeter-wide opening in the figure. On both sides is an open suitcase and in the rear is a staircase with a fountain rushing water down its steps. All of the four elements have a base of an enlarged bronze drain cover with a recessed seascape diorama below the floor level.

The violence of the pierced body is dramatic, shocking and at first glance blasphemous. But in closer analysis it is possible to see an acute vision of the Church by one of its outcast members. The delicate piercing of Mary by celestial light or angelic arrows is part of the painterly tradition in Renaissance Annunciation

paintings.[27] Here the large pipe refers to that piercing and connects to the symbolic context of the visitation of Mary by an angel but in a violent manner inspired by the Readymades of Duchamp (a Virgin Dynamo?) connecting to the deep personal debate of the artist and his conflicted belief in Church. The pipe is also part of the water imagery used throughout the space which in itself is a symbol of cleansing, baptism and rebirth. The central figure exists as both an optimistic view of redemption and an embittered feeling of the void.

The Gober installation (or chapel?) could only exist in a private gallery, and it is tragic that the aesthetic distance separating the expression of faith in the twenty-first century from its most fascinating and talented artists is too large a gap to imagine ever closing.

Robert Gober, installation *Untitled*, 1997, permanently installed at the Schaulager, Basel.

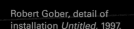

Robert Gober, detail of installation *Untitled*, 1997,

Aerial photo of
Rockefeller Center,
New York, Raymond
Hood, 1931–1939.

Andy Warhol, *Nelson
Rockefeller*, 1972.

It was the perfect combination.
The three women among them had
the resources, the tact and the
knowledge of contemporary art that
the situation required. More to the
point, they had the courage to
advocate the cause of the modern
movement in the face of widespread
division, ignorance and a dark
suspicion that the whole business
was some sort of Bolshevik plot.
**Nelson Rockefeller on the founding
of the Museum of Modern Art**

Nelson Rockefeller, His Artists and His Architects in the Definition of Art in the American Public Realm

Nelson Aldrich Rockefeller (1908–1979)
was one of the third generation of wealthy
descendants of patriarch John D. Rockefeller
Senior, founder of the Standard Oil Company.

He was one of the most dynamic of the
five grandchildren of John D. His activities
in commerce ranged from farming in Venezuela to real estate in New York City. His
achievements in politics ranged from the
Governorship of New York State to his
appointment as Vice President of the United
States. His personal interests and investments
were also diverse but his most focused
involvement was with the world of art.

It is his involvement in that world which
is most important for the way the strange
and alien vision of modern art was extended,
and limited, in America and how that vision
intersected the public world of wealth,
museums and architecture.

Domestication of the Modern

Nelson Rockefeller often referred to the
Museum of Modern Art as "Mother's
Museum" (MoMA sounding very closely
to mama) and with that familiarity the
image of modern art was forever altered.
For in America, the illustration of class
difference is always whitewashed as
merely a (temporary) level of distinction
in taste, education or money. And the
presentation of modern art in America has
always been whitewashed by the clean
gallery spaces of MoMA to be something
that it was not.

Abby Aldrich Rockefeller (Nelson's
mother) was one of the three forceful
women who founded MoMA in 1928
and it is obvious that an imprint of her
family's character exists, even today, in
that institution:

Nelson Rockefeller with
Isamu Noguchi in 1942
at Rockefeller Center.

Nelson Rockefeller
with Frida Kahlo in
Mexico City, 1945.

Nelson Rockefeller
with Naum Gabo in
1970 at Time & Life
Building, New York,
Wallace Harrison, 1959.

Nelson Rockefeller with
Wallace Harrison in
1975 at Empire State
Plaza, Albany, New York,
1978.

a Baptist missionary spirit matched
to a Calvinist cleansing order;
a patrician's generosity combined
with a parent's necessity for control;
an aesthete's desire for beauty contrasted
to an American's fear (fantasy) of sex.

One of the most direct criticisms of
America's, and the world's, finest modern
art collections is that MoMA (exemplified by
its first director Alfred Barr) has taken the
vast variety of expressions of contemporary
artists and reduced them to stylistic
simplicities, ironed out the wrinkles, covered
up the anger and disguised the politics.

The first question one must ask is why
would the obvious representatives of the
ruling class in America devote so much
effort to the production and enshrinement of
radical and often abrasive new art forms?[1]

Many of the easel paintings collected
by Abby and the other founders were at a
simple level not very pretty in the traditional
Edwardian sense. They were involved with
austere spatial ideas, Georges Braque,
or with metaphysical beliefs, Wassily
Kandinsky, or with the violently erotic,
Pablo Picasso. There were many other safer
avenues of aesthetic and cultural interest
to follow: collecting ancient oriental vases,
Chippendale furniture and the patriotic
American folk art.

Why did the Rockefellers nevertheless
collect modern art? One possible answer
is the power of the specific taste of one
person: Abby directing her sons. Another
possibility would be the redefinition of power
in the second and third generation of wealth
in the Rockefeller family. By being entirely
new, modern art around 1900 became a

cultural and philanthropic area where a few
could exert an immense amount of power
and control, and be associated with values of
status and esteem.

Americans are constantly reinventing
culture and status, not by overthrowing
the existing order but by inventing new
and different strata to the layer of human
connections and competition. If the rising
class of new wealth in New York City was
excluded from the existing opera house
or any established private club then the
solution, quite simply, was to construct a
new opera house or private club.

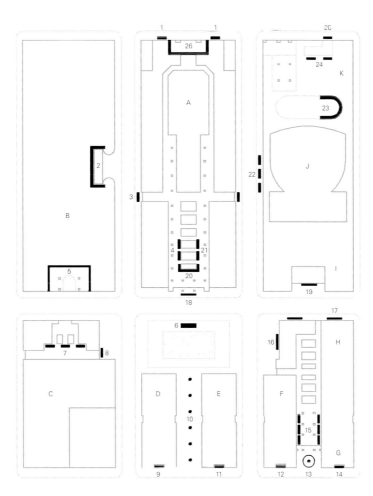

I've never believed in God,
but I believe in Picasso.
Diego Rivera

Rockefeller Center, New
York, Raymond Hood,
1931–1939.

Site plan:
A RCA Building
B 10 Rockefeller Center
C One Rockefeller
   Plaza
D La Maison Française
E British Empire
   Building
F Palazzo d'Italia
G International
   Building North
H International
   Building
I Associated Press
   Building
J Radio City Music
   Hall
K 1270 Avenue of the
   Americas

1 G. Lachaise,
   sculpture *Aspects
   of Mankind*
2 S. LeWitt, mural
3 L. Friedlander, mural
   Transmission
4 José Maria Sert,
   mural *American
   Progress*
5 D. Cornwell, mural
   Transportation
6 P. Manship, sculpture
   Prometheus
7 C. Milles, sculpture
   Man and Nature
8 L. Lawrie, sculpture
   Progress

9 A. Janniot, sculpture
   Friendship
10 R. Chambellan,
   sculpture *Fountain-
   heads*
11 C. Jennewein,
   sculpture *Industries*
12 G. Manzù, sculpture
   Immigrant
13 L. Lawrie, sculpture
   Atlas
14 A. Piccirilli, sculpture
   *Youth Leading
   Industry*
15 M. Ihara, sculpture
   Light and Movement
16 L. Lawrie, sculpture
   Story of Man
17 G. Lachaise,
   sculpture
18 L. Lawrie, sculpture
   *Wisdom with Sound
   and Light*
19 I. Noguchi, sculpture
   News
20 D. Rivera, mural
   *Man at the
   Crossroads*
21 F. Brangwyn, mural
22 H. Meiere, sculpture
   Dance, Drama, Song
23 E. Winter, mural
   Fountain of Youth
24 R. Kushner,
   sculpture *Sentinels*
25 R. Garrison,
   sculpture *Morning,
   Present, Evening*
26 B. Faulkner, tile
   mural *Intelligence
   Awakening Mankind*

The Benign Censorship of Modern Art

If the territory of modern art was the area
chosen to defend, there were limitations
in presenting a challenging artistic force to
the existing conservative powers. The tear
in the seamless values of modified modern
art in the United States is seen in the career
of Nelson Rockefeller who was a central
figure in two of the more famous incidents
of art censorship: the complete destruction
of Diego Rivera's fresco *Man at the Crossroads* in 1934 and the painting over of Andy
Warhol's Mural *Thirteen Most Wanted Men*
in 1964. In both cases the image of the
"other," whether it was the other political
view (communism) or the other sexual view
(homosexuality) were not to be tolerated.

After his college years and his
honeymoon trip around the world Nelson
undertook the biggest urban development in

the States: Rockefeller Center. Built 1931–
1939, during the peak of the Depression,
this project had thirteen buildings on 4.7
hectares in dense midtown Manhattan.
Although Nelson was specifically concerned
with rental sales for the complex he saw
the possibilities of combining large scale
production of labor, capital, advertising,
architecture and art.

Rockefeller Center was more than the
advertising motto of "The city within the
city," it was organized around a marketing
concept appealing to the new media industry
of radio (the RCA Building) connecting to
entertainment (Radio City Music Hall),
retail and culture (the originally planned
new opera house).

The high rise steel framework of the
Center's building construction is clad in a
series of thin layers of nonstructural veneer.

Whether these are stone piers or glass
windows or metal spandrels or bas-relief art
it all exists within the rational ordering of the
construction sequence. The art and artists in
the Center followed this same order. Even the
monumental free-standing sculpture such as
Paul Manship's *Prometheus* was placed against
the wall so as to smooth it out to postcard
flatness. The most successful works of art
in the Center are the numerous shallow bas-
relief carvings of the sculptor Lee Lawrie,
that emphasize the various entries to the
buildings.[2] In publicity statements it was noted
that Lawrie was hired because of his success
in the carving of ornaments for the American
Beaux-Arts masterpiece: the Nebraska State
Capitol building. The aesthetic ideas behind
the Rockefeller Center buildings and artwork
derived from the Beaux-Arts tradition rather
than a completely modern mentality.

Raymond Hood, Wallace Harrison and L. Andrew Reinhard, architects of Rockefeller Center, 1931.

Lee Lawrie supervising carving of his design for bas-relief sculpture for Rockefeller Center.

Bas-relief sculpture *Story of Man* by Lee Lawrie at Rockefeller Center International Building.

Flags snap, high heels tap:
a little sex and aggression,
the city's delights.
Vincent Scully on Rockefeller Center

Being at the very edge of the modern movement in the United States, the Center's main design architects Raymond Hood, Harvey Corbett, Jacques André Fouilhoux and the young Wallace Harrison could not accept the old direction in defining the buildings' lobbies.[3]

Before the 1930s, the lobby walls would have been developed with ornamental panels of plaster, stone or wood but the new "modern" image demanded a smoother and simpler presentation with inspired mechanical touches, new lighting systems and new technologies like escalators. The architects compromised by dividing the walls into two areas. The lobby for the RCA Building consisted of walls with a 2.13-meter-high wainscot of smooth machine polished marble with a vast clean white area above. It is this white area that was most problematic.

RAYMOND HOOD AND THE CRISIS OF THE VERTICAL SURFACE For both the architects and the artists the idea of art in architecture as only ornament represented a crisis, but for separate reasons.

For the architect Hood modern architecture dictated that the façade of a structure should be a direct projection of modern manufactured products, as when he lectured: "In the development of the walls and surfaces that clothe the buildings [...] our twentieth century industry has had an immense influence [...] the result has been an architecture of plain surfaces, with slight ornamentation, the decorative effects being obtained almost wholly by the decorative effects of color, texture and the contrast of materials [...] stone in slab form, for example, direct from the saws with solid masonry and carving reduced almost to the vanishing

point, is the logical, durable and beautiful material for the exterior. In the interiors, where fire control is so strictly imposed by law, wood veneered over steel has a charm [...] But this eliminates heavily carved ornamental work and molded forms cut from the solid and where ornamentation may be needed, it leads almost inevitably to inlays and other such flat surface decorations."[4]

By the time construction reached the interiors the figurative work on the exterior seemed already dated. It was as if the designers were stuck in the middle between the "Horror of Emptiness" that motivated ornament and its opposite: the cost-efficient smooth image of the modern blank wall. In 1935 a concerned and ineffectual effort was made to contract Henri Matisse and Pablo Picasso to produce something that would be more innovative and up-to-the-minute

Lobby of RCA Building with José Maria Sert mural that replaced the Diego Rivera fresco.

Entry to RCA Building with sculpture by Lee Lawrie.

for the lobby. In the adjacent International Building, Nelson Rockefeller and the architect Harrison pushed for the amazing proposal by Fernand Léger for a cine-mural that would be a continuous movie loop projected on the lobby walls. The design would connect the worlds of Cubism and cartoons, with Walt Disney mentioned as a possible co-contributor.[5]

But marketing dictated something more dramatic and newsworthy for the RCA Building lobby. It was at this moment that Abby Aldrich Rockefeller pressed for the Mexican muralist Diego Rivera, who had recently been honored with a show at the Museum of Modern Art.

Rivera was grand and expansive in every way. His fresco work covered huge areas, his themes spanned across time.

His topics ranged from prehistoric geology, to agriculture, to machine production, to politics. His intellectual appetite devoured the world.

His proposal for the Rockefeller fresco established a central figure (a white male worker) at a set of machine controls and from that point two elliptical diagonals broke the wall into several smaller views. The right side portrayed a set of socialist motifs while on the left side were a matching set of capitalist images. When Rivera decided to add the head of Lenin, the managing interests of the Rockefeller Center demanded that Nelson force the artist to change this last-minute propagandistic imposition.

With the distance of history it all seems quite absurd. Nelson's famous letter trying to

negotiate a change. Rivera's blustering and small compromise to put the head of Lincoln opposite that of Lenin. The pay-off of Rivera and his police escort out of the building. Nelson's last-minute attempt to relocate the fresco to MoMA. The final climax of dozens of picketers outside demanding justice. The secret midnight destruction of the fresco and wall with a pickaxe.[6]

DIEGO RIVERA AND THE TWILIGHT OF FILTH AND BLOOD The story of the Diego fresco has all the histrionics worthy of opera, but what was the lesson to be learned? The naiveté of Nelson (and Abby) or the foolishness of Diego? The hypocrisy of the capitalists or the delusion of the socialists? The power of art to change the world or the

Diego Rivera drawing figure outline of lobby mural at Rockefeller Center, 1933. His design was later repainted in the Palacio de Bellas Artes in Mexico City.

The dispute revolves around a simple question: In the decorative scheme shall an artist be permitted to follow his own fancy or shall he work in harmony with the project as planned. With the great majority of people there is no possible doubt.
Rockefeller Center Publicity Statement

powerlessness of the artist to control the use of his work?[7] In retrospect the sweeping declarative utopian gestures of Diego Rivera seem as if from a long distant era while the small painfully intimate confessions of the artist's wife, Frida Kahlo, now seem filled with contemporary importance.

At the very moment that the Diego fresco was pulverized, the Soviet State had completed its long purge of avant-garde ideas as counter-revolutionary. The most radical of the modern art movements, the Russian Constructivists, had been brutally crushed several years before under Stalin and the aesthetic program of a Socialist Realism was forcibly introduced: realist murals with obvious acts that communicated directly with anyone, the illiterate peasant or the literate Comintern, the moral and political

goals to be endorsed. All other voices were imprisoned, condemned or erased. The pickaxe breaking the painted portrait of Lenin in the Diego fresco was a foretelling of the assassin's ice pick shattering the skull of Trotsky years hence in 1940.[8]

But before his death in Mexico City Trotsky wrote a short manifesto, with collaborators Diego Rivera and André Breton. "Towards a Free Revolutionary Art," written in 1938, was meant to be a declaration of revenge and justification of Rivera's stand in New York City. It is a document with three distinct voices. One seems to be Diego justifying his own acts and reactions: "True art, which is not content to play variations on ready-made models but rather insists on expressing the inner needs of man and of mankind in its time – true art is unable not to

be revolutionary, not to aspire to a complete and radical reconstruction of society."

But the villain in the essay is not the United States, capitalism or Nelson Rockefeller but the USSR. And in a voice that is obviously Leon Trotsky's the current Stalinist order is condemned: "The totalitarian regime of the USSR working through the so-called 'cultural' organization it controls in other countries has spread over the entire world a deep twilight hostile to every sort of spiritual value. A twilight of filth and blood."[9] This atmosphere of apprehension and death turned out to be the future foretold as peace became war and the world that seemed open, closed.

Nelson Rockefeller, Philip Johnson and Robert Moses, 1963, at presentation of New York State Pavilion Rendering for the World's Fair.

Roy Lichtenstein's cover for *Art in America* on the World's Fair, 1964.

Aerial photo of New York State Pavilion at World's Fair, 1964.

Kitsch, Art and the Modern World of Tourism

Although Nelson could not be blamed for the destruction of the Diego fresco he was complicit. A role he would repeat in the next example of censorship.

The 1964 New York World's Fair, held at Flushing Meadows Corona Park in Queens, was the creation of Robert Moses, director of the Triborough Bridge and Tunnel Authority and an independent agent for urban reform, bridges and road building. Nelson was at his second term and sixth year of being Governor of the State of New York and was enthused about the participation in the Fair with a permanent pavilion representing the State. He chose Philip Johnson as his architect, who, as the first curator at MoMA, brought the International Style to the States in a slightly adapted and sanitized format.

The architect was an early collector of Warhol works, buying the *Golden Marilyn Monroe* in 1962 and commissioning his own portrait in 1972, so it was natural to have Andy Warhol as part of the collection of New York City artists whose work was placed on the curved blank façade of the New York State Pavilion's Theaterama.[10]

Johnson was very interested in how art and architecture intersect and in 1951 organized a symposium at MoMA titled "How to Combine Architecture, Painting and Sculpture." His placement of the artists at the World's Fair had the appearance of randomness but was organized on a tight compositional order. The selection of ten artists was a rather prejudiced view of the New York City art world of that moment,

88

Exterior view of
Theaterama of World's
Fair New York State
Pavilion with art. From
left to right: Robert
Indiana, *EAT*; Robert
Rauschenberg, *Skyway*;
Alexander Liberman,
Prometheus.

Roy Lichtenstein, *Girl at
Window* at World's Fair
New York State Pavilion.

Alexander Liberman,
Prometheus at World's
Fair New York State
Pavilion.

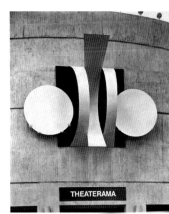

with a set of five painters identified with the Pop Art movement: Andy Warhol, Roy Lichtenstein, Robert Indiana, James Rosenquist and Robert Rauschenberg set against a set of three Minimalist sculptors: Alexander Liberman, Ellsworth Kelly and John Chamberlain.[11]

The strategy for the combination of two different styles and two different mediums was to place an "Invisible Frame" around all the pieces to unify the different artworks and visually tie them to the building. Johnson did this by requiring that each piece fill a 6 × 9 meter invisible outline (the Warhol piece has a blank bottom section to fill out its requirements), matching the ground level column edge to column edge spacing, with the top of the piece beginning at the top

of each invisible frame, thus creating both a vertical and horizontal alignment of each artwork with the building elements.

Due to the huge scale of the pieces and their raised position the Pop Art works played out a literal relationship with their inspirations from advertising and billboards, as shown in the examples of the Rauschenberg newspaper collaged images, Warhol's police poster, Rosenquist's broken billboard images and Indiana's abstract electric word. This relationship was so strong that the Indiana *EAT* art piece was later shut off because the confused public thought it was literally advertising a restaurant. The merging of the American highway billboard and the Greek temple frieze strongly connects the art displayed at this building.

The geometrically severe Minimalist sculptures related to the architecture on a different level, in that they duplicated and elaborated the building's circle motif. For the building with its circular theater, circular covered arena, circular piers and circular observation decks the geometry is always in the plan, and for the sculptures by Liberman and Kelly the circle motif is repeated in both the section and the elevation.

Both sets of artworks allow a complicated reading of the display, shifting back and forth from the sculptures acting as further articulation of the building's pure platonic order and the paintings as advertising the gaudy good times of the upstate high school marching bands inside.

Andy Warhol, silkscreen
on canvas *Thirteen
Most Wanted Men,*
World's Fair New York
State Pavilion.

Philip Johnson and
Andy Warhol, 1979.

Andy so loved the famous, that he
made anyone he met – like me – feel
famous just to talk with him.
Philip Johnson

The irony of this mirror-image of the nightmare that the
American dream had become, in an age of rampant
commercial exploitation and affluence, escaped most of
the nouveau-riche collectors who rejoiced in owning art
that mocked them […] Certainly Warhol's grotesque
portraits of his patrons, playing up every feature of their
vacuous narcissism, his grotesquely made-up Marilyn
Monroe and tearful Jackie Kennedy will stand as an
indictment of American society in the sixties as scathingly
as Goya's merciless portraits of the Spanish Court.
Barbara Rose

**ANDY WARHOL KISSES PHILIP JOHNSON
AND TELLS** The 1964 World's Fair had
several examples of art controversy and
censorship. The billboard-sized image of
Palestine refugees at the Jordanian pavilion
and the mural titled *Tomorrow Forever*
by American kitsch artist Walter Keane in
the arts pavilion were forcible removed.
Michelangelo's 1499 sculpture, the *Pietà*,
was installed in the Vatican pavilion with
tacky Broadway stage theatricality and
soaring recorded music. But the least known
change of all was the painting-over of Andy
Warhol's mural *Thirteen Most Wanted Men*
at the New York State Pavilion.

Installed as a grid of faces from the New
York City Police Department's most wanted
list, the blown-up images of low life thugs

did not amuse Robert Moses, who had
a strong dislike for anything approaching
the underclass, sex or modern art.[12] One
reconstruction of the story is that Moses
told Nelson, Nelson told Johnson, Johnson
told Warhol and the work was painted over
in silver.[13] Unlike the confrontation of Rivera,
the Warhol incident was treated by the artist
with calculated confusion. It was not a point
for protest, but more of a passive aggressive
gesture exemplified by the remaining blank
silver rectangle as an empty question.

The disturbing qualities of Warhol's work
are not in its apparent critique of American
culture but in his embrace of it at the same
time. The *Most Wanted* mural was both a
comical Dick Tracy cartoon of bad guys with
broken noses and a voyeuristic staring at

"rough trade," combining child-like jokes and
dreams of sexual degradation.

Warhol's embrace of wealth, power
and celebrity led him all the way to Ronald
Reagan's inaugural party in Washington.
Wearing his fright wig and bulletproof vest
he was for all appearances the tamed avant-
garde artist put on display to entertain. But
even at that point his work was a potent
subversive force distorting logic, taunting
sexuality and blurring the edges of American
culture.

The Negotiation of Freedom and Censorship in America

Confronting the blunt reality of censorship in America it is necessary to note the traditional perceived function and characteristics of public art (and memorials) in the United States. Public art was meant to justify the values of the social order: it was patriotic, somber, didactic and realistic. Art that was abstract, art that was cynical, art that was frivolous existed as an affront to one class (the citizen-worker) by another (the elite-academics). The idea that modernism has been entirely absorbed by the bourgeoisie is not a reality in the States, but the surface imagery of modern art has been appropriated by advertising, the most powerful arm of propaganda for all of capitalism.

Two powerful images of American public art illustrate the difference between abstract and figurative public art: Richard Serra's *Tilted Arc* in New York City and James Michael Maher's *Ronald Wilson Reagan* in Rapid City, South Dakota.

The collection of life-sized bronze statues at the *City of Presidents* exists as part patriotic and part commercial gimmick. The state of South Dakota is most famous for its Mount Rushmore National Memorial in the Black Hills. The vast carving of the faces of four presidents in the granite cliff of Rushmore Mountain started in 1925 and stopped in 1941. The idea that Washington, Jefferson, Lincoln and Theodore Roosevelt were historic leaders of giant proportions is given a literal demonstration. In contrast *City*

of Presidents in Rapid City shows America's leaders standing 10 centimeters off the sidewalk, some are sitting down, some are staring into space, and some are coming home from work. You pass them going to the laundry, store or restaurant and they appear as trapped in banal everyday drudgery as the living humans nearby.

The severe abstraction of the Richard Serra sculpture *Tilted Arc* in New York City would represent the opposite extreme of public art. The artwork fell victim to a heavily publicized case of censorship and was removed in 1989 from the Federal Office Building Plaza in downtown Manhattan, after being installed for only eight years.

As a political football the sculpture was the perfect shape to throw around. It existed

Richard Serra,
Greenpoint, 1992,
aligned on axis with
the Mueller Tower
at the University of
Nebraska, Lincoln,
Nebraska.

Richard Serra, *Berlin
Junction,* 1987, in front
of Philharmonic Hall,
Berlin, Hans Scharoun,
1963.

not on the safe (or neutral) grounds of a museum or university but in a dreary corner of an overcrowded section of the federal and judicial office complex north of City Hall. By literally bisecting the small plaza in front of the office building it proposed an aggressive juxtaposition: from free access to blocked confrontation.

The project was fascinating for its manipulation of both space and pattern. The ground plan of the arc was opposite but similar to the radius of the circular paving pattern of the plaza – an important relationship because the sculpture's most meaningful viewpoint was from the elevated offices looking down at it.

In terms of space, the most obvious point was the effect of enclosure created by the steel wall, but there was also the visual force of the continuous curved line at the top of the sculpture expanding the scope of the pedestrian's vision.

For too many it was simply a rusting wall collecting debris and imposing a blank confrontation to any pedestrian. One of the artist's arguments was that the object could not be moved because it was site-specific. Some of Serra works are amazingly picturesque in their context. The mirrored paired curved steel plates *Greenpoint*, 1992, in the University of Nebraska frames the axis of the monumental Mueller Tower perfectly; the parallel paired curved steel plates *Berlin Junction*, 1987, mimic the curved swooping profile of the roof of Hans Scharoun's adjacent Berlin Philharmonic Hall, 1963.

Its confrontation, unfortunately, was not only with the powers that be, but also with the office workers of the complex. *Tilted Arc* makes a perfect example of art that is articulating the conflict of power and control in American art. It shows on one hand the artist in the position of what has been called Minimalism's "Rhetoric of Power" and on the other hand the growing conservative voice in American culture.[14]

The Domestication of the Modern

There are many definitions of the term "modern" but none of them contain the word "cozy," yet Nelson Rockefeller was able to tame and transform the work of two of the most famous of modern artists, Pablo Picasso and Piet Mondrian, into something quite domestic.

The first image transformed was from the world of Picasso. Nelson had collected several important works of the artist and had long admired the canvas *Les Desmoiselles d'Avignon*. Here was a work that was the climax of the violent eroticism contained within modernism, consisting of a portrait of four prostitutes with their figures and faces carved away into the angular planes of African tribal masks. After the painting was purchased by the Museum of Modern Art he made a request to the artist (through Madame van Doesburg) to have a copy made in dyed wool as a tapestry.[15]

This canvas, of such explosive quality, was transformed into something softer, tactile, gentle and less threatening. The images of the faces were blurred by the loom's rectangular matrix making the painting's curved line appear out of focus; thus the aggressive figures moved out of the foreground and were less threatening. The colors were slightly altered to be less acidic, to become something almost, but not quite, pretty.[16]

Nelson repeated this process of transformation on almost all the Picassos he donated to MoMA and then on some that he did not own. A total of nineteen tapestries were made from Picasso's artwork with several additional ones made from the works of Fernand Léger, Alexander Calder and Joan Miró. Although each was approved by the artist the changes from one medium to another were not without controversy. In the adaptation of Picasso's stark black and white *Guernica* into a fabric version color was added (green and yellow) which quite confused and upset Alfred Barr, the director of MoMA.[17]

As Thorstein Veblen noted, "We find things beautiful [...] somewhat in proportion as they are costly,"[18] the many tapestries lining the walls of Nelson's art gallery walls in his home at Pocantico Hills show the ability of Americans to adapt and utilize the graphic power of modern art without any worry about its content.

The other artist who was assimilated was Piet Mondrian. Nelson Rockefeller had only one Mondrian painting in his collection but he commissioned, with his architect Wallace Harrison, four murals from one of the artist's most devoted followers, Fritz Glarner.[19] The murals were located in the Empire State Plaza in Albany and in the UN Headquarters, Time & Life Building,

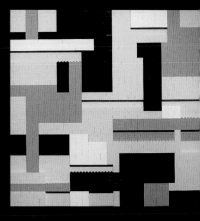

Piet Mondrian, *Salon de Madame B. à Dresden*, 1926, reconstructed at the Fondation Beyeler, Basel, 2001.

Robert Yoder, collage of Lego blocks *Untitled*, 2004.

Dining room in Nelson Rockefeller apartment 810 Fifth Avenue, New York, Fritz Glarner, 1964.

and Nelson's own dining room at his 810 Fifth Avenue apartment, all in New York City.

Glarner, who was Swiss, copied closely not only the visual elements of the Dutch De Stijl movement but also the underlying philosophy of theosophy advocated by Mondrian himself. The austere black grids and primary colored rectangles reflected an equally austere lifestyle devoted to art as a religious force.

Mondrian did design a few interiors that presented a balanced equilibrium between painting and architecture. One 1926 proposal was for collector Ida Bienert titled *Salon de Madame B. à Dresden*. The later reconstructions show the room to be both static and vibrant, with the large primary colored rectangles visually shifting back and forth from the actual plane of the wall.[20] Mondrian hoped for a utopian unification of art and architecture as a greater metaphor for the balance and order that was missing in a Europe still traumatized by the war.

The Nelson Rockefeller dining room was also a complete environment; with the painted canvases attached to all four walls, including the ceiling, it created a tent-like atmosphere. Added to this is the relatively small size of the colored rectangles which made them seem as if they were made from samples of fabric: the grey areas

appeared to have the texture of heavy felt, the red rectangles matched the leather squares on the chairs, the blues and yellows appeared as shiny silk patches, the white zones blended with the linen window curtains. When Nelson added the decorative table setting, Dresden "Swan Service" porcelain, a complete transformation of the Dutch artist's ideals occurred, from a severe European social experiment into a softer American luxury product.[21]

The entire aesthetic of the De Stijl movement was appropriated by American advertising and merchandizing in making ornamental patterns for various products. Till finally the art world itself recycles that abuse as a form of commentary on its own. The contemporary collage constructions of Robert Yoder are an example where the well-worn Mondrian grid and colors are re-imagined and re-constructed, made by children's toy "Legos" into both a commodity and comedy.

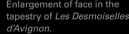

Portrait of Fritz Glarner working on his mural at the Time & Life Building, New York, Wallace Harrison, 1967.

Nelson Rockefeller with Pablo Picasso's *Les Desmoiselles d'Avignon* at the Museum of Modern Art, 1939.

The Marketing of the Modern

In his new 1937 apartment at 810 Fifth Avenue Nelson Rockefeller, with architect Wallace Harrison, achieved a synthesis of the best of two styles: the end of the Art Deco period and the beginning of modern.

The major rooms had smooth continuous walls of polished oak veneer, with curved corners, punctuated by a free-form curved outline as doorways, giving the rooms a flowing quality. Organized into this modern shell was the work of several amazing modern artists and decorative craftsmen. Henri Matisse and Fernand Léger painted murals surrounding two fireplace mantels. The talents of Alberto and Diego Giacometti were concentrated on ironwork at the hearth and light fixtures. And the grand interior designer Jean-Michel Frank supervised the manufacture and placement of the furniture. Full scale canvas room mock-ups were made in Paris for Frank to experiment with the composition of his works.

The organizational model of the *décorateurs-ensembliers* achieved many successful composite modern interiors in the 1930s, uniting the work of artists, architects and craftsmen. The secret of their success is not that they presented a unified style but the opposite, in that the collected art pieces had only a partially shared visual vocabulary. The exact time this was produced was a transition between several styles, and the artists created work inspired by a wide spectrum of influences.

This can be seen in how the art pieces in the Rockefeller apartment interlock in small gestures to each other, while maintaining their own separate identity. The elaborate modern curved entry cutouts in the walls, by Wallace Harrison, match the interior profile line of the legs for the streamlined Louis XV styled chairs, by Jean-Michel Frank. The thick black twisted bronze shafts that the Giacomettis used for the lamps match the thick black lines in the paintings by Pablo Picasso, *Pitcher*

Fernand Léger, painting of the fireplace surround mural for the Nelson Rockefeller apartment, 1937.

and Bowl of Fruit, 1931, and Henri Matisse, Italian Woman, 1915. Also the angular fireplace andirons made by the Giacomettis relate directly to the African tribal art assembled near the mantel. And the mural by Matisse, La Poésie, 1938, in its placement of four chatty guests, inhabits the room at the eye level of the real guests.

It is an extremely successful example of collaboration and an obvious complement to the taste of the patron. But this was not just a place to live; it was a lifestyle image that you too could be part of. Before the fantasy luxury lifestyle advertisements of Ralph Lauren, Calvin Klein or Martha Stewart there was Nelson Rockefeller.

In 1977, after his political career had ended, Nelson announced the beginning of his newest adventure, The Nelson Rockefeller Collections Inc.; its purpose was to offer the highest quality reproductions of artwork, both modern and others, to the general public. The objects came directly from the collection of Nelson and his family. The catalogue for this production was divided into sections that opened with a lush color interior photograph of one of the many Rockefeller homes: the Fifth Avenue apartment is paired with modern art and Art Deco pieces, the colonial Dutch farmhouse is matched to American folk art duplicates, the 1970 Japanese summer home is

connected to Asian art reproduction and the family estate Kykuit near New York is the setting for the sale of imitation eighteenth century porcelain serving sets.

The implication was that one was not just purchasing an injected molded stone/resin duplicate of a marble statue but participating in the glamour of the Rockefeller family.

The company was met with damning criticism from the New York Times, the Art Dealer Association, popular magazines[22] and with the occurrence of Nelson's death it changed ownership twice and disappeared within two years.[23]

One piece of furniture from the Fifth Avenue apartment, the gilded console table by Jean-Michel Frank, was offered as a copy in the catalogue of The Nelson Rockefeller Collections Inc. It was a combination of styles that vaguely links Art Nouveau Paris and Art Deco New York. Being the largest piece reproduced for the marketed collection it seemed as if it was the only survivor from the tragedy of the disassembly of this intensely beautiful room, a strange parallel to its creator's life.

For in July 1940 Frank sent a telegram to Nelson, hoping to get help in escaping the advance of fascist armies. Nelson had written in the upper right hand corner asking for Harrison's comment and finally sent a

short cold note that there was nothing he could do.

Frank made his way out of France, to Spain, to Buenos Aires, to San Francisco and finally to New York City, where, for reasons only guessed at, his losses overwhelmed him and he committed suicide.

In memoriam Jean Cocteau has written: "He undoubtedly leapt out of this period because he found it unlivable and foresaw its formlessness. His death was the ending of the play, the final curtain rundown between a world of light and a world of darkness."[24]

It is the haunting image of the Frank telegram with its 1930s ornament, its stilted language, its forgotten technology, its tragedy and emptiness that leaves us with the unanswered questions of artist rights, the power of the patron and the changing values of the art object in the marketplace.

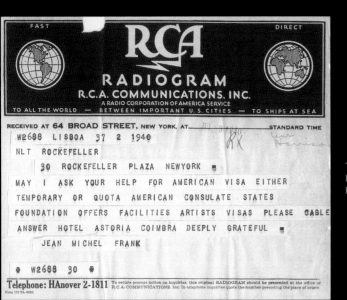

Telegram of Jean-Michel Frank asking Nelson Rockefeller for help, 1940.

Interior of Nelson
Rockefeller living room,
810 Fifth Avenue, Wallace
Harrison, New York, 1937.

Page from catalogue
of Nelson Rockefeller
Collections Inc. with interior
and products, 1979.

I think we're going to see the same
break-through and the democratization
of faithful reproductions of painting and
sculpture that we already have for the
benefit of people today – the great American
people – in music through records and in
the performing arts through cassettes.
That is my objective.
Nelson Rockefeller

6: Gravestones of Modernism

Isamu Noguchi, *The Family,* Connecticut General Life Insurance Company, Bloomfield, Connecticut, Skidmore, Owings & Merrill, 1957.

Traditional cemetery in Japan with gravestones.

The inspiration for many of the abstract vertical stone sculptures by Noguchi can be found in the forms and formal organization of traditional gravestones in Japan. There the stone pylon can be naturalistic or geometric with the carving of the Japanese ideograms vertically organized. The same

semaphore-like images are carved by Noguchi into the Connecticut sculptures. Besides the transposition of abstract forms from one culture to another there is an underlying metaphor of existential reality: the haunting presence of death and isolation in each act of making a marker for art and the artist's life.

Yet sculpture has followed the path sought by Duchamp-Villon, the path leading toward the great light of open air and landscape. He speaks of *la sculpture architecturale de plein air* as the objective of a revision of the whole artistic education; he does not speak of an architectural integration.
A.M. Hammacher

The public sees nothing, absolutely nothing, in these stone fields, tilted arcs, and instant Stonehenges, because it was never meant to. The public is looking at the arcane of the new religion of the educated classes. [i.e. modern art] Tom Wolfe

Monumental Public Sculpture and the Identity of the American Artist

The climax of the American modern public sculpture movement may have been in Chicago during the early 1970s. For there in a straight line moving north across five city blocks, were three major public plazas and their major public art: the Federal Plaza with its Calder, 1974, the Chase Tower Plaza (originally the First National Bank Plaza) with its mosaic *Four Seasons* by Chagall, 1974, and the Daley Plaza (originally the Chicago Civic Center) with its Picasso, 1967. The specifics may be different but the effects were duplicated at this time in every major city in the United States.

All monumental, but monuments to what exactly? Not to mark a successful battle, an honored citizen or the death of a lost cause, but, at its simplest, to establish a front door location and welcome mat to enormous office buildings.

The symbolism and narrative tradition of representative public sculpture was replaced, not by the usual visual explanation of a non-representative abstraction (art for art's sake), but by the autobiographical and personal symbolism of the artist. And it is from this viewpoint that the connection (and separation) between the monumental art and the architecture can be described.

Added to this argument is the way the personal brand image of the artist's name defines the very nature of art in America. For, in the United States, artists are typecast in very specific ways. And if artists are thought about at all by Americans (and American architects) it is within these limits. In the two sculptors connected to the Chicago plazas this can be seen in the simple labels used to describe them in the Chicago press: Alexander Calder as the clowning child and

The mind which plunges into Surrealism, relives with burning excitement the best part of childhood. Childhood comes closest to one's real life – childhood – where everything conspires to bring about the effect: risk-free possession of oneself.
André Breton

Portrait of Alexander Calder with mask by Saul Steinberg, 1959.

Alexander Calder, drawing *Circus*, 1932. The figures against the verticals of the curtain are the same composition as Calder's *Flamingo* against the repeated mullions of the Mies office buildings.

Pablo Picasso as the dangerous (communist) genius.

Another public artist that was given a label is Isamu Noguchi and his work at Yale University. Throughout his career Noguchi can be seen as typecast in the press as the unknowable outsider.

Each of these artists will be described in a specific selection of his public work, its connection to the surrounding buildings and his public identity.

Alexander Calder in the Role of the Clowning Child

Alexander Calder represents the most accessible image of modern art to the American public. His work is big, colorful and active. And, most importantly, it is always vaguely representative, whether seen in the titles to the art pieces (*Snow Flurry; Lobster Trap and Fish Tail)* or in other works in the anthropomorphic shapes themselves (legs, tails, trunks, penises, heads, noses and mouths) which all seem somewhat recognizable.

Calder came from a family of successful academic artists: his father, Alexander Stirling Calder (1870–1945) and his grandfather, Alexander Milne Calder (1846–1923). Both men produced monumental heroic figures. The father sculpted the figure

of George Washington for the Washington Arch in New York City, and the grandfather created the monumental figure of William Penn for the pinnacle of Philadelphia City Hall. This established a precedent for the youngest Calder to understand the possibilities of collaboration between artists and architects.[1] But, in fact Calder's "participation" was extremely limited: he never visited the site of some of his monumental sculptures even after the installation of the work.

An example would be Calder's sculpture in Grand Rapids, Michigan, about which the writer Miwon Kwon has noted: "It is important to note that Calder never saw, nor did he feel it necessary to visit the plaza before the sculpture's installation. Like a good modernist, he operated under

Riddle:
Why did the chicken cross the road?

Answer:
Alexander Calder (Alexander called her).

the assumptions of an artwork's autonomy. The site, in the case of this project, then, was conceived as a kind of abstract blankness awaiting some marker (i.e. art, sculpture) to give it what could be claimed an authentic identity, even if that identity was created through the logic of a logo."[2]

Early in his life Calder wandered through many odd jobs only to find his way back to the family path of being an artist. His work in Paris in the 1930s started with cartoon-like wire caricatures and moved on to the avant-garde idea of motorized and moving geometric shapes. Calder's dramatic innovation came when he made bi-morphic shapes derived from the paintings of Miró, in sheet metal placed at the ends of long wires that, in turn, were counter-weighted

by another larger sheet metal form about a central pivot. The delicate balance and loose interlocking allowed the assembly to move in the wind. The invention of these moving sculptures, titled *Mobiles*, brought Calder fame and fortune.

Later he expanded the articulation of the plinth-like base of the mobiles and developed an independent set of sculptural forms that his friend Jean Arp titled *Stabiles*. These objects were all made of sheet metal folded or joined in such a way as to make a free-standing series of cutout silhouettes. At the inception of the pieces' first exhibition at Pierre Matisse's gallery in New York City in 1937, Calder proposed them as ranging in scale from the hand held to the monumental. The Chicago Calder is the climax of the artist's work since that time.

In Chicago, the Calder sculpture is the city's most prominent public artwork, if only by its color and size. The Chicago stabile consists of cut sheets of 19-millimeter-thick plate steel in two sets of shapes, the first are two partial elliptical forms and the second are three sets of angular diamond-shaped forms. All five pieces touch the ground at the bottom and connect to a common squarish central plate at their other ends. The entire assembly was erected at the site with construction cranes and reaches the height of 16 meters. It is painted an orange-red color, titled *Calder Red*, it was from the color and the curve of the largest ellipse (like the curve of a long necked tropical bird reaching down) that Calder titled the piece: *Flamingo*.[3] The published reviews of the work have revealingly

Riddle:
What bird can
lift the heaviest
weight?

Answer:
The crane.

The three maquettes
sent to Chicago in
1973 by the Klaus Perls
Gallery for the selection
of the artwork for the
Federal Plaza.

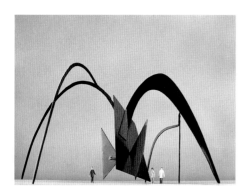

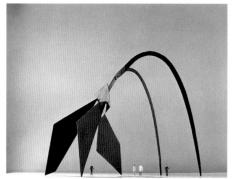

mentioned the words "playful," "fun," and "toy-like," corresponding to the accepted image of this artist in the role of the precocious child.[4]

The history of the selection of the stabile for the Federal Plaza in front of Ludwig Mies van der Rohe's Federal Center illustrates the problems of collaboration within the arts. As one of the first art objects to be paid for by the American Federal Government's One Percent for Art program it was an innovation. But it also represented the least involvement of the artist with the architect in the development of the composition between the work of art and the buildings.

The selection process was an exercise in connoisseurship, not collaboration. It began in 1973 with a phone call from the team of architects to Klaus Perls, Calder's New York gallery, requesting a sampling of

possible sculptures by an American artist to be enlarged for use in the plaza. When three of Calder's maquettes arrived in the mail, the architects, Gene Summers, Carter Manny and others quickly selected one. Mies was not a participant for he had died in 1969, and his partners, along with the various associated architects, had supervised the construction of his design for the three Federal Center buildings.[5]

The three buildings of the complex, one an office, one a courthouse and one a post-office, are carefully placed in an asymmetric layout to define a fully enclosed urban space. The placement of the Calder sculpture on the granite paved plaza was slightly off-center against the office building. The team of architects decided to leave the plaza's center open so that it could be used for public events and ceremonies, and

to allow for a pedestrian diagonal short-cut across the plaza. In fact it seems as if Calder's only involvement in the entire process was limited to his review of the factory construction of the sculpture and his appearance at the opening ceremony.

There is a surprising similarity of Mies' past interests in art and the design of the Chicago Federal Center.[6] In 1930 Mies produced a series of freehand sketches for Berlin courtyard housing and the architect always placed a scribble outlining a statue of a reclining figure in the courtyards. The Chicago Federal Plaza seems almost carved from the solid masses of the surrounding forty-story buildings, making a cubic void with the same visual characteristics of Mies' early courtyard houses, and with strangely similar proportions between the enclosing walls and the artwork.

Riddle:
Why did the
lion spit out
the Clown?

Answer:
Because he tasted
something funny.

It is worth noting that the same extraordinary ingenuity which now marks the conception and creation of these monumental pieces has been characteristic of Calder almost from early childhood. **Robert Osborn**

Downtown Chicago (Loop)

Site plan:
A Daley Plaza,
  C. F. Murphy Architects
B Chase Plaza,
  Perkins & Will
C Inland Steel Building,
  Skidmore, Owings &
  Merrill
D Federal Plaza, Office of
  Mies van der Rohe

1 P. Picasso, sculpture, 1967
2 J. Miró, sculpture, 1981
3 M. Chagall, tile mural
  Four Seasons, 1974
4 A. Calder, sculpture
  Flamingo, 1964
5 R. Lippold, sculpture
  Radiant I, 1958
6 E. Anderson, sculpture
  Dirksen bust
7 S. LeWitt, mural *Lines in
  Four Directions*, 1985

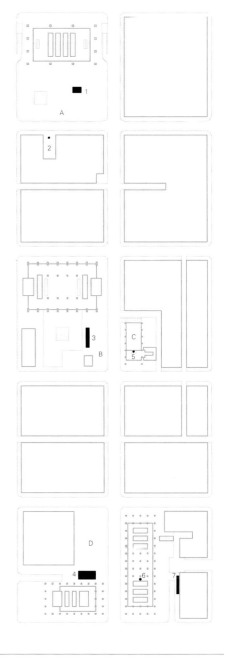

The potential dialogue between art and architecture in Chicago was still possible even if the participating architect was no longer living and the participating artist was physically absent. This can be seen in how the black planar gridded office slabs of Mies become a perfect backdrop for the silhouette of the Calder sculpture. Calder started his career doing three-dimensional caricatures from thick wire, which created a sharp graphic outline of a person or animal profile. To view these thin black objects with any clarity the background had to be blank and white. Following from his earliest work it is obvious that the strength of Calder's sculpture is in its outline, not in its volume, and the compositional interlocking between the art to the architecture is not about the building framing the art but the building acting as an engaged backdrop, removing

the visual confusion that would occur if the Calder work stood alone within a chaotic urban streetscape.[7]

The Chicago Calder also connects to themes repeated by the artist. It is possible to ignore the title *Flamingo*, given to the piece by its color, and to see the same composition as the artist's *Circus* drawings. The drawings play the repeated line work of the vertical bars of the cage against the free-form figures of the animals, an exact parallel to the vertical mullions of the Mies buildings and the curved Calder sculpture.

The circus was an obsession with Calder. It represented a world that he wanted to make his own: a mobile society, a family of artists, a continuous set of performances and a specific group of character types. Those characters, that he would draw and model over and over again, in both realist and

abstract forms, were the balancing acrobat, the baggy pants clown, the monumental elephant and the caged lion. Those types were also the roles that he would play: the artist balancing art on a wire, the artist with ribald humor, the artist with expanding girth, the artist restlessly pacing at his enclosure.

The Chicago Calder can be understood as an avatar of Calder himself and the repeated abstract animal figures that became his substitute. Not that they were representative portraits of Calder, but they were the mechanism through which Calder could project himself.

It is both fitting and bittersweet that the dedication ceremonies of the Calder sculpture in Chicago in October 1974 was orchestrated as a circus-like event. The forty-horse wagon of the Schlitz Milwaukee Brewing Company carried Calder, family and

Frontal view of the
Chicago Picasso,
1967, in the context
of the Daley Plaza,
behind is the Richard
J. Daley Center, C. F.
Murphy Architects and
Skidmore, Owings &
Merrill, 1965.

A partial rear view of
the Chicago Picasso.

Picasso's oeuvre – and this is a given –
is purely, entirely erotic.
Jean Clair

circus band down Adams Street as part
of a parade with ten unicyclists, eight
clowns, seven flag girls, five midgets and
four circus wagons, the last containing a
caged actor in a gorilla costume. The master
of ceremonies was the organizing architect,
Carter Manny of C. F. Murphy Architects,
dressed in the costume of a circus ring-
master, top hat and all.

There, on the raised dais, before the
crowds and politicians, the final image of
collaboration of the arts in Chicago was that
of the architect as lion tamer and the artist as
the beast caged by the city.

**Pablo Picasso and the Image of the
Dangerous Genius**

If Calder represents the most accessible
modern artist to Americans then Pablo
Picasso represents the most famous and the
most confusing. As the undisputed heavy
weight champion of modern art, the inventor
of Cubism, the destroyer of beauty, the
communist radical bohemian, the source of
joke cartoons, he is feared and ridiculed, he
is seen as both a genius and a charlatan.

The Chicago Picasso of 1967 was one of
the first in the monumental modern public
arts sculptures in America. Being one of the
first it is also one of the most controversial
objects. The idea of an 18-meter-tall steel
object of abstract shape representing
nothing seemed unbelievable to the general
population. The lack of a narrative was
not just unnerving, it was considered by

many insulting. For that reason, over the
years, this icon has been "dressed" with
meaning: a huge baseball cap for the World
Series of Baseball, Santa's red velvet hat for
Christmas, on and on.

The official explanation is that the Picasso
piece is simply the abstracted shape of a
woman's face.[8] A series of design sketches,
starting in 1962, shows the evolution of
the theme of a monumental sculpture
starting from a woman's profile; it is a
perfect example of the articulated symbols
of traditional public art transferred to the
introspective, private and autobiographical
world of the modern artist.

The front of the sculpture represents a
female face. One can identify the features
with the two circles, in a lens-shaped
surround at the top of the center element,
as two eyes and the two circles at the

Pablo Picasso, painting
Head of a Woman, 1962.

Detail of Chicago
Picasso, 1967.

Ivory statuette Venus
of Lespugue, approx.
25,000 BC.

Portrait of Pablo Picasso
with bull's head *Picasso
Toro*, photo by Edward
Quinn, circa 1950.

bottom of the same piece as the nostrils, the angular vertical piece in the sculpture is the symmetric outline of a mouth, with lips extended, and the two large curved figures in the back act as the hair of the subject.[9]

But if we take an object in Picasso's personal collection, the plaster cast of the Venus of Lespugue made from the original at the Musée des Antiquités nationales, it is possible to propose an extended metaphor to the official Chicago story. This prehistoric fetish is the exaggerated image of the female form as a fertility idol; with its suggestive head, its exaggerated curved hips, and the legs tapering to a triangular point referring to the pudendum, the venus was for Picasso a distortion of reality that told a greater truth.

The other element of importance is Picasso's obsession with the concept of transformation. In this case transformation is the similarity of forms exaggerated for poetic power: the shape of a teardrop transforms to the shape of the eye, the head of a bird morphs into the head of a man, the almond shape of a woman's mouth is made equal to the shape of her genitals.

With the Venus as our guide, and the idea of transformation, it is possible to see the rear view of the Chicago Picasso as being equal in importance to the front. For if the front is an abstracted female face than the back is the abstracted genitals. The transformation of form which so obsessed Picasso can be seen in the transformation of the sculpture's curved blades which in the front shape a woman's flowing hair and from the back become the exaggerated hip and pelvic bones of another Venus idol. The rods that connect the front piece to the back further define the shape of the vagina. And

the vertical face piece as viewed from the back presents an obvious phallic character.[10]

The previously tame picturesque portrait of a woman's face now becomes something more powerful and worthy as the symbol of the Metropolis. Picasso presented Chicago, the city that he knew as a tough town filled with gangsters and stockyards, with a mystical form, a fertility goddess, a savage idol to the most primal force that he knew: sex.

Picasso acted as transformer, magician, and divine genius, and it is through his art that his private world becomes an entry to the power of the universe.

A purely cold abstraction doesn't
interest me too much. Art has to have
some kind of humanly touching and
memorable quality. It has to recall
something which moves a person –
a recollection, a recognition of his
loneliness, or tragedy.
Isamu Noguchi

Isamu Noguchi Wearing the Mask
of the Unknowable Outsider

The public sculpture of the artist Isamu
Noguchi is not part of the Chicago plazas
discussed previously, but Noguchi is
important to this discussion because one of
the most productive artistic collaborations
of the 1970s was between that artist and
the architect Gordon Bunshaft.

Bunshaft was a design partner in the
large corporate architectural office of
Skidmore, Owings & Merrill, and was in a
position to offer an artist large commissions
to complement the office buildings produced
by his firm. With Noguchi he organized a total
of twelve separate design proposals of which
seven were built and, from those, fifteen
individual sculptures were produced.

Yet, despite their extensive collaboration,
there seemed an obvious abrasion between

these two driven characters. They matched
each other in their determination to produce
design excellence and in the process left a
trail of dramatic arguments.[11]

Bunshaft presented himself as a
crude, direct, aggressive character with
an almost illiterate design strategy. When
discussing public sculpture Bunshaft has
blankly stated: "Sculpture serves the owner
to enrich his building, just as he is by good
furniture."[12] Yet his passion for modern
art was notable: he established a major
collection and was a committed board
member for the Museum of Modern Art,
to which he donated many of his prized
possessions. He also commissioned several
site-specific works from other important
artists such as Henry Moore, Alexander
Calder and Harry Bertoia. Bunshaft was an
enigma wrapped in a scowl.

Noguchi was hard to typecast. He
produced realistic portraits and extreme
abstractions, socialist murals and science
fiction fantasies, low art product design
and high art monuments, western flavored
oriental gardens and eastern influenced
modern sculpture. With an American mother
separated from his Japanese father he
traveled between two worlds his entire
existence. His young life was a dramatic
juxtaposition of two identities: one in
America as Sam Gilmore (Gilmore being his
mother's maiden name) and another in Japan
as Isamu Noguchi (his father was the poet
Yone Noguchi). Noguchi was a man with two
nationalities and he could play the image of
"the other" to his advantage as he saw fit.

In working with Bunshaft, Noguchi
presented himself as temperamental,
stubborn and combative. His options in

these collaborations were obviously limited
by the fact that Bunshaft was the patron
and Isamu could only push his ideas so far.
But in the composition of the three figures
making the sculpture *The Family* (the use
of three figures representing the father,
mother and son will return in other of his
works), installed for the Connecticut General
Life Insurance Company, 1957, Noguchi
succeeded in locating his sculpture assembly
away from the buildings and far down the
meadow. The resulting period photograph
shows the sculpture in the foreground
looming over the illusion of a visually smaller
building, far in the background. This was
Noguchi correcting the power relations
between artist and architect.

The collaborative work of Bunshaft and
Noguchi can be divided into two types: one
being the traditional asymmetric placement
of a free-standing sculpture at a building's
entry plaza, and the second being a garden
design for the building's courtyard.

For the first type, as in the sculptures
for 140 Broadway in New York City and the
John Hancock Building in New Orleans, the
most important compositional connection
between them was that Noguchi could
produce art objects that were not only
physically large, but also evoked a much
larger scale. This was necessary for the art to
be noticed in front of Bunshaft's extremely
long suburban office buildings or extremely
tall urban skyscrapers.

Most of the free-standing sculptures
were traditional solutions of a visual
balancing act between the large gridded
mass of the building and a smaller highly
figurative art piece. The more innovative
works are the courtyard garden designs. In

many ways Noguchi's sculptural work was
already treated (unconsciously) by architects
as if they were landscape elements. And in
the case of the Crown Zellerbach Building in
San Francisco, Noguchi's rejected sculpture
proposal was easily replaced with a less
costly planting of specimen trees.

The most intriguing faux garden produced
by the union of these two minds was the
one located within the Beinecke Rare Book
and Manuscript Library at Yale University
in 1964. The building consists of a granite
and marble gridded façade covering a large
Vierendeel truss system that allows the
exterior box of the building to be supported
on only four corner columns. Inside the
exterior marble box is an interior glass box
which holds the collection of rare books in
a free-standing multi-floor bookcase. The
overall impression is funereal with the

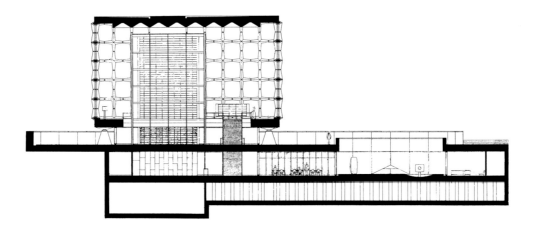

tomb-like exterior and the sealed glass interior. The glowing glass center has an ominous appearance; one gets the feeling that removing a book from its sarcophagus of climate control would cause it to crumble into dust. Added to this monument to the wealth of its donors is the art piece by Noguchi. Located in a sunken rectangular court, it operates as a lightwell bringing sunlight into the subterranean reading rooms.

There are some immediate and superficial pairings between the building and the artwork. Both use the same white Vermont marble. Both have a severe geometric vocabulary. And both exist adjacent but in separate planes of vision. This separation allows the view looking down on the sculpture to act like a fifth elevation of the four-sided library.

The Noguchi faux garden consists of three abstract marble objects in a field of marble paving. Many would say that abstract art needs no more than the visual strength of its forms to justify its existence, but because of Noguchi's specific comments regarding his work, the obvious associative values of these shapes speak of a larger metaphor and allegory.

The three objects operate on several levels of complexity and symbolism. For the first level each of the sculptural figures are derived from one of the three basic geometric blocks: the pyramid from the triangle, the torus from the circle, the rotated cube from the square. These are platonic universals, but they make a weak metaphor for the ancient classical texts stored in the library.

The second level of metaphor comes directly from the artist. Noguchi gave quick short titles to explain his forms: the torus was energy, the cube was chance and the pyramid was the earth.[13] But it isn't obvious why this trio adds up to a greater meaning or what is their connection to the symbols of a library or the composition of the building. These are a token set of symbols for this public building and the artist's explanation is merely a rhetorical gesture.

The dissatisfaction with these dislocated and simple metaphorical images leads me to propose a different extended metaphor for the art piece. This third level of metaphor attempts to connect deeper to the biography of the artist and disregards any reason to attach to the artwork the traditional public symbols of heroic self-sacrifice, genius, patriotism or cosmic imagery. The operating

assumption is that these objects are directly related as symbols to the artist's personal life.

The rotated cube or die is a symbol that Noguchi has personally identified with more than once.[14] The idea of chance, of change, of motion, of instability are all images that Noguchi has used to describe himself and attributes of the rotated cube. The image of motion connects with his movement back and forth in a conflicted allegiance between his heritage in both Japan and America. The cube, in its general proportions, can also be seen as representing a human head, for Noguchi was a prolific portrait sculptor, and it becomes another self-portrait in a Minimalist manner.

The torus, the thickened circle, also has associations of motion and is the direct metaphor of the sun, but not exactly the way Noguchi has described, because the most

important sun metaphor for the artist is the national symbol of Japan: the rising sun. The symbol of that country is also the symbol of his Japanese father. Both the father and the torus are images of strength and also of unstable motion; the marble circle appears to be ready to roll away at any moment and be as distant as his father.

The pyramid is the most stable of all the pieces and can be seen in multiple symbolic images: an image of the earth, of the pitched roof of home, of the pointed breast of nourishment for the child, of Noguchi's American mother in this family equation of the three forms representing father, mother and son. Noguchi has written on this garden: "The cube on its point may be said to contain both earthly square and solar radiance."[15] This is a perfect description of the rotated cube as a symbol of the child born from the

union of the earthly pyramid (square in plan) and the circular sun. In total, this design is an image of the static emptiness and forced emotional separation of the individuals in this dysfunctional family.

Further proof of this conjecture – that these geometric forms represent people – would be found in the other table-like sculptures that Noguchi made over the years. One of the most relevant is *Bed* of 1946, long before the Beinecke Library work at Yale, a bronze tablet that has geometric recesses and protuberances that abstract simple body parts of a man and woman lying next to each other.

Other artworks of a similar imaginary landscape tablet composition would be the *Tortured Earth* of 1943. There is a repeated "table" motif through several of Noguchi's works that all start with a horizontal slab-like

Isamu Noguchi,
sculpture *Bed*, 1946.

Alberto Giacometti,
sculpture *No More
Play*, 1932.

Isamu Noguchi, early
study for Beinecke
Library, 1962.

form and develop recesses and swellings in multiple variations. The works range from actual table designs, to relief sculpture, to architectural models. The simplest way to classify them is with the label *tableaux*, a word that would cover the use of the dominant table form (a variation of the sculpture base) and the carefully arranged frozen positions of the various shapes on the horizontal surface.[16] I am proposing that the Beinecke Library courtyard is separate from Noguchi's other garden designs, which have other priorities and attributes (the most important one being the procession through space), and that the work at Yale can be described as part of the series of *tableaux* works.[17]

The few remaining photographs of the early studies for the Beinecke Library show that the origin of the design was directly

related to the early work seen in other *tableaux* sculpture. The initial two studies show a simple variation of a positive mound shape and a negative crater shape. The project developed and these two forms remained in the finished design as the two overlapping circles in the paving pattern.

The final set of metaphors connects to the influence of other artists and themes. Noguchi has long been associated with the sculptor Brâncuşi, whose minimal and highly crafted work inspired him. The fact that Noguchi worked as a stone cutter for Brâncuşi in 1927 justifies those associations.

But it is possible to see the influence of the French Surrealists in Noguchi's work as well, particularly the early work of Alberto Giacometti.[18] Giacometti's work has long been identified with the elongated and gaunt bronze figures of his later period, but before

that he produced a wide range of objects under the spell of the Surrealists in Paris. I would say that Giacometti produced *tableaux* sculptures that are both precedent and unacknowledged inspiration for Noguchi's work at Yale. The art pieces *Man, Woman and Child* of 1931 and *No More Play* of 1932 show the same themes as Noguchi's work. It is the sculpture *No More Play* that shows a strange combination of a child's board game and a cratered battlefield. The value of the exploration done by Giacometti is not just formal as in the rhythm of the curved recesses contrasted to the hard edged rectangle of the block but also symbolic. Here is an amazingly brilliant explication on the theme of death seen in the twisted anguish of the figures that act as pawns and in the directionless motion of the player through the game of life. This metaphor

Alberto Giacometti,
sculpture *Head/Skull*,
1934.

Noguchi sculpture
Red Cube with Marine
Midland Bank building
at 140 Broadway, New
York, Gordon Bunshaft,
Skidmore, Owings &
Merrill, 1968.

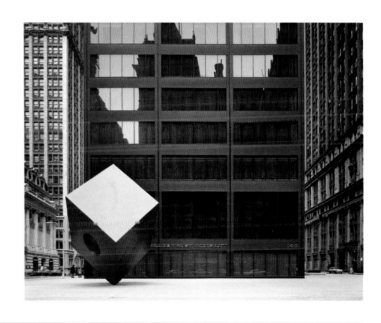

derives directly from the Surrealist tradition in the meditation on death, its immediacy and its existential power. Noguchi's penultimate study for the Beinecke Library shows in the model photos to have the cube, not yet rotated, floating above a curved recess. Noguchi's figure of the cube becomes exactly the same figure of anguish above a curved recess in the Giacometti work.

The force of Giacometti as an unacknowledged inspiration can be seen in the *Red Cube* in front of the Marine Midland Bank building at 140 Broadway in New York City, a Noguchi public sculpture which was also a collaboration with the architect Gordon Bunshaft of Skidmore, Owings & Merrill. Comparing Giacometti's *Head/Skull*, 1934, to Noguchi's *Red Cube*, 1968, there is the similarity of the Surrealist faceted cube-like form approximating a human skull reduced

by Noguchi to one more step of abstraction.[19] The circular recesses in Giacometti's object are the same as the cylindrical cutouts in Noguchi's cube making the two circular eyes of the skull. The urban plaza becomes a memento mori still life. Taken together with the previously discussed association of Noguchi with the symbol of the rolling die and its uneasy imbalance, it is not hard to project a theme of death with the cube as the skull; not necessarily representing the death of the artist, but the end of an uneasy alliance between the architect and the sculptor. For this work was the last completed collaboration between Noguchi and Bunshaft.

Like the Shelley poem on the ruined monumental sculptured head of the ancient king Ozymandias, the monumental *Red Cube* ("Red Skull" in this interpretation) of

Noguchi, at 140 Broadway, marks one more gravestone of the collaborative ideals of modernism and the escape of the artist to a larger world of his own making.

Olafur Eliasson, *The Weather Project,* an installation at the Tate Modern, London, 2003.

Gordon Matta-Clark, *Conical Intersection,* Paris, 1975.

The true avant-garde of architecture, the adventurous, risk-taking, experimenting, problem seeking, redefining fringe, is not in architecture. It is in the jetties, towers, tunnels, walls, rooms, bridges, ramps, mounds, ziggurats, the buildings and landscapes, structures and constructions of environmental art.

Michael McDonough

Artists Making Environments Without Architects or Against Architecture

There was in America, during the late 1960s through the 1970s, a symbolic rebellion by a select group of artists against architecture as a form of authority and political control. In the short span of six years starting in 1968 the sculptor Robert Smithson proposed a series of artworks on the scale of an airport in Texas; the artists Christo and Jeanne-Claude wrapped their first building, the Kunsthalle in Bern, Switzerland, also in 1968; in the next year Michael Heizer blasted and bulldozed two megalithic gashes in the Nevada desert, and in 1974 the artist/architect Gordon Matta-Clark cut an Englewood, New Jersey, residence in two for an artwork he called *Splitting.*

Each of these art projects could be called "Anti-architecture." Robert Smithson used the term "Dearchitectured" and Gordon Matta-Clark "Anarchitecture"[1] (combined from

anarchy and architecture). Together these works represent the expansion of the definition of sculpture into the new areas of performance, photography, ecology and installation.[2]

I believe these artists were not only attracted to a wider vision but driven out of an established, and faltering, zone of activity. The progress of contemporary art in the 1970s was spurred on by its failure to find a creative place for expression and innovation in galleries and public structures. This movement of "Anti-architecture" came about at the same time as the birth of monumental public art in the One Percent for Art programs in America's municipal buildings. This was a program which should have allowed public art to flourish but in practice, because of political limitations, denied a place to the most innovative artists and thus helped drive them in a new direction.[3]

Robert Smithson,
*Wandering Earth
Mounds and Gravel
Paths*, Dallas/Fort Worth
Regional Airport, 1967
(unbuilt).

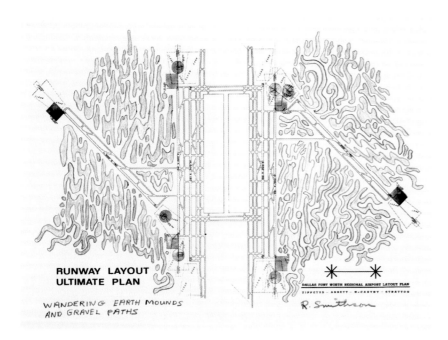

RUNWAY LAYOUT
ULTIMATE PLAN

WANDERING EARTH MOUNDS
AND GRAVEL PATHS

One consequence was that many artists moved on and engaged architectural themes without working with architects or working against the order represented by architecture.

Amongst the results of this process rank Earthworks, Land Art, Environmental Art and site-specific art. One of the more unusual examples is Smithson's sculpted earth mound, a construction that is part ancient burial tomb, part monumental sculpture and part landscape design that by its size and weight equals or overshadows nearby buildings and man-made objects.

The unusual unbuilt design made by Robert Smithson for the Dallas/Fort Worth Regional Airport in 1968 (with the engineering firm TAMS) is one of the first examples of Earth Art. The airport is among the largest in the United States covering an area of 202 hectares. Smithson's simple idea was that artwork at an airport should express the vast scale of air travel itself. He proposed a series of sculpted mounds and patterns in various geometric (or non-geometric) shapes that could be viewed from airplanes flying overhead.

In a similar theme during 1947 Isamu Noguchi had imagined an artwork that could be seen from the stratosphere with his unrealized proposal *Sculpture to Be Seen from Mars (Memorial to Man)*. The piece would have been a series of mounds that made an abstract human face as large as a mountain range in order to send a message to observers from outer space.

Although there are a number of recently completed airports that include an integral art program at the very beginning of their design none have proposed anything as radical as Smithson's scheme. A short list would be the Ronald Reagan National Airport in Washington, DC, by Cesar Pelli & Associates with thirty art pieces in 1997, the Pearson International Airport in Toronto by Skidmore, Owings & Merrill in 2004 with ten artists and the 2005 addition of Terminal D at the Dallas/Fort Worth Regional Airport by HKS with ten artists. In all cases the architects and art directors have made an extremely conservative use of the artists and the artworks. The exact purpose of the art program is still ambiguous; visual delight, civic pride or directional markers?

Because of his studies of existing types of airports for the Dallas project Smithson developed the idea of using the construction process in his art. The huge earth moving machinery that alter the landscape became Smithson's proposed tools. The final

Three views of Michael
Heizer, *Double Negative*,
Nevada, 1969.

Isamu Noguchi, *Memorial
to Man,* 1947.

presentation included placement of finished work by Robert Morris, Carl Andre and Sol LeWitt. By strict chronology this design is the first Earthwork (although titled *Aerial Art* by Smithson), for later that same year a group exhibition at the Dwan Gallery in New York started the use of that term.

In 1967, Smithson produced several different types of site designs for Dallas; the first was a series of ascending square asphalt "pavements" which later became the rectangular spiral reflecting pool *Clear Zone*. He then created the *Three Earth Windows*, a back lighted grid of broken glass. Further, he proposed a network of walkways that made a pattern, *Web of White Gravel Paths Surrounding Water Storage Tanks*, he then envisioned a random collection of landscape squiggles *Wandering Earth*

Mounds, and lastly *Aerial Map*, a series of interlocking concrete geometric shapes forming a monumental spiral.

None of these designs employed such traditional transportation images as gateways, direction markers, message boards or warning signs to the airplanes. They all engaged the geometry and scale of the runways and airport structures. The vast empty scrub grass areas were altered from an empty field to one of a series of figures.

In Smithson's words: "The world seen from the air is abstract and illusive. From the window of an airplane one can see drastic changes of scale, as one ascends and descends. The effect takes one from the dazzling to the monotonous in a short space of time – from the shrinking terminal to the obstructing clouds."[4]

The final unbuilt project consisted of a series of arithmetically decreasing concrete triangles that assembled to make a larger spiral shape. There is no record of where the piece would have been located, but the elegance of the form is a direct precedent for Smithson's most famous work, *The Spiral Jetty*, in the Great Salt Lake in Utah.

The proposal by Gordon Matta-Clark for the Museum of Modern Art in New York City is another example of an artist moving against architecture. Matta-Clark wished to attack a 1960s addition to the museum slated for demolition in 1978. The proposed target was the building designed by Philip Johnson and would be subjected to a series of surgical carvings through the tissue of built walls, slabs and façades. He was never able to convince the museum in New York to

Sol LeWitt, *Wall Drawing # 1100, Concentric Bands*, Terminal 1 at the Pearson International Airport, Toronto, Skidmore, Owings & Merrill and Moshe Safdie, 2004. Besides the sympathetic pattern corresponding to the geometry of the building the LeWitt mural connects to the larger imagery of the oculus skylight as a celestial eye.

Robert Smithson, *Spiral Jetty*, Great Salt Lake, Utah, 1970.

Sol LeWitt, *Untitled*, Dallas/Fort Worth International Airport, HKS Architects, 1999.

The space around my work is critical to it.
Donald Judd

Gordon Matta-Clark,
Splitting, photo collage,
1974.

Gordon Matta-Clark,
Splitting, Englewood,
New Jersey, 1970
(destroyed).

Why hang things on the wall
when the wall itself is so much
more a challenging medium?
Gordon Matta-Clark

undertake this but he followed through with this idea in two separate projects: one in Paris, *Conical Intersection,* 1975, and one for the Museum of Contemporary Art in Chicago, *Circus – The Caribbean Orange,* 1978.

The attack on architecture by Matta-Clark is aggressive and confrontational. The entire attitude of collaboration has been replaced with the term *détournement* which might be simply defined as "the reuse of pre-existing artistic elements in a new ensemble."[5]

The MoMA scheme takes a façade drawing of the six-story Miesian style building and proposes removing precisely cut sections of the building by a set of curved slices that create five floating circular remnants within a field of a large arc.

What was Matta-Clark trying to achieve? Was he making a critical comment on the power of the museum? A joke on the

seriousness of the architect? Creating a style game directed to the same art audience it proposes to displace? Did he propose politically radical communal spaces or stage sets for mass entertainment? Was he subversive or submissive?

There are no remaining carved buildings by Matta-Clark. But the artist's photographic series of montages of his destroyed projects show the amazing complexity of the layered planes revealed by geometric openings. They were both abstract, geometric and architectural (completely rational) while simultaneously being Surrealist in the juxta-position of dangerous voids at unexpected locations (completely dream-like).

The design is not a simplistic attack because one motif continues throughout from Matta-Clark's carving of the addition's façade to the adjacent original building of

1929: the 1.8-meter-diameter circular cutouts of both the Matta-Clark intervention and the existing MoMA top floor cornice.

For Edward Durrell Stone, the designer of the original MoMA building, cutting the circles in the cornice was both an artistic motif which he later developed into a trade-mark and an acceptable geometric ornament on an early presentation of modernism to America. Matta-Clark used circles of the same size as at the MoMA roof terrace, act-ing like bullet holes shot into his victim (as the artist had done in another work). How-ever, one must bear in mind that the exact cutting of the existing tempered glass in the windows would have been technologically impossible (the glass would just shatter).

It is one of the most confrontational collaborations between art and architecture, with the MoMA building standing in for a

What you see is what you see
Frank Stella

A thing is a hole in a thing it is not.
Carl Andre

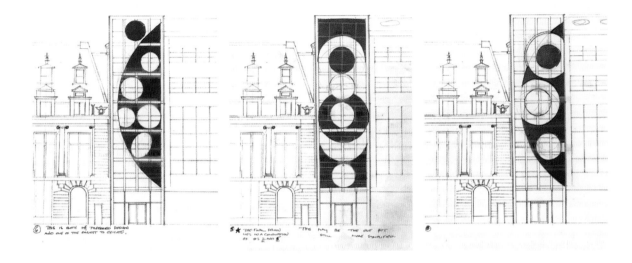

shot-to-death corpse. The targets of Matta-Clark's work were always buildings just short of demolition. They were vacant and available for examination and dissection with the most precise of construction tools. But they also represented, as all architecture does, an existing power structure. And Matta-Clark's attack on these buildings represented many themes on power: one of rebellion against the artist's architectural education, against the political establishment, against the art world market, against his famous artist father Roberto Matta (represented in the museum's collection). It is these intense psychologically charged elements that make the project one of the best "suspended conflicts."

The theme of the death of an "Architecture" is also found in the next artists; Christo and Jeanne-Claude. Famous for their work of wrapping large structures,

encircling islands and occupying vast landscapes, the artists' work many times evokes a Surrealistic reframing of an object, building or property. To examine the imagery of the wrappings by the artists it is possible to bring associations of veils, shrouds, mysterious packages and bundles of rags. Other critics have noted that, "carrying irony and dark humor to absurd extremes, Christo imbues his ephemeral monuments with more than a trace of imperious grandeur."[6] But the artists Christo and Jeanne-Claude reject any of these obvious metaphors and insist on the idea of wrapping as a method of evoking a pleasant abstract form with the repeated phrase "We want to create forms of joy and beauty", which is, however, not always a believable argument.[7]

One of their early works, the proposed MoMA wrapping, was commissioned as

a one day closing event on June 8, 1968, for the *Dada, Surrealism and Their Heritage* exhibition at the Museum. The metaphor of death (and dreams) is an important theme in Surrealist art and this project would have been a fitting conclusion for that show. The installation was not realized because New York City public officials were too anxious that such a spectacle would attract civic unrest, an unbiased interpretation of the high degree of anxiety produced by the design, and all we have to examine are the poster, model and drawings done by Christo. The pencil renderings by the artist show a realist perspective, on a photograph of the street, with a dark and brooding quality while the model is a corpse constructed of wood, twine, burlap and plastic; neither is a colorful explication of joy.

I often say, "Our work is a scream of freedom."
Christo and Jeanne-Claude

The proposal with its haphazard rope ties, bulging lumpy surfaces and indistinct scale is a match for the construction scaffolding found on any demolition site in New York City. The protective covering during the process of dismantling existing buildings is a dull colored screen material that hangs floor to floor billowing out in irregular forms creating ghost forms of the encapsulated structure behind.

The production of the vast and monumental works by these artists requires the same compromises that an architect would confront in making any public structure. One of those compromises is limiting the negative publicity on any event. At the time of its proposal the nature of institutions whether government or cultural was seriously questioned. But it is not possible to engage in the public world of monumental construction and criticize the sponsoring institutions at the same time.

Even though it was never realized, the Christo and Jeanne-Claude MoMA proposal is clearly an amazingly beautiful and articulate critical commentary on the institution, the building and the scheduled event.

The artists Smithson, Heizer, Matta-Clark and Christo/Jeanne-Claude present a range of ideas on expanding the scope of sculpture in more directions than illustrated here. But with these selected projects the path of artists moving away from architects can be traced and documented as a valid artistic direction in itself.

Anti-Architecture Art Absorbed

The inheritor of the ground work of these Environmental Art pioneers would be the contemporary Danish-Icelandic artist Olafur Eliasson. This artist has worked with themes of illusion, lighting, technology and at a scale that matches the previously mentioned artworks.

Eliasson's first major project, *The Weather Project*, 2003, was organized in the main turbine hall of the renovated Tate Modern gallery in London and was one step beyond the definition of monumental to being labeled celestial. The artist assembled a vast array of high intensity mono-frequency light fixtures behind a 9-meter-diameter translucent diffuser half circle, along with a ceiling mirror (making the image of a whole circle) and some special effects mist machines, with the resulting illusion of

Olafur Eliasson, *The Weather Project,* an installation at the Tate Modern, London, 2003.

Olafur Eliasson, *New York Waterfalls,* an installation on the East River (Brooklyn Bridge segment illustrated), New York, 2008.

You could say that I'm trying to put the body in the mind and the mind in the body. **Olafur Eliasson**

sunset so close you could touch it. The effect operated at two levels, one was the public amazement and amusement of a day at the beach inside the building and the second, visually connected to the remnant industrial elements of the power plant, was of an ominous science fiction stage-set dream.

More recently in his project called *The New York Waterfalls,* 2008, a collection of four scaffolding structures placed within communal sight along the East River in New York City support a powerful set of water pumps that recreate the rushing power of a massive waterfall. Set within Brooklyn's manufacturing sheds, ship piers and bridges this cascade of water seems both a tourist attraction of a freak of nature in the city and also more ominously of an industrial accident leaking at a destructive explosive gush.

Eliasson has developed "spectacles" that bring in the enormous scale of natural wonders, rainbows, fog, rain, waterfalls, sunsets, glaciers and volcanic lava, into an urban space or gallery. The juxtaposition of the natural/art phenomena in the context of the cultural/architecture container is a major component of the visual success of these projects. The, once daring, component of scale in the environmental artists has been absorbed into Eliasson's vocabulary without the necessity of its anti-commercial or anti-architectural associations.

All the power of the sun was fitted neatly into the Tate Modern and all the wildness of a waterfall installed at the base of the Brooklyn Bridge. The technology and philosophy of the artist's work has been elaborated on but never the emotional content of his work.

The fade-out of the environmental artists in the 1980s could have been seen as a result of tragic early death (Smithson died in 1973 and Gordon Matta-Clark died in 1978, both at the age of thirty-five) or a validation of their uncommercial (anti-architectural) rhetoric or the extreme difficulty (and cost) in producing artworks at that vast scale, Christo and Jeanne Claude's *Central Park Gates* taking over twenty-five years to complete, Michael Heizer's *The City* still being developed after thirty years and James Turrell's construction at the *Roden Crater* continuing after thirty-five years. But within one generation their work has been re-examined by young artists like Eliasson, and although the utopian rhetoric of the past has been discarded the anxiety and apprehension has not.

The Merging of Land Art, Landscape Architecture and Architecture

Perhaps the most publicized conflict between an artist and architect is the one filmed in 1997 for the central garden at the J. Paul Getty Center, a vast hilltop museum complex in Los Angeles.[8] Here the artist Robert Irwin and the architect Richard Meier were separated by the dividing line that plagues most collaboration: order versus expression, unity against variety, who is in control and who has authorship.

Richard Meier is an architect of great reputation with a specific style of buildings, a "white" design vocabulary developed from mixing the early and late work of the French/Swiss architect Le Corbusier. Certainly one of the most used words in the architect's vocabulary is "heroic" and the image of the Parthenon on the Acropolis was a major organizing concept for the Getty Center. The point of contention between artist and architect was the central garden, originally designed by Meier's office as a stone stair connecting across a pergola to a series of monumental circular rings that stepped down to a terrace overlooking the ravine and the view of the city beyond. It is this section of the project that was given to the artist Robert Irwin.

Robert Irwin is a conceptual artist who has experimented with a wide range of mediums: painting, sculpture, installation, sound art, Land Art and public art. The variety of his explorations shows in his workings on the central garden for the Getty Center. Instead of a logical geometric order there is a desire by the artist to produce an impulsive and sensuous experience not bound by one central theme.

The problem was that the architect could not give up control of the last designed area of the complex to any of the chosen landscape architects, so the client chose a feisty artist to add some diversity to a stylistic monolithic and monochromatic scheme.[9] The climax to this filmed argument is when the design architect (in the background) has his substitute criticize the artist's work and records Irwin's direct response: "Bull…shit!", shocking and amusing the audience of polite museum staff.

In his own published version of the events Meier noted: "What was most difficult for me in this whole affair was that Irwin was being treated as an artist while I was being relegated to the secondary status of architect. His creative work was regarded as sacrosanct and subject to only token cost control, while my contribution was fair game for everyone."[10]

The Irwin garden consists of zigzag paths that ramp down to the main space below. The area on the way down is planted extensively with numerous flowering species and has a water channel with boulders continuing to the bottom. The final destination is a series of circular enclosures that first start with rows of deciduous trees and bougainvillea arbors, then continuing with more ramps to rings of low plantings and a central pool with an elaborate geometric three circle labyrinth of shrubs.

What is strange about the Irwin garden is how opposed it is to traditional landscape ideas of functionality: the central azalea maze is in the middle of a pool and therefore unwalkable, the plant selection was out of the normal species for the climate and requires seasonal replanting and the elevation of the main portion of the garden is below sight lines to the ravine below. It is these and many other distinctions that make this artwork separate from a traditional garden and places it into the classification of Land Art.

It is true that the Irwin garden eliminates the image of a stone base for the complex, the walls of the acropolis, but it connects to other themes in the buildings as the circular atrium of the nearby Research Institute. The motif of the circle appears in several places in the garden: the ramps, trellis and labyrinths. It is this adjustment to the geometry of one of the existing buildings that places this most debated garden in an unacknowledged sympathetic context to the architecture. Also because of the grade drop the central garden is eased into an acceptable separate world of natural color and texture, out of any conflict with the architecture above.

This story illustrates the generic problem with collaboration in the visual arts, but the final results may grow (literally) to be one of the most successful and sympathetic installations of Land Art within modern architecture.

Robert Irwin, sculpture *Tilted Plane*, 1999, in foreground of Rachofsky House, Dallas,

Aerial view of the J. Paul Getty Center, Los Angeles, Richard Meier, 1997.

Robert Irwin, Getty Center central garden, 1997.

Getty Research Institute's curved entry terrace at the J. Paul Getty Center.

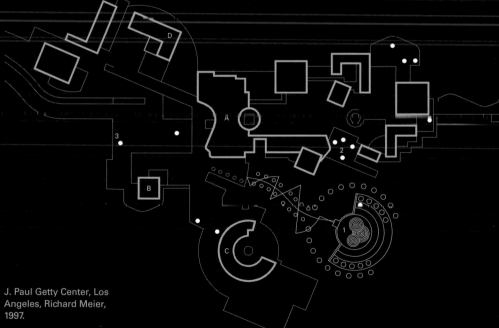

J. Paul Getty Center, Los Angeles, Richard Meier, 1997.

Site plan:
A J. Paul Getty Museum
B Restaurant and cafe
C Getty Research Institute
D Getty Administration and
   Trust

1 R. Irwin, central garden
2 Fran and Ray Stark
   Sculpture Garden
3 M. Puryear, sculpture
   That Profile

8: Sculptural Space Becomes Architectural Space

Until lately art has been one thing and everything else something else.
Donald Judd

In the Baroque, the center would be multiple, in the vortex there is no center nor centers but merely the relative tension established around multiple differential surfaces.
Greg Lynn

Blobs in Bilbao and Boxes in Berlin

Recently we have seen the adaptation in contemporary architecture of using the curved and convoluted surfaces of abstract sculpture in the construction of avant-garde buildings. One of the immediate justifications for this development is the availability of computer software that allows for rendering elaborate shapes and the translation of those forms to dimensioned sections producing buildable orthogonal coordinates. Some have labeled these new forms as "Blobs"[1] and the resulting interior as "Warped Space."[2] The question is how can art, whose basis is figurative, work with (or against) a setting that is also figurative? The traditional relationship of art in architecture was one of figure to ground and now has been changed, in this setting, to one of figure to figure.

And in a parallel development a contemporary style of architecture evolving directly from the International Style of the 1930s has been labeled as "Minimal Architecture." The name originates from the buildings' formal simplicity, austere rectangular forms, and points to its predecessor in the art world of "Minimalism."[3]

When these two meet, Minimal Architecture proposes a relationship with Minimal Art that instead of the traditional visual *gestalt* of figure to ground has been changed to one of ground to ground. What is the formal relationship (or conflict) between two objects whose visual vocabularies are both based on repetition, industrial materials and planar monochromatic surfaces?

In this case the Minimal Art world defined by the artist Donald Judd as producing "specific objects"[4] overlaps with the vision of architect Mies van der Rohe for his buildings that he described as "almost nothing" (beinahe nichts).

Each of these two architectural movements, Digital Form and Minimalism, is illustrated with a pair of examples that shows the limitation, possibilities and strategies of collaboration between the contemporary arts.

Richard Serra, sculpture *Torqued Ellipses*, Dia Center for the Arts, New York, 1997. The sculpture was shown in Gallery 104 at the Guggenheim Museum Bilbao in 1999.

Exterior of Guggenheim Museum Bilbao with "Fish" Gallery 104 in foreground, 1997.

I would hope that architects could accept the fact that they are architects and useful as architects and could stop flirting with the notion of being both artist and architect.
Richard Serra

Part I: The Adaptation of Architecture to Warped Sculptural Space

Artists and Architects at the Guggenheim Museum Bilbao

Two examples of the millennial "Warped Space" buildings that attempt to integrate art into their compositions are the elaborate bent and twisted Guggenheim Museum Bilbao in Spain and the smooth curved interior of the Ibirapuera Auditorium in Brazil.

The Guggenheim Museum Bilbao, 1997, by the architect Frank Gehry is infamous for demonstrating an intuitive and irrational new form vocabulary for modernism. But the building was not a pure unfunctional sculptural expression; it can be reduced to a "flower diagram" that has its entry at the major vertical space and its galleries extending radially from that central point. The main mass of the structure is broken into rectilinear sections at the south, relating to the existing city grid, and the elaborate twisted volumes at the north, connecting to an imagery of curved boat forms against the river. Part of its original program was the necessity to incorporate the work of two sculptures in the museum: Claes Oldenburg's and Coosje van Bruggen's *Soft Shuttlecock* and Richard Serra's construction *Snake*.[5]

The Oldenburg/van Bruggen piece *Soft Shuttlecock* is located in the main entry volume at the vertical center to the entire complex with angular glass walls intersecting curved plaster volumes. The figurative enlarged badminton piece with its droopy feathers is lost within the tangle of weaving elements in the lobby. The Surrealist juxtaposition between the confines of the normal world and the inflated reality of Oldenburg's artwork is lost here, and the work seems to dissolve into the walls of the lobby. This is a perfect example of the severe

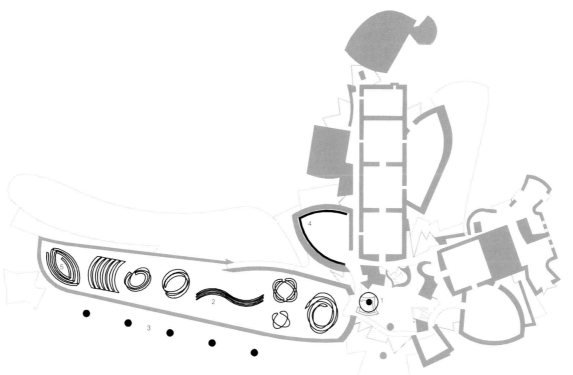

Guggenheim Museum
Bilbao, Frank Gehry,
1997.

Second floor plan:
1 C. Oldenburg, C. van
  Bruggen, sculpture
  Soft Shuttlecock
2 R. Serra, sculpture
  Snake
3 Y. Klein, sculpture
  Fire Fountain
4 S. LeWitt, mural
  Mural # 831
5 R. Serra, sculpture
  Blind Spot Reversed

I am for an art that is political-erotical-
mystical, that does something other
then sit on its ass in a museum.
Claes Oldenburg

limitations of the interaction between art
and the aggression of warped space forms
that surround it. The metaphor of the artist's
flaccid droopy feathered "cock" surrendering
in impotence to the architect's soaring phallic
forms in the atrium is a theater script playing
out the power of architecture against art.

Gehry worked with the artist Richard
Serra as early as 1981 in the New York
Architectural League exhibition titled
Collaboration; Artists and Architects. They
submitted a bridge design with two pylons;
one end of the bridge held up by Gehry
in the form of an angled gigantic fish and
the other by Serra with an enormous tilted
steel slab. The project is a literal tug of war
between the artist and the architect. This
juxtaposition also shows the beginning of
the repeated use of the image of a fish and a
snake by the architect.

The repeated motifs used by Gehry of
the elongated fish and the coiled snake
translate into two general typological forms;
the linear shed and the point pavilion.[6] The
fish/shed motif can be seen in the earlier
type of the nineteenth century train shed,
which is a long fish form with exposed
structural skeleton and fish-like scales in its
glass skylight roof. The snake/pavilion motif
can be related to a number of centralized
buildings such as a bilaterally symmetric
domed church.

The Guggenheim Museum Bilbao has
both form types in a developed state.
The curvy galleries clad in titanium scales
derive from the fish form studies, and the
centralized vertical atrium consisting of
fragmented glass curtain wall segments
derives its inspiration from the original
cylindrical snake form.

The location for the Serra sculpture
Snake is at the main floor Gallery 104
(named the "Fish"), an enormous volume of
approximately 131 meters in length and 25
meters in width with a varying ceiling height
going from 15 to 23 meters. The room was
designed structurally to hold the weight of
Richard Serra's massive sculpture *Snake*
consisting of three units of weathering steel
conical sections at 15.8 meters in length,
4 meters in height and 180 metric tonnes
in weight. Gehry's strategy to engage the
proposed sculptures is to keep the floor
as a neutral base for the display of the art
and distort the shapes of the ceiling with
selectively exposed radial beams and molded
skylights in order to create an active but
distant background.

The challenge of the architecture to
the art is in the scale of the room and the

Frank Gehry, fish and snake sculpture *Prison*, Leo Castelli Gallery, New York, 1992.

Richard Serra, sculpture *Snake*, and Lawrence Weiner, installation *Reduced*, at Gallery 104, Guggenheim Museum Bilbao.

The brief for Bilbao was there are dead artists and we should make classical galleries for them and there are live artists and we should make galleries that will confront them.
Frank Gehry

distortion of the ceiling. It is a fairly regular white box gallery space with a literal twist, in the distortion of the ceiling plane. For this installation it is as if the art and architecture have traded responsibility for the room, since the art is top-less by the consistent straight cut-off height of the steel walls while the architecture, in its top-heavy skylights, establishes a visual substitute of what the art is missing.

The original Serra sculpture *Snake* was later added to and became an assembly of eight pieces that occupied the entire gallery. With the Serra work establishing not only surface volume but internal volume as well, the group becomes the equivalent of a series of small rooms built within the larger gallery volume. The sequence from entry to end is a series of three sets of concentric sculptures alternating with a

set of linear sculptures. The decreasing arithmetic sequence of spacing the sculpture along the long gallery space turns out to be: 3 Concentric – 1 Linear – 2 Concentric – 1 Linear – 1 Concentric. A strange coded message from the artist to the architect using the same general form types in the building: the linear "fish" and the concentric "snake."

The play-off of one curved steel plane to another gives another compositional element to the total works. But for this essay the inflection of the last work to the building is the most telling. The last sculpture titled *Blind Spot Reversed*, 2005, takes the concentric spiral motif of the other pieces and distorts it from a circle to an almond shape that matches exactly the adjacent curve of the end gallery walls, making a perfect fit.

The assembly of all eight sculptures is given unity by the fact that this is the work of one phase of one artist. All the objects relate by their similarity of materials, colors, heights and curved shapes. Also they are unified by the fact that all can be seen in a totality from the balcony of the next floor.

Interestingly, the most theatrical displays of Serra sculpture have been in interior spaces slightly too small for the object displayed.[7] Unlike the evenly spaced perimeter around each artwork at the Bilbao installation, the tall twisted massive steel plates are more imposing when they consensually work against their enclosure. The best example would be the object titled *Union of the Torus and the Sphere*, 2001, squeezed within the small column spans and rectangular walls of an old factory in the Dia:Beacon Gallery near New York.

Interior of Dia:Beacon
Gallery, New York, and
*Union of the Torus and
the Sphere* by Richard
Serra, 2001.

Interior of Gallery 104
with view from upper
balcony looking onto
sculpture *Torqued
Spiral* in foreground by
Richard Serra, 2004.

If anything, this century in architecture
will be marked by the demise of the
right angle [...] How will this proceed
from my work, if at all? Probably by
misinterpretation.
Richard Serra

The slight geometric warping of the
surface becomes emotional and tactile in the
immediate visual and volumetric pressure
between it and the enclosing walls.

At the Bilbao Guggenheim the floating
of the dark rust red art in the soft white
plaster volume presents a clear distinction
between the textures of the container and
the contained, but it does nothing to match
the benefits of claustrophobic juxtaposition
to the formal elements of the art in other
more successful displays.

Artists and Architects in the Modernist Brazilian Baroque

The architect Oscar Niemeyer has always
involved artists in the production of his Latin
American buildings. His work has gradually
evolved from the strict rectangular grids of
the International Style to a free-flowing and
free-form curvilinear structure. Although he
cannot be considered part of the generation
of architects doing computer aided Warped
Space his work can show how artistic
collaboration in similar spaces is possible.

Three of the most notable commissioned
artworks for his buildings are in the
Auditorium built in the Ibirapuera Park at São
Paulo, Brazil, 2003. The Auditorium building
is part of a complex that was designed by
Niemeyer fifty years ago. It is a trapezoid in
plan and a triangle in section, which allows
for the assembly of spaces to proceed in

sequence by height from the lowest to the
tallest: entry, lobby, auditorium and stage
with overhead scenery space.

Inside this hard geometry are three art
pieces: the entry canopy *Flame (Labareda)*
by Niemeyer himself, the lobby sculpture
Untitled by Tomie Ohtake and a mural titled
Orchestra Rehearsal (Ensaio de orquestra) in
the lower level music school by Luis Antônio
Vallandro Keating, both from 2003.

The lobby is a single open volume
with curved edges at the walls and ceilings;
although it is not a complicated curved
surface the calculated effects of the up-
lights from the floor (not from the ceiling)
gives the windowless room a soft
ambiguous form.

The painted plaster sculpture *Untitled*
by Ohtake seems to be a gestural single
paint stroke blown up to enormous size. The

[...] the Baroque
is defined by the
fold that goes out
to infinity [...]
Gilles Deleuze

Exterior entry of
Ibirapuera Auditorium,
São Paulo, Oscar
Niemeyer, designed
1955, completed 2003.

These are mountains that look like
women's bodies lying down and they
were designed by God the day that
God thought he was Niemeyer.
Eduardo Galeano

The building appears to be a platonic
solid having oral sex with the sky.
Robert Storr

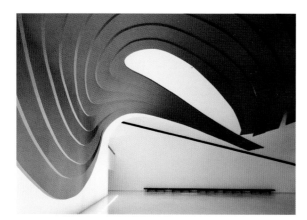

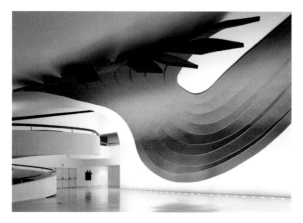

S-shaped sculpture exists both at the wall and ceiling of the lobby and directly over the spiral stair to the balcony seats. With both the main entrance and the theater entrance recessed and almost hidden, the artwork and stair act as the main focus for the room.

The original 1950s organization of the room was altered by Niemeyer as a response to the recent proposed artwork. The architect moved the spiral stair off-center of the lobby to better engage the artwork and to tilt the visual weight of the room to contradict the basic axial procession from the exterior entry to the theater entry.[8] It is one of the few examples of a productive dialogue between architect and artist in an engaged artwork addition.

The sculpture acts as a subdivision of the empty all-white room which in itself has been simplified with the artwork in mind.

The Bilbao Guggenheim and the Ibirapuera Auditorium by Comparison

The Guggenheim at Bilbao makes a compromise between artist and architect by splitting the responsibility for the qualities of the room. The "Fish" gallery by Gehry distorts the traditional white box by its vast scale and ceiling articulation. The artwork by Serra commands the other qualities of the room by having its walls as the only dynamic vertical surfaces in the gallery. Although the collection of eight separate artworks is unique, the sum of experience does not match the drama of other displays of the same artist's work where the enclosure and artwork are in much more of a conflict.

By contrast, the Niemeyer/Ohtake collaboration presents a much more generous gesture by the architect to the artist. The example in São Paulo is one

where Niemeyer makes the curved white walls and ceiling a neutral element, allowing the colored sculpture to command the enclosure and engage the off-center spiral stair as an extension of its influence and movement. Added to this is the generous homage the architect has paid the artist by taking the imagery and color of her sculpture as the basis for his own design for the entry canopy of the building.

Aerial view of the
Chichu Art Museum,
Naoshima Island,
Japan, Tadao Ando,
2004.

The main thing wrong with painting
is that it is a rectangular plane placed
flat against the wall. **Donald Judd**

Part II: The Difference between Minimal Architecture and Minimal Art

Is it possible that even though the attributes of Minimal Art and Minimal Architecture are similar, the same clean, austere, rectangular volumes, the objectives of the artist and the architect are not?

Minimal Art was defined in 1964 with the works of artists as Donald Judd, Carl Andre, Walter De Maria and others. The common characteristics of the artworks were an austere simplicity using repetition and industrial materials. The start of Minimalism in architecture happened much later in the 1970s when young architects in London and Japan were producing small shops and restaurants.[9]

Some visual elements are similar, but in the artworks there is a polemical aggressive confrontational quality that is not found in the architecture of a decade later. The buildings do not present a dramatic philosophic break with the previous image of modernism, but instead offer a refined stylistic version of the original International Style. This is best illustrated by the fact that many of the first Minimalist spaces were fashion showrooms.

The strategies for collaboration with these artists and architects would seem relatively easy at first glance, but an effective and engaging union of the arts is more complicated.

This can be demonstrated by looking at buildings by Tadao Ando that concentrated on an artistic unity with others and the reverse condition where the artist Donald Judd produced the surrounding for his own art alone.

Since the very beginning of his career the Japanese architect Tadao Ando has taken the Le Corbusier influenced post-war Japanese modernism and directed it to a

Within the simplicity of the box you discover qualities that make you aware of the specialness of the space or the things around you. **Tadao Ando**

geometric austerity that has been compared to the spirituality of both Zen Buddhism and western Minimal art.

But for all that is eliminated in the elements of traditional comfort and habitation in his work it still develops with a theme of the theatrical and sensuous.

Ando's many museums allow him to interact with a number of contemporary artists, patrons and curators. The strategy for collaboration that the architect uses is a simple adaptation of his trademark of long blank walls and expansive empty outdoor spaces. Unlike Mies van der Rohe, whose manipulation of artworks transforms them to the characteristics of walls and columns, Ando's placement of art is to allocate one piece of art in its own special room, an idea similar to the Japanese *tokonoma*, the ancient decorative alcove for the display of

a single precious item in the ceremonial tea pavilion. The art is not so much framed as it is sanctified in its own temple for worship.

The perfect example of this is the Chichu Art Museum, 2004, at the isolated island of Naoshima in Japan. Here the work of the three artists Walter De Maria, James Turrell and Claude Monet are placed in individual underground rooms linked to courtyards open to the sky. The literal translation for the Japanese name Chichu Bijutsukan is "Art Museum in the Earth." The installation of the De Maria work *Time/Timeless/No Time*, 2004, is the most extreme. The artist is known for his installations and conceptual works that take up the entire volume of a gallery with simple elements: metal rods, scrim walls, dirt and other materials. For the Japanese museum he proposed gold finished rods in sets of three placed in equal

separation around the suggested cube-like room with the center dominated by a 1.8-meter-diameter stone sphere. The stage set appearance of the installation is emphasized by the monumental staircase filling the center of the room, leading nowhere. The entire assembly of art and architecture seems ready for a religious performance of an exotic cult. It is easily mistaken for a place of worship to the deity of modern art.

The other unique condition in the Chichu Art Museum is the outdoor courtyards with the basic geometric shapes of circle, square and triangle. In any other place these would be seen as a perfect location to display the individual piece of sculpture, but here they remain unused, intentionally designed as inaccessible, but visible, spaces. They are the indulgence of the architect making an artistic signature.

Pulitzer Foundation
for the Arts, St. Louis,
Missouri, Tadao Ando,
2001.

Entry façade of the
Pulitzer Foundation
for the Arts.

Ground floor plan:
1 R. Serra, sculpture
  Joe
2 E. Kelly, sculpture
  Blue Black
3 S. Burton, sculpture
  Rock Settee
4 K. Smith, sculpture
  Pee Body

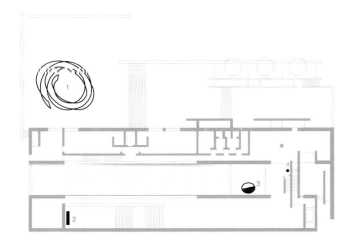

Artist and Architect at the Pulitzer Foundation for the Arts

Ando has produced another building in direct collaboration with modern artists at the Pulitzer Foundation for the Arts in St. Louis, Missouri, 2001. This work has more development in the same interaction of the arts.

The artist Ellsworth Kelly has had early experience in producing monumental abstract artwork within an architectural setting. His first mural was for the Philadelphia Bus Terminal building in 1957, now located in the MoMA in New York, a range of four rows of geometric shapes in front of four rows behind. Like a basket woven with strips of primary colors the mural *Sculpture for a Large Wall*, 1957, animates the wall with a metaphor of movement for a frantically busy lobby.

For the Pulitzer Foundation he was assigned a wall that ended a long rectangular gallery with a wide set of steps in front of it. It was obviously a point of central focus but not a symmetric position. Kelly proposed a flat rectangular "sculpture" divided into two by a pair of dark colors: blue and black.

It at first appears simplistic to the point of absurdity, a rectangle within a rectangle, but the connectiveness here between the art and the architecture brings up a rich set of compositional relationships.

The Kelly artwork *Blue Black* is a sculpture on an aluminum panel monumentally sized at 8.5 × 1.8 meters, giving the proportions of a rectangle almost exactly similar to the wall that it is mounted on (subdivided by the balustrade). The width of the painting is the same as the side rectangular cutout opening in the wall, which makes a parallel rectangle two thirds the height of the artwork. Interestingly, the architect lowered the height of the opening on request by Kelly so as to visually control these two parallel rectangles: art and architecture.[10] The value of this rectangle within rectangles is how in this environment small relationships of proportion, orientation and size give a resonating connection of the artwork and its enclosure. The art very successfully becomes a detail of the architecture, and simultaneously the wall becomes an extension of the sculpture in the image of the stepped squares in the *Homage to the Square* painting series of Josef Albers, a teacher of Kelly.

The Richard Serra sculpture, titled *Joe*, 2000, located on an exterior courtyard of the Pulitzer Foundation is one of the first torqued spirals that the artist had produced. It is a set of rolled Corten steel plates of enormous size that are welded together to make a

Josef Albers, *Homage to the Square*, 1951.

Ellsworth Kelly, wall sculpture *Blue Black*, 2001, Pulitzer Foundation for the Arts.

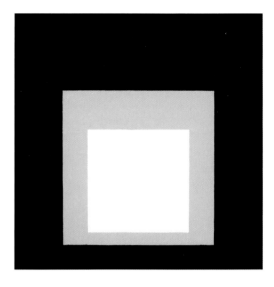

I know that when I was in Europe I wanted to come back to America and paint huge paintings that covered the outsides of buildings. But now I feel I want to make things in my studio – and let anything bigger grow out of that.
Ellsworth Kelly

constantly weaving spiral wall. It is literally
sculpture in the round and stands dead
center in the exterior courtyard of the Pulitzer
Foundation. The artist and architect chose a
simple and conservative placement of the
artwork contrasting one to the other: rust red
sculpture to white concrete building, curved
art to straight walls and a discrete walking
space separating the object from any building
part. For Serra with his "site-specific"
inclination this is a disappointment. Unlike
the sculpture *Axis*, 1988, which matches the
cubic mass of the adjacent Philip Johnson
designed *Kunsthalle* in Bielefeld, 1968, or
Serra's sculpture *Tilted Spheres,* 2006, at
the Toronto Pearson International Airport that
mimics the scalloped roof profile, the work
at the Pulitzer Foundation seems disengaged
from its surroundings and could have easily
been located by the curator in any place.

Installations in Marfa, Texas

The next example to pair with the Ando work
is the private enclave built and rehabilitated
by the artist Donald Judd. He was certainly
the most articulate of the Minimalist artists
during the 1960s. Judd produced paintings,
sculpture, extensive art criticism, invented
the definitive Minimalist phrase "specific
objects" and hated being called a Minimalist
artist.

With a loft building as a base in the New
York City art world, Judd chose an extremely
isolated area of southwest Texas to start a
series of habitable experiments with art,
architecture and the desert landscape. After
purchasing the abandoned army base Fort
D. A. Russell with its 138 hectares of land
in 1973, Judd proceeded to transform the
area into one of the world's most unique and
eccentric demonstrations on uniting art in

architecture. The airplane hangars, machine
sheds, artillery buildings, barracks, offices
were transformed into vast empty volumes
with only the barest necessities left to hold
up and contain the space within. Their new
purpose was to display his monumentally
scaled sculpture and the works he collected
with the same strategy that Ando used where
the Minimal artwork stands alone within its
own dedicated free-standing pavilion.

The Marfa complex takes this one step
further than Ando by taking advantage
of the existing structures and presenting
the same industrial materials used in the
artwork for the building framing around the
artwork: rusting steel girders and pitted
corrugated siding for the crushed cars of
artist John Chamberlain and raw concrete,
common brick and plywood for Judd's own
works. The other compositional element

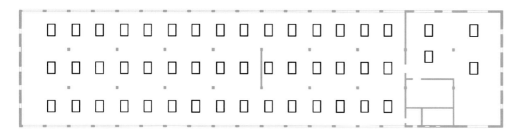

is the enormous scale of the rooms. As if a cure for the claustrophobia of New York City, one room for the Judd works in the artillery shed is 18.9 x 42.7 meters, another for Chamberlain's art pieces is 23.2 x 45.7 meters.

The two buildings that are the most important to demonstrate Judd's contribution of placing art in the composition of modern architecture are the artillery buildings. These two identical short span shed structures were re-roofed with metal vaults and hold Judd's *100 Untitled Works in Mill Aluminum*, 1986. The 6.1 × 8.5 meter bay size defined by concrete columns holds two of the total of fifty metal Judd sculptures in each building.

Judd's rectangular metal boxes, 1.04 x 1.30 x 1.83 meters, stand within a similarly proportioned rectangular box of columns and beams. The metal boxes are not exactly identical; each contains some variation of an open or closed side and the position of a central metal piece: high or low, straight or slanted, parallel or perpendicular. Also the pair of boxes are not centered in each bay but consistently pushed to one side implying a direction of movement through the space. The multiple bays imply an infinite repeating series with the artist expanding his artwork into the building, then into the world.

Once again the Albers proto-minimal painting *Homage to the Square* becomes an organizing image for the placement of Minimal Art. The rectangles of the Judd artwork visually command the space around them blocked out by the concrete work, which then sits within the larger rectangle of the building itself. Like the Albers painting the value of the installation is in the subtlety of the visual relations between the rectangles. The slight off-center of Albers squares implies a perspectival shift making a constant visual break from the obvious flat zoned paint to an implied depth.

For Judd the envelope of the architecture bows to the nature of the sculpture enclosed: the Chamberlain sculptures of ruinous car crashes within the derelict metal warehouse, and the Judd serial assemblies of rectangular boxes in lockstep with a repeated structural framework followed by the equal rhythm of the windows.

Donald Judd,
*100 Untitled Works
in Mill Aluminum,*
1982–1986, detail.

Donald Judd, sculpture
Untitled, 1992.

It takes a great deal of time and
thought to install work carefully.
Donald Judd

Minimal Architecture and
Minimal Art in Comparison

The aggressive shape making for avant-
garde buildings of the new millennium
is an obvious attempt to make a clear
separation of this time and the twentieth
century. The visual disjunction of a blob
building to its surroundings is severe, that
is part of its marketing appeal. But with
the hyper-articulated forms there is little
place for the other arts except in a regressive
placement of the sculpture detached from
the building, standing guard at the entrance
lawn.

But counter-intuitively, with the severe
rectangular Minimal architecture, that started
similar to Minimal Art in name only, there is
a great potential for an active engagement of
the arts.

The potential for the articulation of a
framing system would come from the
Minimal Art and not the building. In effect
because of the relatively neutral setting
from the architect the artist is forced to take
command of a larger scope of design than
for the artwork itself.

Some Aspects of the Color Blue: the Sky, the Sea, the Void

Two European artists famous for their extreme minimal presentations have both produced mystical artwork in the context of modern buildings. The first would be the French painter Yves Klein, considered a reactionary against the abstract Expressionist paintings of the 1960s; Klein produced monochromatic installations by applying fire, water or painted nudes against his canvas.[11] One painting series he developed was with a saturated, turquoise tinted, blue that became his visual trademark and was even patented by him as "International Klein Blue."

His largest work in that series was in 1959 for six commissioned murals at the Musiktheater im Revier in Gelsenkirchen, Germany, by the architect Werner Ruhnau.[12] Four of the vast murals (the largest is 7 × 20 meters) symmetrically cover two sides of the lobby and consist of an application of the Klein Blue over a range of hundreds of sponges fastened to the wall. The work is mystical in its blank silence, dominating the room by its size and pulsing color. It is immediately tempting to associate the sponges and the color blue as a metaphor for the sea or the saturation of the color as a gesture to an illusionist spatial depth. But for this artist, who had studied eastern religions, the imagery might be more emotional in the symbolism of emptiness and modern anomie.

But for our purposes the Klein mural fits into the composition of the building by being one of three commissioned art objects (by artists Norbert Kricke, Yves Klein, Robert Adams) that are all long rectangular works placed against horizontal blank rectangular surfaces. Although made of different materials (metal rods, sponges and precast concrete) and styles (Constructivist, Pre-Minimal and Brutalist), they operate as part of the architecture by being articulated horizontal bands (like decorative moldings): in the first case visually extending the small theater to the larger (Kricke), secondly connecting one lobby to its other side (Klein) and lastly linking the south entry to the north entry (Adams).

The other artist is the German Gerhard Merz, a Minimalist painter with an intense interest in the forms and images of modern architecture who titles his work as "Archi-Painting."

Yves Klein mixing paint during construction, 1959.

Yves Klein, mural at the upper lobby of Musiktheater im Revier.

Merz has produced proposals for the Marx-Engels-Forum in Berlin, a Miesian pavilion for the 2000 Hanover World Exhibition and an amazing interaction with the architect Hans Kollhoff in the renovation of the former Reichsbank in Berlin, originally built in 1940 to a design of Heinrich Wolff, for part of the new Federal Foreign Office.

The artist was commissioned to produce three artworks in the former Reichsbank building: a new ceiling in the lobby, a new movable partition wall at the conference hall and a painting at the entry to the board room.

The lobby was transformed into an expansive blue ceiling with its perimeter "triglyph-like" fluorescent tubes. Here as well the blue seems to be a metaphor for the expansive sky above, but in the context of the building's history it connects to a larger theme. The building was of course the banking headquarters for the National Socialist regime and then the seat of the East German Communist Party Politbüro and Central Committee; later with the unification of the two Germanys the building and an addition were to become the Foreign Ministry. History, politics and power are not the usual themes for Minimal Art, which is presented to be without symbolism, but there are interpretations that see the inevitable figurative element in even this art form. The associations of endless repetition, hard geometry and an unremitting order can be seen as a symbol of a controlling political order. Added to this is the erasure of the building's original artwork consisting of exterior figurative relief sculpture at each ground floor window panel and the large imperial eagle in the entry vestibule. What makes the Merz installation so brilliant is that it operates (and comments) on the decorative, functional and metaphorical level. The expanse of the blue ceiling wipes cleans all previous ornaments.

The historian Anna Chave noted: "The blank face of minimalism may come into focus as the face of capital, the face of authority, the face of the father"[13] or the face (façade) of a building. If the work of Donald Judd depended on (or engaged) the space of its presentation, then the work of Gerhard Merz depends on the erasure of architecture (and memory) within its presentation.

Gerhard Merz, lobby installation at former Reichsbank, Berlin, 1934, renovated for the Federal Foreign Office by Hans Kollhoff, 1999.

Exterior of the Musiktheater im Revier, Gelsenkirchen, Germany, Werner Ruhnau, 1959, with Norbert Kricke's sculpture Large Horizontal on Two Planes (Röhrendickicht) at the adjacent small theater.

Exterior of Musiktheater im Revier

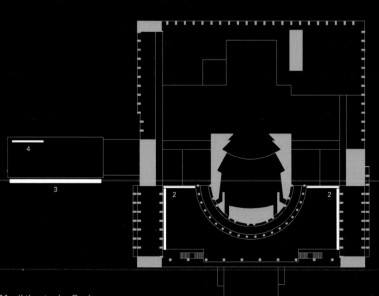

Musiktheater im Revier, Gelsenkirchen, Germany, Werner Ruhnau, 1959.

Second floor plan:
1 R. Adams, sculpture
2 Y. Klein, mural
3 N. Kricke, sculpture
4 J. Tinguely, mobile

9: Conclusion: What Shall We Do Now?

Peter Eisenman,
*Memorial to the
Murdered Jews of
Europe*, Berlin, 2005.

Sigfried Giedion,
*Space, Time and
Architecture*, 1941,
double page spread of
Pablo Picasso painting
and Walter Gropius'
Bauhaus building.

Art is a lie that makes us
realize the truth.
Pablo Picasso

The visionary lies to himself,
the liar only to others.
Friedrich Nietzsche

Two Possible Comparisons for Consideration

One of the earliest attempts to make a connection between the ideas of modern art and modern architecture is seen in the paired images from the 1941 book *Space, Time and Architecture*. The author, Sigfried Giedion, proposes a comparison of Picasso's Cubist painting *L'Arlésienne*, 1912, and a photograph of Walter Gropius' Bauhaus building in Dessau, Germany, 1926. He argues that Cubism with its transparency of overlapping planes creates a duality of spatial experience (overlapping of frontal and profile views) which resembles the all-glass corner of the Bauhaus workshop wing (interior and exterior spaces being interchangeable).[1]

I believe that this comparison is forced and deceptive, made believable by a set of unstated visual similarities between these two images that have nothing to do with the argument. The Cubist figure is seen in fragmented profile, the L-shaped nose, or multiple noses, looks the same as the several L-shaped corner mullions of the window. The painting's major diagonal lines are parallel with the perspective diagonals of the building's floor slabs, and the grid of paint marks at the upper left of the painting recalls the glint of light off the grid of small glass panes on the building. Out of all the Cubist paintings to choose from, Giedion selected a work that had multiple superficial similarities to this one specific Bauhaus photograph, supporting his argument at the subconscious level.

With his unstable analogy Giedion meant to attach the aesthetic and philosophical status of analytic Cubism to the visually impoverished modern architecture and so link the two arts within his narrow definition of the Spirit of the Age.

The limitations of Giedion's weak visual juxtaposition have been elaborated on by other authors.[2] I want to add another set of comparisons to illustrate how such linkages may point a different direction for further investigation, one direction that I believe predicts an optimistic future for work between the arts.

Pablo Picasso, *Still Life with Chair Caning*, 1912.

Krzysztof Wodiczko, projection on the Hirshhorn Museum, Washington, DC, October 25–27, 1988.

I suggest pairing another Picasso, *Still Life with Chair Caning*, 1912, representing the technique of collage, with the photographic projections in 1988 of the artist Krzysztof Wodiczko on the façade of the Hirshhorn Museum in Washington, DC, by the architect Gordon Bunshaft of Skidmore, Owings & Merrill, built in 1974.

With his projected images on the surface of monuments, buildings and other structures, Wodiczko has made modern architecture into a medium of expression, producing unexpected anthropomorphic similarities and perhaps an unintended public symbolism. The projections done for the Hirshhorn Museum were a provocative juxtaposition of a male right hand holding a revolver, a left hand (with a gold wedding band) holding a lit candle and below in the center a line of four microphones.

The huge cylindrical blank façade of the museum and its singular balcony opening become a strange helmet with its eye slit (or the squinting eyes of U.S. President George H.W. Bush). This projection was done a week before the American national elections in 1988 and the images of violence, fidelity, religion, culture, media, politics and power cannot be unraveled into one simple sentence. The juxtaposition of contradictory elements creates the tension in the artwork.

In his painting Picasso transforms lost bits and debris from life. The rope around the canvas is like an architectural molding around a window or the decorative edge of a table. The painted reality of the bottles and cups, with their own shadows, contrasts with the photographic reality of the rattan caning wallpaper. The physically flattest object has the greatest visual depth and vice versa.

Taken as a whole, the picture is a substitute for the almond-shaped eye of the artist and his unique vision.

The Picasso painting has some obvious similarities to the Hirshhorn projection, the painting's roundel format matches the round plan of the building, Picasso's contrast between painted reality and photographic reality is similar to Wodiczko's projection showing the real building against the photographic hands. The headline of the journal in the Picasso can be compared to the microphones in the Wodiczko. The wide range of ideas and images evoked by this comparison make it stronger and more relevant to today than the previous pair of images used by Giedion.

Irrational thoughts should be
followed absolutely and logically.
Sol LeWitt

Three Possible Strategies to Act On

After examining many collaborations,
including some successful engagements
between artist and architect at the highest
level, I would like to make these simple
observations.

A single unified image of the arts will
never be possible in a diverse, capitalistic
and democratic society. As noted by Guy
Debord: "It is the historical moment in which
we are caught."[3] If the artists and architects
of our time wish to collaborate they must
make use of the aesthetic flexibility of
"collage," the multi-discipline language of
"architectural fragments" and the strategy of
critique in *"détournement."*

COLLAGE

The word "collage" derives from the French
coller meaning to glue; the willful juxtaposition of different elements of contrasting
materials, scale or imagery is an aesthetic
formula that allows the artist to deal flexibly
with a wide range of limiting conditions.

The installation *Clothed House* by Matej
Andraz Vogrinčič for the Venice Biennale
1999 covers the façade of a historic building
that was once used as an orphanage. The
central sculptural figure of the Madonna
stretching her cloak around "the children"
become reflected in the word play and visual
ambiguity of the installation. The clothing,
mostly female, establishes a grid of color
and texture that highlights the surface of
the building and simultaneously completely
transforms it. The work establishes
associations with the past history and

past lives of the previous occupants of the
building. The artist inhabits the structure with
his collage done at the same scale of the
building and engages it fully.

The artist Jeff Koons has proposed a
collage sculpture, *Train*, for the center of
the Los Angeles County Museum of Art
(LACMA) campus designed by the architect
Renzo Piano. The artwork takes an actual
Liebherr LR 1750 lattice boom crane and
uses it as the support for a suspended
replica of a 1943 Baldwin 2900 class
steam locomotive. The sculpture presents
a mocking viewpoint on the articulated
construction methods of the architect
famous for exposing structure, mechanical
and construction elements by making the
steel lattice crane arm a permanent part of
the exhibition. The Piano Building Workshop
has built a similar derrick structure for the

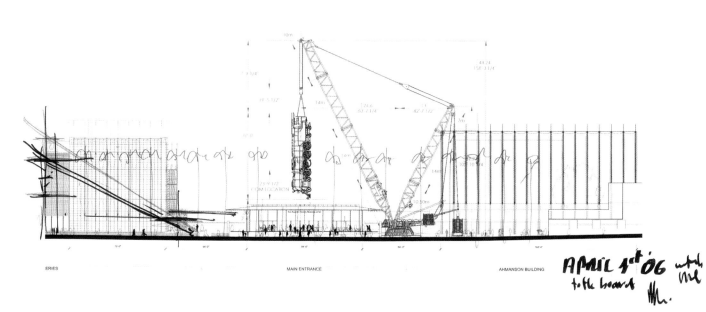

Drawing of LACMA extension by Renzo Piano Building Workshop with Jeff Koons' *Train*.

Jeff Koons, model of installation *Train*, 2011 (planned completion date), LACMA extension, Los Angeles, California, Renzo Piano Building Workshop, 2009.

Claes Oldenburg and Coosje van Bruggen, sculpture *Binoculars* for the Chiat/Day Building, Frank Gehry, Venice, California, 1991.

Claes Oldenburg, proposal for Chicago Stock Exchange, 1961.

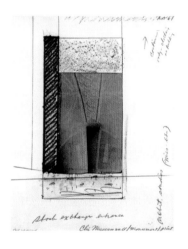

old harbor in Genoa, Italy, in 1992 to hold a tourist ride elevator called *Bigo*. The Koons locomotive will have a programmed set of motions that has the wheels move, the engine smoke and the whistle screech three times a day. Here the engine is like a captured Duchamp "Bachelor Machine" that huffs and puffs; its pistons pump up and down, while finally climaxing with an orgasmic moan for the entire city to hear.

The Chiat/Day Building in Venice, Los Angeles, by Frank Gehry with the sculpture *Binoculars* by Claes Oldenburg and Coosje van Bruggen shows how the idea of collage as used by the architect and artist can produce a building that mimics how a city is built with all the associated compositional and visual richness. The low rise office building is divided into three sections: parking garage, entry and offices.

The suggestion to use the juxtaposition of the monumental binocular form came from the architect by reusing a sculptural element from Oldenburg's proposal for a previous collaborative effort.[4] The paired cylinders of the 13.75-meter-tall entry sculpture act as the traditional gateway of doubled columnar forms. But it also creates an openly sexual image of penetrating an opening between paired legs, a metaphor acknowledged by both the artist and the architect and seen in Oldenburg's similar proposal for the Chicago Stock Exchange. With closer examination it is possible to see that the *Binoculars* are a pivoting point in the architect's career from geometric to increasingly curvilinear elements.

Contrasting the monumental Pop sculpture of Oldenburg with the monumental Socialist Realist Karl Marx Monument by Lew Kerbel in Chemnitz, Germany, is instructive

about the different uses of collage pieces of various scales. The 7.5-meter-tall bronze head of the German philosopher Karl Marx is visually tied to the adjacent office building by a full building height bronze placard with the inscription "workers of all countries unite" in four languages. The six-story building with its continuous horizontal banded windows and stone spandrels gives an abstract background (without human scale) enforcing the monumental scale of the sculpture.

Strangely both objects, the binoculars and the portrait, are so dramatically inflated that they do not seem threatening but more toy-like, which would explain the sentimental attachment the local population has for the preserved Marx sculpture, even with the default of its political content, now with the nickname: the "Nischel" (Saxon term for "head").

Low Kerbel, Karl Marx Monument, Chemnitz, Germany, 1971.

Claude Monet, *Water Lilies: Morning*, 1914–1918, copied on enamel metal panels and placed underwater at the Garden of Fine Arts, Kyoto, Tadao Ando, 1994.

Max Lingner, mural *Building the Republic*, Berlin, 1952.

In Berlin, a set of three art objects – Wolfgang Rüppel's *Memorial for the Uprising of June 17, 1953*, installed in 2000, the former Ministry of Aviation and the Max Lingner mural *Building the Republic*, 1952 – a building, a mural and a glass image on the ground, seem to float unattached to each other but at the same time subtly engage as a series of historically overlapping collage pieces. The building was designed by the architect Ernst Sagebiel (assistant to the modernist architect Erich Mendelsohn) in 1936 for the fascist Third Reich and consists of an extreme simplified Classicism. The most interesting details are the honorific windows at the piano nobile with their articulated solid stone rectangles of head, jambs, sill and aligned brackets. Their austerity, weight, repetition and geometry are both sophisticated and militarist. At

the main entry, courtyards and sides are rectangular colonnades at which one has a 16.75-meter-long glazed tile mural titled *Building the Republic (Aufbau der Republik)* by the artist Max Lingner, installed after the war by the new communist government of the German Democratic Republic. Added to that is another layer constructed after the fall of the East German government during the renovation of the building, serving now as the Ministry of Finance, a memorial pool for the *Uprising of June 17, 1953 (Aufstand des 17. Juni 1953)*. This long horizontal photo mural by the artist Wolfgang Rüppel is the same length and carefully aligned with the old mural and centered on the older façade.

The artworks and building become a set of adjacent symbols for three political eras: National Socialism, communism and democracy. They are subtly aligned in a visual

dialogue that seems ready to accept the declaration of the next new world order.

An image is added for comparison from the Garden of Fine Arts, 1994, by the architect Tadao Ando in Kyoto, where a number of iconic western artworks are copied in enameled metal panels and displayed in a setting open to the weather. Ando has placed an indestructible copy of Claude Monet's 12.5-meter-long *Water Lilies: Morning (Nymphéas)*, 1914–1918, horizontally under a pool of water so that the visitor can see the painting in, his interpretation, their most sympathetic location. The architect is intentionally playing with the transformation of a cultural treasure from one society to be utilized as a collage piece, altering its meaning from an idea about the abstraction of form to a comment about the alien occidental world.

Rachel Whiteread, *Untitled Monument (Inverted Plinth)*, Trafalgar Square, London, 2001 (removed).

Winged Victory of Samothrace at top of the Daru stairs, Louvre, Paris. I.M. Pei, architect of the Louvre entry glass pyramid, 1989, proposed to relocate the sculpture there.

The conflict between modern sculpture and the plinth (or pedestal) can be seen as similar to the conflict between modern sculpture and its position in modern architecture. Many sculptors struggled with the pedestal as part of their composition, Auguste Rodin lowered it to bring pathos and direct human contact to his *Burghers of Calais (Les Bourgeois de Calais)*, 1886; Tony Smith replaced it with a 2 centimeter gap allowing his steel sculpture *Die*, 1962, to float with a machine mysticism; Brâncuşi absorbed the plinth as an extension of the sculpture itself. In all three cases the artists manipulated the idea of the plinth as the friction point between architecture with its tradition of isolating sculpture and con-temporary sculpture that extends itself into the landscape and interacts with its context.

The eleven tonne clear resin duplicate of a Neoclassic plinth in Trafalgar Square in London, named *Untitled Monument (Inverted Plinth)*, 2001, is a critical work of the artist Rachel Whiteread that shows the elements of an architectural vocabulary literally inverted and altered in a comment on the architecture itself and the powers behind it (the square commemorates the famous sea battle).

Another temporary installation in Lon-don is the *Event Horizon*, 2007, by Antony Gormley which consisted of thirty-one cast iron molds of the artist's body placed on various rooftops all facing toward the Hayward Gallery, where a retrospective of the artist was taking place. The success of this composition is the random and asymmetric placement of the figures using

a variety of buildings claimed as the sculpture's various plinths.

By contrast, the architect I.M. Pei's proposal to relocate the ancient sculpture Winged Victory of Samothrace to be part of his new entry lobby at the Louvre Pyramid shows a more traditional view of collage. Here one of the iconic artworks of the museum was to be removed from its location at the top of the Daru Stairs, acting as the symbol of the Louvre itself, and placed on top of a modern concrete column. The proposal is one more step in the constant expropriation of art from its original site through wars and conquests to be relocated once more as a trophy.

Antony Gormley, *Event Horizon*, Hayward Gallery, London, 2007 (removed).

Anselm Kiefer, *Jericho*,
Royal Academy of
Arts, London, 2007
(removed).

GERMANIA

Installation by the artist Hans Haacke, *Germania – Bottomless*, German Pavilion during the 45th Venice Biennale, 1993.

Anselm Kiefer, *To the Unknown Painter*, 1990.

Rendering of the Monument for Otto von Bismarck by Ludwig Mies van der Rohe, 1910.

ARCHITECTURAL FRAGMENTS

The words "architectural fragments" have associations with ruins, items broken or unfinished, the exact opposite of a unified or complete work. Also the establishment of a multiple repetition of similar elements implies that the existing artwork is a fragment of a larger open-ended whole that could extend itself further. The acceptance of the dystopian incompleteness of any composition allows the artist or architect to adjust to the limitations of contemporary construction.

The construction titled *Jericho*, 2007, by the artist Anselm Kiefer at the Royal Academy of Arts in London consists of a set of used precast concrete components stacked in imitation of a tower or apartment building. Although the slabs are usually a concealed part of a building the construction

perfectly illustrates the many meanings of the architectural fragment. The broken concrete pieces are literally "fragments" of another construction project, but also they represent "fragments" of larger ordering systems. The vertical ribbing mocks the ornament fluting in the square fascist classical columns seen in Kiefer's painting *To the Unknown Painter*, 1998. The repeated forms echo the precast concrete panels of modern apartment buildings in the 1970s.

Paired with this is another literal ruin and architectural fragment as seen in the installation *Germania – Bottomless (Germania – Bodenlos)* by the artist Hans Haacke for the German Pavilion of the 1993 Venice Biennale that commented on the power of architecture and its connection to politics. A new wall was added to make an apse of the existing gallery with the austere

lettering "Germania", the female figure standing as a national allegory for Germany, and then the artist proceeded to destroy the existing marble floor in the room. The rubble, which visitors walked over, created an emotive ruin within the rectangular order of the existing building shell and represented the artist's intense response to the memory of the 1934 meeting of Hitler and Mussolini at the Biennale.

Both Kiefer's and Haacke's work can be compared to an early unbuilt competition project by the architect Ludwig Mies van der Rohe. The traditional imagery of the political hero memorialized as a massive bronze figure surrounded by the crescendo of an endless colonnade was the strategy used by Mies in his early work on the memorial competition for Otto von Bismarck in 1910. In this project the architecture completely

Alberto Burri, *Cretto*
(memorial to the 1968
earthquake), Gibellina,
Sicily, 1985.

Richard Serra, *Eleva-
tional Mass*, 2006.

overwhelms the sculpture in the apse which unintentionally matches the theme of power described by the previous artworks.

The term architectural fragment can also apply to an artwork that by elaborate repetition implies that it can be extended on and on, thus making it a piece (fragment) of a larger implied whole. This is the logic for classifying the Berlin *Memorial to the Murdered Jews of Europe* by Peter Eisenman as a fragment and examining it from that direction.

The Eisenman design for this memorial was first developed with the artist Richard Serra and although that partnership did not last, the influence of the artist's vocabulary on the architect is evident. The use of thick large slabs of steel plate is the identifying image of the artist Richard Serra. That image is here transformed in the over two thousand

precast concrete slabs in an obvious, but disputed, metaphor of tombstones in a graveyard. The value of the assembly is in its ambiguity: the muteness of the austere prisms and their incalculable scale. All of which leads to the image of a fragment of an endless necropolis.

The memorial in Berlin can be related to another memorial, *Cretto,* in Gibellina, Sicily, by the artist Alberto Burri. Here the town, which was destroyed in an earthquake in 1968, is recalled in a ghost-like set of concrete plinths that match the medieval street pattern. The composition presents a minimum amount of information that allows for the visitors to reassemble the town in their own memory. Compared to the Berlin memorial the work by Burri is crude and unrefined, but it still implies a larger order both physically and metaphorically.

Fragments can be articulated in the most banal of situations, like the functional and drab corridor. One amazing example can be found at the Arp Museum at Rolandseck, Germany, designed by the architect Richard Meier, located on a cliff site with a concrete tunnel to get to the main level of the complex housed in a historic train station. It is a fragment of the entire processional sequence of the new linked museum buildings. What the artist Barbara Trautmann in her light installation *Kaa*, 2007, has done is shape the repetition of dozens of neon rings to light the long space in a way that makes another cylindrical tunnel in the vaulted space and distorts the perception of the larger space.

This can be compared to two other light installations done by the artist James Turrell at the Museum of Fine Arts in

Peter Eisenman,
*Memorial to the
Murdered Jews of
Europe*, Berlin, 2005.

Barbara Trautmann,
light installation *Kaa*
at the Arp Museum,
Rolandseck, Germany,
Richard Meier, 2007.

James Turrell, light installation *The Light Inside,* 1999, in the tunnel connecting the Ludwig Mies van der Rohe building of the Museum of Fine Arts, Houston, Texas, with the extension by Rafael Moneo, 2000.

Keith Sonnier, light installation *Connection RedBlueYellow (Verbindung RotBlauGelb)* Munich Re Headquarters, Baumschlager & Eberle, 2002.

Sarah Morris, installation *Robert Towne,* 2006, at the Lever House, New York, Gordon Bunshaft, Skidmore, Owings & Merrill, 1952.

Isamu Noguchi's proposed sculptures for the Lever House garden in 1952.

Leo Villareal, *Light Matrix*, 2006, at the Albright-Knox Art Gallery, Buffalo, New York, Gordon Bunshaft, Skidmore, Owings & Merrill, 1963.

Houston, Texas (William Ward Watkin, 1924; Ludwig Mies van der Rohe, 1958/1974; Rafael Moneo, 2000) and Keith Sonnier for the Munich Re Headquarters building (Baumschlager & Eberle, 2002)

For the artist Turrell the saturation of the space with an unseen even color source allows the strictly geometric volume to be transformed into an intense optical illusion (resulting from the lack of any spatial keys for the spectator) that confuses the visitor's perception of exact depth.

For the artist Sonnier the long space is broken into smaller segments of color and pattern that results in a flattening out of the space making it a pulsating abstract painting.

For both artists the corridor as a functional fragment of the whole complex is manipulated with such success that it achieves a dramatic architectural identity of its own.

The idea of the architectural fragment can be used to induce an element of anarchy by taking an isolated piece of the building's system or logic and using it to oppose the regular order; in the following two cases the artists, while opposing the modern glass box, create new links across the structures.

The Lever House in New York by the architect Gordon Bunshaft of Skidmore, Owings & Merrill, 1952, has had a number of proposed and temporary art installations that operate in different ways. The original proposal was for the artist Isamu Noguchi to install several abstract sculptures in the courtyard and one relief sculpture in the lobby interior. The proposed placement of the artwork reveals the awkwardness of the concept of a public courtyard hidden from view. The ground floor open area and second floor base serve only as a dramatic horizontal

visual separation of the vertical building from the street. The proposed Noguchi sculptures would have been hidden from both pedestrians on Park Avenue and the residents of the building's interior.

The installation *Robert Towne*, 2006, by the artist Sarah Morris takes the ceiling of the open covered plaza and introduces a series of conflicting grids and colors. The overhead mural takes the modular grid of the building and distorts it to present another layer of activity. The logic and order of the office layout dimension of a repeated 1.5 meter division gives way to the impulsive illogic of fragmented disorder, successfully matching the random circulation of the pedestrians through the space.

The installation *Light Matrix*, 2006, by the artist Leo Villareal on the black glass box which is the modernist addition to the

Neoclassic Albright-Knox Art Gallery in Buffalo, New York, also designed by Gordon Bunshaft, presents a different interpretation. The syncopated flashing lights face from the addition to the main building and are most visible from an upper gallery. The artist has appropriated the architecture as a frame for his own work, making one more small fragmented step in a link between the old building and the new.

The flexibility of the idea of fragments can be found in artwork that establishes itself so linked into the motifs, colors and shapes of the main structure that it becomes like a small crystal replica containing in miniature an entire summary of the main structure.

The new National Opera House for Oslo by the architecture firm Snøhetta, is a clear diagram of the functions of the program that breaks down into the performance spaces and their public circulation ("the Wave Wall"), the back of the house ("the Factory") and the exterior cladding and plaza ("the Carpet").

Each has a separate coding of materials and shapes: the exterior of the building is both angular and white, whether it is aluminum panels, marble pavers or granite surfaces, while the auditorium and its immediate enclosure is an assembly of vertical slats of warm brown oak. The interesting development is that the artists have selected their works to become fragments of these organizing architectural motifs.

The computerized ceramic patterned surface in the main lobby by the artist Olafur Eliasson encloses the coat rack room. It is a complicated set of backlit intersecting diamond shapes that alter their proportions from the top of the wall to the bottom. It is by its location, under the plaza and behind the white angled columns, that makes it part of the white service container for the central brown theater.

Certainly the most interesting art object is the digitized photo of a reflective crushed angular aluminum foil used for the woven fabric stage curtain by the artist Pae White. It serves a wide range of performances by making itself a mystical image that is about an illusion (a flat surface which appears as a metal screen with depth) that itself opens on to the world of illusion in the stage sets of the operas. This connects to the tradition of the illusionistic stage curtain at the nineteenth century Paris Opera which creates an illusion of a deep multilayered curtain in its flat woven surface.

The tapestry by White seems a contradiction to the idea of an alliance of the artwork in the organization of the building because it is white and angular in the wrong place. But if the third element of the architects' explanation is included ("the Factory"), which is the low metal clad building facing the street and containing the offices, scenery shops and mechanical services, then the stage curtain becomes one part of that metal façade and a clear separation between the audience and the performers. When the curtain rises you are not just looking onto a stage but into the work-a-day world of the artists and their building.

The last fragment discussed is an artwork by the American artist Andrea Blum, *Split Pavilion*, 1992, which combines various elements of the previous examples. The artist produced an installation at the Pacific ocean in Carlsbad, California, which utilizes its awkward triangular site to its advantage.

Located on a zone parallel to the ocean, but between areas of parking and retail, the artist's design of long rectangular strips of benches, paving, sand and planting gets prematurely sliced off by the angles of the site and, as a fragment, implies the extension of this new order across the natural barriers. It is small but implies a renovation to the entire water front.

Another feature is the small fountain that starts a channel and extends between two pavilions and empties into a small pool. This simple arrangement plays with the idea of the fragment recalling the memory of another larger order. In this case the Salk Institute and its monumental courtyard by the architect Louis I. Kahn is evoked, farther down the coast, looking out into the same ocean. At the Kahn building the narrow water channel has a mystical image of the small flow of water to the endless horizon.

It is tragic that this charming and benign artwork was destroyed because of a real estate argument in this conservative Republican town.

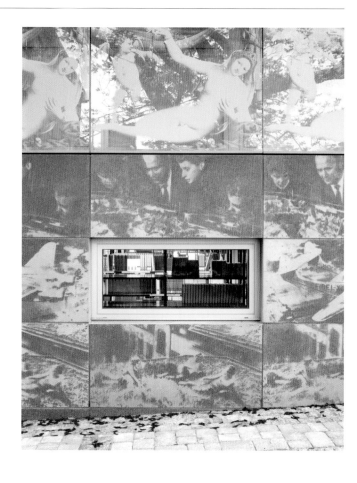

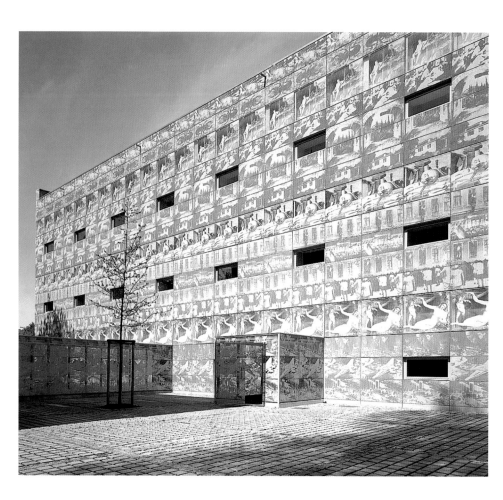

DÉTOURNEMENT

The word "détournement" can roughly be translated as "turnaround." The word was adopted by the French Situationalists in the 1970s to mean an artist's reuse of well-known cultural images in a new and subversive way. Originally the term was used for the political vandalism of billboard advertisements that altered the text or image to mock the product illustrated. But it can also be part of the operational strategy of art engaging architecture. It is a tool for the artist using the existing architectural vocabulary or media syntax of the setting for his work to engage it in a critical manner.

The idea of "turnaround," in which one element of the public media is misused to distort or alter the meaning of the original message, can be applied to the collaboration between artists and architects, if we

consider as source material both the new public electronic media and the old visual language of architecture in its history. At the Library at the University of Applied Sciences in Eberswalde, Germany, by Herzog & de Meuron, 1999, the architectural trope of putting a literary label on the façade of a library is altered and twisted around by artist Thomas Ruff. At the Parisian Bibliothèque Sainte-Geneviève, by Henri Labrouste, 1851, for example, the names of the authors on the façade were directly behind the book stacks; at Eberswalde the exterior is lined with bands of photographic reproductions from newspapers, magazines and books. The use of image-transfer lithography on concrete and glass allows the work of the artist and architect to be unified in an object where both are fused together. The associations with the multiple images on

a reel of movie film or the multiple images of an Andy Warhol Pop Art painting create a tension between the text of the façade as an art object on the one hand and as a commentary on the function of the building on the other.

Another library whose interior ornament engages in a twisting of the idea of text as a symbol is the Public Library in Usera, near Madrid, by the architects Ábalos & Herreros. Here the artist Peter Halley digitally manipulates scanned images of the pages from a short story by Jorge Luis Borges entitled *The Library of Babel* to make a large scale wallpaper that covers not only the walls of the reading room but also the interior surfaces of the exterior sun screens on the façade. The unreadable text seems more like a transcribed Morse code of dots and dashes than words and sentences, which then

becomes an illustration of the transformation of the written word into digital information of ones and zeros.

The signs and symbols in church architecture are as articulate as a contemporary billboard advertisement. The "turning around" of the symbolic colored light of divine radiance from traditional stained-glass windows by the use of colored neon tubing in the light installation *Tears for Saint Francis*, 2002, is a powerful statement in the small suburban church St. Franziskus in Steyr-Resthof, Austria, by architects Riepl Riepl. The artist Keith Sonnier has had a long history of claiming space with his artwork whether it is in metal, as a sound piece or a light installation. This artwork does not light directly the worship space but acts as both a "billboard" sign for the church and as a precisely framed art object. The installation

with its delicate and playful curvilinear nature limits the industrial and commercial association of the neon tubing.

For the installation *Within Reach* for the British Pavilion for the Venice Biennale in 2003, the artist Chris Ofili cooperated with architect David Adjaye. In a series of paintings the artist limits himself to a theme of three colors, the red, black and green of Marcus Garvey's Black Nationalist flag, which is then used as the basis of all other colors and materials in the gallery.[5] The carpets, walls and most importantly the architect-designed skylight *Afro Kaleidoscope* are elaborations on the theme. The strategy sounds like a potential disaster, but it is saved by the fact that the whole pavilion is lit to be an overall dark space with intense spot lights on the paintings. The gallery's dark saturated colors act like an extension

of the enveloping jungle paradise theme illustrated in the background of the paintings. The room itself has become absorbed into the paintings but is still secondary in prominence to the artwork.

The refurbishment by Norman Foster of the damaged and long abandoned Reichstag in Berlin for the new German Parliament Building included an extensive art installation program. With a history that covers the monarchy, the Weimar Republic and the National Socialist regime it was obvious that the current government wished to restore the building as well as stake its claim on it. The art and modern architectural additions did that by including various well-known avant-garde artists as Georg Baselitz, Joseph Beuys, Christian Boltanski, Jenny Holzer, Anselm Kiefer and others.

Keith Sonnier, light
installation *Tears for
Saint Francis* at the
Church St. Franziskus,
Steyr-Resthof, Austria,
Riepl Riepl, 2002.

We turn in circles during the night
and are consumed by fire.
Guy Debord

Chris Ofili, painting
Afro Apparition in the
British Pavilion for the
Venice Biennale, 2003.
Skylight covering and
interior by the architect
David Adjaye.

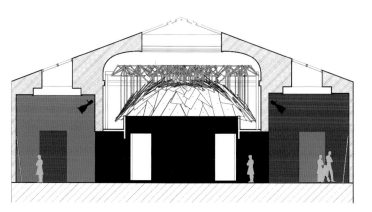

Section through existing British Pavilion, David Adjaye, 2003.

Rem Koolhaas, proposal for *European Union Flag*, 2002.

Gerhard Richter, mural study *126 Colors* for the German Parliament Building, Berlin, Norman Foster, 1997.

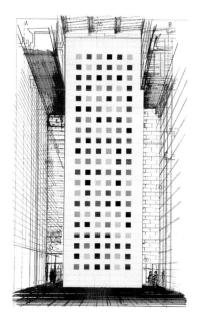

Although the mural study by Gerhard Richter titled *126 Colors* did not meet approval and a more conservative mural by the same artist, titled *Black-Red-Gold*, was installed in 1997, the first design is more interesting in its manipulation of decorative elements in an architectural context. The motif of a grid of various colors has been used previously by the artist in a series of stained-glass windows and interior blind windows.[6] The success of this design is in the ambiguity of the image. The German flag colors are "turned around" in a mix of many other colors, sometimes organized correctly and sometimes not, seeming like an enormous crossword puzzle. The mixed color grid has symbolic implications for the national identity of the German people and its current mix of cultures and immigrants.

One Possible Explanation for Examination

Jacques Rancière, in his writings on political art, talks about "crossing borders and blurring the distribution of roles" in the production of art.[7] I feel that the collaborative work of the modern artist and the modern architect is best seen when each can speak the other's language and engage the other's ideas. I do not mean to suggest that artists must be architects and architects act like artists, but that each can expand beyond the previous definition and limitation of his or her role and identity to create public works of a greater whole by means of debate, what Rancière has called "the creation of formal structures within which one may operate with anarchic equality."[8]

Architecture is many times locked into supporting the status quo by virtue of its clients and through financial restraints, but within the building itself the artist can bring a tolerated critique of everything that the architect cannot. It is this debate between the formal structure of architecture and the anarchy of art that gives an opportunity for engagement and exploration.

Earlier the word "composition" was defined in the narrow sense of art speaking in the language of architecture, and the word "collaboration" was opened up to the widest possible interpretation as in any interaction between the arts. I believe that the future for the collective voice of modern arts is in the redefinition of two other words, namely "collusion," a secret agreement between foes, and "resistance," (as, for instance, in the French Résistance) the secret struggle against a foe, so that these opposites can be interlocked and interchanged. How that is achieved is a perfect riddle for our time.

Guest house *Yu-un*
by Tadao Ando with
installation of ceramic
tiles by Olafur Eliasson,
Kyoto, Japan, 2006.

The reason you bring artists in is
so that you can actually propose
a different type of space in the
architecture, or a different type of
time, or a different type of ideology,
if you don't have access to that then
there's no point. **Jorge Pardo**

The following list of over one hundred artist
and architect interactions is by necessity
incomplete and arbitrary. It itemizes artworks conceived or chosen specifically
for buildings of five architects discussed
earlier in this book, selected for their international presence, their long-standing
involvement with art and their range of
built work. Collaborations treated already in
the chapters of this book are not repeated
here but can be found through the index.
The list is organized chronologically by the
architects' buildings.

The works of art represent three types
of interaction.

COLLABORATION: The artist and architect
had direct involvement in placing the work.
(This also illustrates the phenomenon of
artists favored by the architect regardless
of site or program, such as the repeated
collaborations of Gehry/Oldenburg, Foster/
Clarke, or Piano/Shingu.)

ARCHITECT'S CHOICE: The architect selected
and placed the artwork without consulting
with the artist. In some cases, the architect
also opted to create his own artwork for his
building.

CURATOR INSTALLATION: In a museum
setting the curator (or owner) has placed
artwork engaging the specific building
context.

Tadao Ando

Walter De Maria, installation *Seen/Unseen Known/Unknown*, 2000; Benesse House, Naoshima, Japan, 1992 ARCHITECT'S CHOICE

Richard Long, installation *Full Moon Stone Circle*, 1997; Benesse House, Naoshima, Japan, 1992 COLLABORATION

Bruce Nauman, neon sculpture *100 Live or Die*, 1984; Benesse House, Naoshima, Japan, 1992 ARCHITECT'S CHOICE

Tatsuo Miyajima, installation *Sea of Time '98*, 1998; Benesse House, Naoshima, Japan, 1992 COLLABORATION

Hiroshi Sugimoto, photograph *Time Exposed*, 1991; Benesse House, Naoshima, Japan, 1992 ARCHITECT'S CHOICE

Kan Yasuda, sculpture *The Secret of the Sky*, 1996; Benesse House, Naoshima, Japan, 1992 COLLABORATION

Claes Oldenburg and Coosje van Bruggen, sculpture *Balancing Tools*, 1984; Vitra Conference Center, Weil am Rhein, Germany, 1993 CURATOR INSTALLATION

Susumu Shingu, sculpture *The Memory of the Wave*, 1994; Suntory Museum, Osaka, Japan, 1994 COLLABORATION

Leonardo da Vinci, painting *The Last Supper*, 1498 (copy); Garden of Fine Arts, Kyoto, Japan, 1994 ARCHITECT'S CHOICE

Michelangelo Buonarroti, painting *The Last Judgement*, 1541 (copy); Garden of Fine Arts, Kyoto, Japan, 1994 ARCHITECT'S CHOICE

Vincent van Gogh, painting *Road with Cypress and Star*, 1890 (copy); Garden of Fine Arts, Kyoto, Japan, 1994 ARCHITECT'S CHOICE

James Turrell, installation *Backside of the Moon*, 1999; Minami-dera, Naoshima, Japan, 1999 COLLABORATION

Yamaguchi Makio, sculpture *Saddle in the Sun*, 1975; Hyogo Prefectural Museum of Art, Kobe, Japan, 2001 CURATOR INSTALLATION

Jonathan Borofsky, installation *Self Portrait with Big Ears (Learning to be Free)*, 1994; Modern Art Museum of Fort Worth, Texas, USA, 2002 CURATOR INSTALLATION

Joseph Havel, sculpture *Drape*, 1999; Modern Art Museum of Fort Worth, Texas, USA, 2002 CURATOR INSTALLATION

Anselm Kiefer, sculpture *Book with Wings (Buch mit Flügeln)*, 1994; Modern Art Museum of Fort Worth, Texas, USA, 2002 ARCHITECT'S CHOICE

Michelangelo Pistoletto, sculpture *The Etruscan*, 1976; Modern Art Museum of Fort Worth, Texas, USA, 2002 CURATOR INSTALLATION

George Segal, sculpture *Chance Meeting*, 1989; Modern Art Museum of Fort Worth, Texas, USA, 2002 CURATOR INSTALLATION

Richard Serra, sculpture *Vortex*, 2002; Modern Art Museum of Fort Worth, Texas, USA, 2002 CURATOR INSTALLATION

Alexander Calder, sculpture *The Red Tripod*, 1954; Chichu Art Museum, Naoshima, Japan, 2004 CURATOR INSTALLATION

Claude Monet, painting *Water-Lily Pond*, 1915–1926; Chichu Art Museum, Naoshima, Japan, 2004 ARCHITECT'S CHOICE

James Turrell, installation *Open Sky*, 2004; Chichu Art Museum, Naoshima, Japan, 2004 COLLABORATION

Tatsuo Miyajima and Tadao Ando, installation *Iced Time Tunnel*, at the Snow Show, Kemi, Finland, 2004 (melted) COLLABORATION

Tokujin Yoshioka, sculpture *Waterfall*, 2006; Yu-un, Kyoto, Japan, 2006 COLLABORATION

Olafur Eliasson, installation *Tile for Yu-un*, 2006; Yu-un, Kyoto, Japan, 2006 COLLABORATION

Norman Foster

Brian Clarke, tapestry, *Site Plan II*, 1997; Willis Faber and Dumas Headquarters, Ipswich, UK, 1975 COLLABORATION

Ben Johnson, mobile, 1991; atrium, ITN Headquarters, London, UK, 1991 COLLABORATION

Ben Johnson, photo installation with Norman Foster at 44th Venice Biennale, Venice, Italy, 1991 COLLABORATION

Brian Clarke, stained-glass installation, 1991; Stansted Airport, Essex, UK, 1992 COLLABORATION

Per Arnoldi, color scheme, paintings and sculptures, 1997; Commerzbank Headquarters, Frankfurt, Germany, 1997 COLLABORATION

Brian Clarke, stained-glass installation, 1998; Chek Lap Kok Airport, Hong Kong, China, 1998 COLLABORATION

Per Arnoldi, color scheme, 1997; Reichstag, Berlin, Germany, 1999 COLLABORATION

Christian Boltanski, installation *Reichstag Archives (Archiv der deutschen Abgeordneten)*, 1999; Reichstag, Berlin, Germany, 1999 CURATOR INSTALLATION

Norman Foster, sculpture *Eagle (Bundesadler)*, 1999; Reichstag, Berlin, Germany, 1999 ARCHITECT'S CHOICE

Reichstag original architect Paul Wallot, 1894, the addition of the façade inscription *For the German People (Dem Deutschen Volke)* by Peter Behrens, 1916, renovation by Norman Foster, 1999.

Reichstag renovation courtyard installation by Hans Haacke with inscription *For the People (Der Bevölkerung)*, 2000.

Hans Haacke, installation *For the People (Der Bevölkerung)*, 2000; Reichstag, Berlin, Germany, 1999 COLLABORATION

Bernhard Heisig, painting *Time and Life (Zeit und Leben)*, 1999; Reichstag, Berlin, Germany, 1999 CURATOR INSTALLATION

Jenny Holzer, Installation for the Reichstag Building, 1999; Reichstag, Berlin, Germany, 1999 COLLABORATION

Anselm Kiefer, mural *Only with Wind, with Time and with Sound (Nur mit Wind mit Zeit und mit Klang)*, 1999; Reichstag, Berlin, Germany, 1999 CURATOR INSTALLATION

Sigmar Polke, installation *Five Light Boxes (Fünf Leuchtkästen)*, 1999; Reichstag, Berlin, Germany, 1999 COLLABORATION

Günther Uecker, installation in chapel, 1999; Reichstag, Berlin, Germany, 1999 COLLABORATION

Anthony Caro, co-design of Millennium Bridge, London, UK, 2000 COLLABORATION

Brian Clarke, stained-glass installation, 2000; Al Faisaliah Centre, Riyadh, Saudi Arabia, 2000 COLLABORATION

Per Arnoldi, color scheme and paintings, 2001; Imperial College, Flowers Building, London, UK, 2001 COLLABORATION

Per Arnoldi, co-design of National Police Memorial, London, UK, 2005 COLLABORATION

Jaume Plensa and Norman Foster, installation *Snow Show* at Turin Winter Olympics, Italy, 2006 COLLABORATION

James Carpenter, fountain *Ice Fall*, 2006; Hearst Headquarters, New York, New York, USA, 2006 COLLABORATION

Richard Long, mural *Riverlines*, 2006; Hearst Headquarters, New York, New York, USA, 2006 COLLABORATION

Brian Clarke, stained-glass installation, 2005; Pyramid of Peace, Astana, Kazakhstan, 2008 COLLABORATION

Frank Gehry

Larry Bell, sculpture (not realized); Rouse Company Headquarters, Columbia, Maryland, USA, 1974 COLLABORATION

Frank Gehry, sculpture *Fish*, 1981; Smith House extension, Bel Air, California, USA, 1981 (unbuilt) ARCHITECT'S CHOICE

Richard Serra, co-design of bridge, 1981; Architectural League proposal, New York, New York, USA, 1981 (unbuilt) COLLABORATION

Claes Oldenburg and Coosje van Bruggen, sculpture *Milk Can*, 1984; Camp Good Time, Santa Monica Mountains, California, USA, 1984 (unbuilt) COLLABORATION

Claes Oldenburg and Coosje van Bruggen, sculpture *Toppling Ladder with Spilling Paint*, 1986; Loyola Law School, Los Angeles, California, USA, 1987 COLLABORATION

Frank Gehry, sculpture *Fish*, 1987; Fish Dance Restaurant, Kobe, Japan, 1987 ARCHITECT'S CHOICE

Billy Al Bengston, carpet, 1990 (not realized); Chiat/Day Building, Venice, California, USA, 1991 COLLABORATION

Kenneth Price, installation *Tile Washrooms*, 1991 (not realized); Chiat/Day Building, Venice, California, USA, 1991 COLLABORATION

Frank Gehry, sculpture *Fish*; Vila Olímpica multi-use complex, Barcelona, Spain, Skidmore, Owings & Merrill/Frank Gehry, 1992 ARCHITECT'S CHOICE

Frank Gehry, sculpture *Fish*, 1995; Lewis House, Cleveland, Ohio, USA, 1995 (unbuilt) ARCHITECT'S CHOICE

Frank Gehry, sculpture *Horse's Head*, 1995; Lewis House, Cleveland, Ohio, USA, 1995 (unbuilt) ARCHITECT'S CHOICE

Maggie Keswick Jencks, landscape design; Lewis House, Cleveland, Ohio, USA, 1995 (unbuilt) COLLABORATION

Philip Johnson, guest house sculpture *Octopus*, 1994; Lewis House, Cleveland, Ohio, USA, 1995 (unbuilt) COLLABORATION

Claes Oldenburg and Coosje van Bruggen, sculpture *Golf Clubs*, 1995; Lewis House, Cleveland, Ohio, USA, 1995 (unbuilt) COLLABORATION

Richard Serra, co-design Millennium Bridge competition, 1996; London, UK, 1996 (unbuilt) COLLABORATION

Francesco Clemente, installation *Mother's Room (La stanza della madre)*, 1996; Guggenheim Museum Bilbao, Bilbao, Spain, 1997 CURATOR INSTALLATION

Jenny Holzer, Installation for the Guggenheim Museum Bilbao, 1997; Guggenheim Museum Bilbao, Bilbao, Spain, 1997 COLLABORATION

Office building by Frank Gehry with architect's design *Horse's Head* in atrium, Berlin, Germany, 2002.

Yves Klein, fountain *Fire Fountain*, 1961; Guggenheim Museum Bilbao, Bilbao, Spain, 1997 CURATOR INSTALLATION

Jeff Koons, sculpture *Puppy*, 1992; Guggenheim Museum Bilbao, Bilbao, Spain, 1997 CURATOR INSTALLATION

Richard Serra, installation *Matter of Time*, 2005; Guggenheim Museum Bilbao, Bilbao, Spain, 1997 COLLABORATION

Sol Le Witt, mural *Wall Drawing #831*, 1997, Guggenheim Museum Bilbao, Bilbao, Spain, 1997 CURATOR INSTALLATION

Frank Gehry, sculpture *Horse's Head*, 2000; Conference room, DZ Bank, Berlin, Germany, 2000 ARCHITECT'S CHOICE

Nikolas Weinstein, sculpture *PP3 Chandelier*, 2000; DZ Bank, Berlin, Germany, 2000 COLLABORATION

Alejandro Gehry, mural *Untitled*, 2001; Issey Miyake showroom, New York, New York, USA, 2001 COLLABORATION

Claes Oldenburg and Coosje van Bruggen, sculpture *Collar and Bow*, 2003 (destroyed 2009); Walt Disney Concert Hall, Los Angeles, California, USA, 2003 COLLABORATION

Tomas Osinski, co-design, fountain *A Rose for Lily*, 2003; Walt Disney Concert Hall, Los Angeles, California, USA, 2003 COLLABORATION

Frank Gehry, sculpture *Horse's Head*, 2005; Conference room, Lewis-Sigler Institute, Princeton University, Princeton, New Jersey, USA, Rafael Viñoly Architects, 2005 ARCHITECT'S CHOICE

Paolo Chiasera, sculpture *www.tupac project.it*, 2008; MARTa, Herford, Germany, 2008 CURATOR INSTALLATION

Luciano Fabro, sculpture *The Ball (Der Ball)*, 2008; MARTa, Herford, Germany, 2008 CURATOR INSTALLATION

Richard Serra, sculpture *The Hedgehog and the Fox*, 2000; Peter B. Lewis Library, Princeton University, Princeton, New Jersey, USA, 2008 ARCHITECT'S CHOICE

Frank Stella, sculpture, 2008; Restaurant Frank, Art Gallery of Ontario, Toronto, Canada, 2008 COLLABORATION

Robert Wilson, installation *Eisenhower Memorial*, Washington, DC, USA, 2010 COLLABORATION

Jacques Herzog
Pierre de Meuron

Karl Blossfeldt, photograph mural *Achillea Umbellata*, 1928; Ricola Storage Building, Mulhouse, France, 1993 ARCHITECT'S CHOICE

Helmut Federle, color concept, 1992; Housing Pilotengasse, Vienna, Austria, 1992 COLLABORATION

Rémy Zaugg, master plan for student housing, University of Burgundy, Dijon, France, 1992 COLLABORATION

Dieter Kienast, sculpture *Green Water Pool*, 1993; SUVA House, Basel, Switzerland, 1993 COLLABORATION

Thomas Ruff, photography excerpt of starry sky, 1993; SUVA House, Basel, Switzerland, 1993 COLLABORATION

Adrian Schiess, mural *Color Plates*, 1993; SUVA House, Basel, Switzerland, 1993 COLLABORATION

Michael Craig-Martin, installation *Swiss Light*, 1999 (removed); Tate Modern, London, UK, 2000 CURATOR INSTALLATION

Rosemarie Trockel/Adrian Schiess, color concept, 1998; Ricola Marketing Building, Laufen, Switzerland, 1999 COLLABORATION

Rémy Zaugg, color concept, 1998; Roche Pharma Research Building, Basel, Switzerland, 2000 COLLABORATION

Carsten Höller, installation *Test Site*, 2006 (removed); Tate Modern, London, UK, 2000 CURATOR INSTALLATION

Rachel Whiteread, installation *Embankment*, 2006 (removed); Tate Modern, London, UK, 2000 CURATOR INSTALLATION

Michael Craig-Martin, color concept, 2003; Laban Dance Centre, London, UK, 2003 COLLABORATION

Olafur Eliasson, sculpture *Sphere*, 2003; Fünf Höfe shopping mall, Munich, Germany, 2003 COLLABORATION

Andy Goldsworthy, sculpture *Drawn Stone*, 2005; M. H. de Young Memorial Museum, San Francisco, California, USA, 2005 CURATOR INSTALLATION

Jorge Pardo, cafeteria installation, (not realized); M. H. de Young Museum, San Francisco, California, USA, 2005 COLLABORATION

Gerhard Richter, mural *Strontium*, 2005; M. H. de Young Memorial Museum, San Francisco, California, USA, 2005 COLLABORATION

Kiki Smith, installation *Near*, 2005; M. H. de Young Memorial Museum, San Francisco, California, USA, 2005 CURATOR INSTALLATION

Cai Guo-Qiang, installation *Fireworks*, 2008; National Stadium, Beijing, China, 2008 CURATOR INSTALLATION

Anish Kapoor, sculpture at 56 Leonard Street Apartment Building, Herzog & de Meuron, New York, USA 2011.

Ai Weiwei, design concept for "Bird's Nest" National Stadium, Beijing, China, 2008 COLLABORATION

Ai Weiwei, installation *Mock-up Beijing*, at 11th Venice Architecture Biennale, Venice, Italy, 2008 (removed) COLLABORATION

Igor Mitoraj, sculpture *Ikaria*, 1996 (removed); Caixa Forum, Madrid, Spain, 2008 CURATOR INSTALLATION

Renate Buser, installation; 1111 Lincoln Road, Miami Beach, Florida, USA, 2010 COLLABORATION

Anish Kapoor, sculpture at 56 Leonard Street Apartment Building, New York, New York, USA, 2011 COLLABORATION

Renzo Piano

Michael Heizer, sculpture *Charmstone*, 1991; The Menil Collection, Houston, Texas, USA, 1986 CURATOR INSTALLATION

Michael Heizer, sculpture *Isolated Mass/Circumflex #2*, 1972; The Menil Collection, Houston, Texas, USA, 1986 CURATOR INSTALLATION

Xaxier Veilhan, installation *The Inhabitants*, 2007; Cité Internationale, Lyon, France, 1986 CURATOR INSTALLATION

Susumu Shingu, sculpture *Resonance of the Sea*, 1995; The Renzo Piano Building Workshop office, Genoa, Italy, 1989 ARCHITECT'S CHOICE

Susumu Shingu, sculpture *Columbus' Wind*, 1992; Port of Genoa, Genoa, Italy, 1992 COLLABORATION

Susumu Shingu, sculpture *Boundless Sky*, 1994; Kansai International Airport, Osaka, Japan, 1994 COLLABORATION

Cy Twombly, painting *Untitled (Say Goodbye, Catullus, to the Shores of Asia Minor)*, 1994; Cy Twombly Pavilion, Houston, Texas, USA, 1995 CURATOR INSTALLATION

Susumu Shingu, sculpture *Locus of Rain*, 1995; Lingotto Exhibition Center, Turin, Italy, 1995 COLLABORATION

Susumu Shingu, sculpture *Dialogue with Clouds*, 1998, Meridiana Center, Lecco, Italy, 1998 COLLABORATION

Christo and Jeanne-Claude, installation *Wrapped Trees*, 1998 (removed); Fondation Beyeler, Riehen, Switzerland, 1998 CURATOR INSTALLATION

Susumu Shingu, sculpture *Water-flowers*, 1999; Banco Popolare di Lodi, Lodi, Italy, 1999 COLLABORATION

Tim Prentice, installation *Three Wheels*, 2000; Aurora Place, Sydney, Australia, 2000 COLLABORATION

Kan Yasuda, sculpture *Touchstones*, 2000; Aurora Place, Sydney, Australia, 2000 ARCHITECT'S CHOICE

Mark Di Suvero, sculpture, *For Bartok (Galileo)*, 1996; Quartier Daimler, Potsdamer Platz, Berlin, Germany, 2000 CURATOR INSTALLATION

Susumu Shingu, sculpture *Hommage au Cosmos*, 2001; Maison Hermès, Tokyo, Japan, 2001 COLLABORATION

François Morellet, installation *Light Blue*, 2002; Debis Tower, Potsdamer Platz, Berlin, Germany, 2002 COLLABORATION

Robert Rauschenberg, stained-glass window *Apocalypse of Saint John*, 2004; San Giovanni Rotondo, Foggia, Italy, 2004 COLLABORATION

Susumu Shingu, sculpture *Cloud of Light*, 2004; Il Sole 24 Ore Headquarters, Milan, Italy 2004 COLLABORATION

Ben Rubin and Mark Hansen, video installation *Movable Type*, 2007; The New York Times Tower, New York, New York, USA, 2007 COLLABORATION

John Baldessari, photo mural *LACMA Grows*, 2008; Broad Contemporary Art Museum at LACMA, Los Angeles, California, USA, 2008 COLLABORATION

Chris Burden, sculpture *Urban Light*, 2008; Broad Contemporary Art Museum at LACMA, Los Angeles, California, USA, 2008 COLLABORATION

Maya Lin, sculpture *Where the Land Meets the Sea*, 2008; California Academy of Sciences, San Francisco, California, USA, 2008 COLLABORATION

Chris Burden, installation *Urban Light* at the LACMA, Los Angeles, California, USA, 2008.

Notes

1: Introduction

1. Ruskin's list consists of the lamps of sacrifice, truth, power, beauty, life, memory and obedience.

2. Colin Rowe, "Character and Composition; or Some Vicissitudes of Architectural Vocabulary in the Nineteenth Century," *Oppositions*, no. 2, 1974, and Alan Colquhoun, "Composition versus the Project," *Casabella*, no. 50, 1986.

3. The malleable uses for the word "composition" overlap other terms such as formalism, a concept that stresses rule-governed relationships rather than relationships of cause and effect. See Colquhoun, ibid.

4. Anon., *Architectural Record*, May 1960, pp. 145–156, and Lewis Mumford, "UNESCO House: the Hidden Treasure," *The Highway and the City*, London, Secker & Warburg, 1963, pp. 95–103.

5. The term Brutalism is derived from "béton brute," French for raw concrete.

6. James Ackerman, *The Architecture of Michelangelo*, London, Pelican Books, 1971.

7. J. Strachan, "Henry Moore's UNESCO Statue," *Studio*, December 1958, pp. 170–175, and David Finn, *Henry Moore. Sculpture and Environment*, New York, Abrams, 1976.

8. The initial UNESCO title of Picasso's mural was *The Forces of Life and the Mind Triumphing over Evil*, the final title *The Fall of Icarus* was given by Georges Salles.

9. Marie-Laure Bernadac, "Picasso 1953–1972: Paintings as Model," *Late Picasso. Paintings, Sculpture, Drawings, Prints 1953–1972*, London, The Tate Gallery, 1988, pp. 64–69.

10. James Thrall Soby, *Joan Miró*, New York, MoMA, 1968, pp. 138 and 140. Miró says of the artwork: "The very forms of the buildings [UNESCO], their spatial organization, the conditions of light, have suggested the forms and colors of my walls. I wished to incorporate my work with the ensemble, while seeking a contrast with the architecture. Thus in reaction against the concrete slabs which surround it, the idea of a huge disk in powerful red occurred to me for the large wall. Its rejoinder on the small wall would be a blue crescent, dictated by the more restrained and intimate space for which it was

intended. These two forms, which I wanted to be intense in color, had to be still further reinforced by hollowed-out passages. Detailed elements of the construction, such as the placing of the windows, have inspired me to create checkered compositions and figures. I sought a brutal expression in the large wall, a more poetic one in the small. Within each composition I sought at the same time a contrast by opposing to the black, ferocious and dynamic drawing, calm colored forms, flat or in squares."

11. Brian O'Doherty, *Inside the White Cube. The Ideology of the Gallery Space*, Los Angeles, Lapis Press, 1986, p. 15: "A gallery is constructed along laws as rigorous as those for building a medieval church. The outside world must not come in, so windows are usually sealed off. Walls are painted white. The ceiling becomes the source of light [...] the art is free, as the saying used to go 'to take on its own life'."

12. Neil Levine, "The Significance of Facts: Mies Collages Up Close & Personal," *Assemblage*, no. 37, 1998, pp. 82–84. Levine describes the Resor House collage as follows: "The sense of disorientation and displacement is physically reinforced by the deliberate play on distance and perspective."

13. Anon., "New Buildings for 1941," *Architectural Forum*, no. 78, May 1943, pp. 84–85.

14. *Kurt Schwitters*, exhibition catalogue, UCLA Art Galleries, 1965, p. 9: "I called my new way of creation with any material 'Merz.' This is the second syllable of "Kommerz" (commerce). The name originated from the "Merzbild," a picture in which the word 'merz' could be read in between abstract forms [...]" (original statement 1927). A reconstruction of one of the rooms of the Merzbau is on view in the Sprengel Museum in Hanover, Germany, as a permanent installation.

15. Werner Schmalenbach, *Kurt Schwitters*, New York, Harry N. Abrams, 1967, p. 60.

16. Vivian Endicott Barnett, "The Architect as Collector," Phyllis Lambert (ed.), *Mies in America*, New York, Harry N. Abrams, 2001, p. 90.

2: The Red of the Sky, not the Burning House

1. The first use of the term is by Michel Carrouges with the publication of *Les machines célibataires*, Paris, Arcanes, 1954. Carrouges extended the definition beyond Duchamp to include Franz Kafka's torture machine from the *Penal Colony* and other autoerotic

robotic images. English translation: Michel Carrouges, "Directions for Use," Harald Szeeman (ed.), *The Bachelor Machines/Le Macchine Celibi*, Venice, Alfieri Edizioni d'Arte, 1975, pp. 21–48.

2. Henry Adams, *The Education of Henry Adams. An Autobiography*, completed 1907 but published posthumously in New York, Houghton & Mifflin Co., 1918, chapter 25.

3. A. Ferrand, *Les dynamos et les transformateurs à l'Exposition Universelle de 1900*, Paris, E. Bernard, 1902.

4. Thomas Creighton, "Walter Gropius and the Arts," *Four Great Makers of Modern Architecture*, New York, Columbia University, 1962, pp. 247–258.

5. Frank Whitford, *The Bauhaus. Masters and Students by Themselves*, London, Conran Octopus, 1992, pp. 106–111.

6. The figure in the *Nude Descending a Staircase* is usually seen as a woman but has been interpreted as a male masturbating; see Joseph Mashick, *Marcel Duchamp in Perspective*, New York, Prentice-Hall, 1975, p. 7.

7. A. Lehman (ed.), *Oskar Schlemmer*, exhibition catalogue, Baltimore Museum of Art, 1987, pp. 115–117.

8. Peter Pfankuch, *Adolf Rading. Bauten, Entwürfe und Erläuterungen*, Berlin, Akademie der Künste, 1970, pp. 82–91.

9. Richard Lippold, *Memories*, unpublished, 1990, p. 6. (Archive of Richard Lippold Foundation, Locust Valley, New York)

10. Isaiah Berlin, *The Hedgehog and the Fox. An Essay on Tolstoy's View of History*, London, Weidenfeld & Nicolson, 1953. The text presents the world of Russian literature as written by two types of authors: the Fox who knows many things, travels many roads and accepts the idea that there can be different, equally valid but mutually incompatible concepts of how to live; the Hedgehog, on the other hand, needs only one principle that directs its life.

11. R. R. Fuchs, *Claes Oldenburg. Large Scale Projects 1977–1980*, New York, Rizzoli, 1980, pp. 68–75.

12. Sigfried Giedion, *Walter Gropius*, New York, Dover Publications, 1955, pp. 47–48. Sigfried Giedion, *Space Time and Architecture. The Growth of a New Tradition*, Cambridge, Harvard University Press, 1944, pp. 392–393: "The staircase, relieved of its accustomed shell, now seemed to hover in space." See also the same general view in Nikolaus Pevsner's *Pioneers of*

the Modern Movement, New York, Fredrik A. Stokes, 1936.

13. This omission included artists Gerhard Marcks, Richard Scheibe, Moissey Kogan, Otto Hettner, Hans Blanke and Hermann Haller.

14. Adolf Loos, "Ornament and Crime," Ulrich Conrads (ed.), *Programs and Manifestos on 20th Century Architecture*, Cambridge, MIT Press, 1970, p. 47: "The urge to ornament one's face and everything within reach is the start of plastic art [...] all art is erotic."

15. Mathieu Beauséjour, *Document sur papier archive*, published in *Parachute. Contemporary Art*, no. 115, 2004.

16. Allan Doig, *Theo van Doesburg. Painting into Architecture, Theory into Practice*, London, Cambridge University Press, 1986, p. 175. The Aubette was built in 1767 as a military headquarters, and the name originated from the fact that the soldiers were mustered there at dawn ("l'aube").

17. Theo Wolters, "L'Aubette, expression monumentale Du Stijl," *Cimaise*, no. 99, November–December 1970, pp. 55–56.

18. Herta Wescher, "Entretien avec Nelly van Doesburg," *Cimaise*, no. 99, November–December 1970, p. 41.

3: Symmetric Identities

1. The theme of the mirror image also appears in the many observations which noted Eero's ability to write backwards so as to have his comments read only in a mirror.

2. Finland was declared an independent republic in 1917.

3. Manfredo Tafuri and Francesco Dal Co, *Modern Architecture*, New York, Harry N. Abrams, 1979, p. 378: "[...] a bold structuralism utilized as an advertising technique"; Mark Lamster, *The TWA Terminal*, New York, Princeton Architectural Press, 1999, p. 3: "Like any good ad-man [Saarinen] intuitively grasped the importance of the paired values of visibility and immersion."

4. Ringborn Sixten, "Stone, Style and Truth. The Vogue for Natural Stone in Nordic Architecture 1880–1910," *Finnish Antiquarian Society*, no. 91, Helsinki, 1987.

5. Kirsten Benson, *The Finnish Pavilion in Paris 1900. A Culmination of Finland's Quest for National Identity*, unpublished thesis, Department of Art History, School of the Art Institute of Chicago, 1994.

6. In 1900 Lenin was in Switzerland, publishing the magazine *Iskra* (The Spark) and writing the text "What is to be done?"

7. Marika Hausen, "Eliel Saarinen. Projects," *Saarinen in Finland*, Helsinki, Museum of Finnish Architecture, 1984, p. 72: "One can notice a particular liking for semi-abstract human figures in his monumental buildings which merge into the building [...] The lantern bearers of the Helsinki railway station are the most conspicuous but these have many descendants with lanterns, swords or circular wreaths between their hands."

8. For observations on this effect in the sculpture of Lee Lawrie, labeled "engaged sculpture," see Frederick C. Luebke, *The Nebraska State Capitol. A Harmony of Arts*, Lincoln, University of Nebraska Press, 1990.

9. Sigmund Freud, "Lecture XXII. Some Thoughts on Development and Regression. Aetiology," *Introductory Lectures on Psycho-Analysis*, New York, W.W. Norton & Co., reprint 1989, p. 441.

10. Marika Hausen, op. cit., p. 79.

11. Line from the poem titled "Olga and Carl Milles' Will" carved in stone at Millesgården, Stockholm, Sweden. Until 1931 the home of Olga and Carl Milles, Millesgården today is a sculpture park and museum.

12. Craig Miller, "Interior Design and Furniture," *Design in America. The Cranbrook Vision 1925–1950*, New York, Harry N. Abrams, 1983, p. 82. Eero is listed as having his first art commission, in 1928 and at the age of eighteen, with a series of sculptural designs for the Kingswood boys school in Cranbrook. The work was a series of ceramic grotesque faces for ornamenting the exterior wall and a series of relief tiles of athletes surrounding the fireplace at Hoey Hall.

13. The Académie de la Grande Chaumière (which still exists in the same Paris location) is not a school in the traditional sense, it is more an open set of studio spaces that anyone can pay an admission to and where one can participate in sketching from models.

14. Transference is used here in its psychoanalytic definition. In this case the designer (the patient) relocates his love obsession from the emotional world of art and sculpture (the mother) to another, the ordered world of architecture (the father). Eero's mother, Loja, was trained first as a sculptor at the Académie Colarossi in Paris and later became involved in weaving. See Dennis Barrie, *Artists in Michigan. 1900–1976*, Detroit, Wayne State University Press, 1989, pp. 201–202.

15. Other art at the General Motors Technical Center includes a painting dealing with industrial research by Charles Sheeler; a large oil painting by Jimmy Ernst, suggesting changing relationships of form in space; a stainless steel mural, 9 × 4.5 meters, by Buell Mullen; a fountain sculpture by members of the design section. *Architectural Summary of the GM Technical Center*, Eero Saarinen Architects, undated, p. 13. (Saarinen Collection at Yale University Library)

16. Kevin Roche (design director of the Saarinen office) is given the design credit for both monumental open stairs in the complex. But Saarinen is assumed to have been involved in its approval and development. Anon., "For Men and Women of Industry, Contemporary Design, Tech. Center," *The Birmingham Eccentric*, May 17, 1956, section 2, p. 1.

17. John Peter, *The Oral History of Modern Architecture*, New York, Harry N. Abrams, 1994, p. 198.

18. Letter to Costantino Nivola from Eero Saarinen, November 2, 1959: "In other words, I'm not looking for one piece of sculpture, nor am I looking for just wall decoration, I'm looking for a whole atmosphere created by sculpture and bas relief in relation to the architecture" (Archives of American Art, Nivola Collection, Washington, DC).

19. Mark Lamster, op. cit., p. 5: "Despite Saarinen's proclamations regarding the primacy of 'structure' in his architectural philosophy, with the TWA Terminal he forced a formal solution on Ammann & Whitney, his structural engineers."

20. Anon., *The Saarinen Door. Eliel Saarinen Architect and Designer at Cranbrook*, Bloomfield Hills, Cranbrook Academy of Art, 1963. The door ornament is placed on the cover with the title "Saarinen Door."

21. The word "verschrieben" (miswritten) could be applied here as well and would join Freud's lexicon of labels identifying obvious mistakes and evidence of the workings of the subconscious (Parapraxis). Other well-known terms are "Verlesen" (misreading) and the more famous "Versprecher" (mis-speaking) translated into English as "a slip of the tongue."

22. *The Baldwinian*, Baldwin High School Yearbook, Birmingham, Michigan, 1927, p. 69.

23. Sigmund Freud (James Strachey, series editor), *Leonardo da Vinci and a Memory of His Childhood*, New York, W.W. Norton & Co., reprint 1989, footnote 13, p. 73: "But what appears to a critic's eye as a fault, as a defect in composition, is vindicated in the eyes of the analysis by reference to its secret meaning. It seems that for the artist the two mothers of his childhood were melted into a single form."

24. The term has been used also in modern poetry when Stéphane Mallarmé scattered words across the page in the poem "Un coup de dés jamais n'abolira le hasard" (A throw of the dice will never abolish chance) in 1897.

25. Anna C. Chave, *Constantin Brâncuşi. Shifting the Bases of Art*, New Haven, Yale University Press, 1993, p. 276: "This sense of an always provisional order and calm prevailing amid disarray bordering on chaos, impressed on the visitors as well."

26. Lynn Gamwell (ed.) *Sigmund Freud and Art. His Personal Collection of Antiquities*, Binghampton, State University of New York, 1989.

4: Minotaur in the Labyrinth and Christ on the Cross

1. Another church that is part of the movement would be the Church of the Sacred Heart in Audincourt, France, 1953. Included by many would be the Dominican monastery La Tourette by Le Corbusier. Couturier was also involved in the modern stained-glass windows that were installed in the Cathedral of Notre Dame de Paris in 1937 and after causing great controversy were immediately removed.

2. Anon., "'Errant' Modern Art," *The Commonweal*, August 1, 1952, p. 406.

3. Marie-Alain Couturier, foreword by Marcel Billot, *Sacred Art*, Houston, University of Texas Press 1989, p. 52.

4. Anon., "Ecclesiastical Art," *Architectural Association Journal*, May 1956, p. 265.

5. Anon., "Removal at Assy," *Time*, April 23, 1951. The statue has since been relocated back to the altar.

6. William Rubin, *Modern Sacred Art and the Church of Assy*, New York, Columbia University Press, 1961, p. 55.

7. Richard Moor, "Alchemical and Mythical Themes in the Poem of the Right Angle," *Oppositions*, no. 19/20, pp. 110–139.

8. Stuart Cohen and Steven Hurt, "The Pilgrimage Chapel at Ronchamp," *Oppositions*, no. 19/20, pp. 142–157.

9. John Jacobus, *Twentieth Century Architecture. The Middle Years*, New York, Praeger, 1966, p. 86.

10. James Stirling, "Ronchamp and the Crisis of Rationalism," *Architectural Review*, March 1956, pp. 155–161.

11. Alan Colquhoun, "Displacement of Concepts," *AD–Architectural Design*, April 1972.

12. Stanislaus von Moos, "Cartesian Curves", *AD–Architectural Design*, April 1972, pp. 237–239: "For Le Corbusier, the three arts remained independent, yet connected by a common ground of plastic notions. Consider for example, the formal analogies between Purist painting of 1925 and certain contemporary house plans. Think of the towers of Ronchamp, based on a series of pictorial studies (in particular on *Ozon*, a series of sculptures of 1946)."

13. Colin Rowe and Robert Slutzky, "Transparency: Literal and Phenomenal," *Perspecta,* no. 8, 1964 (original text 1955). Bernhard Hoesli's comparison can be found in this edition: Colin Rowe and Robert Slutzky, *Transparency*, Basel, Birkhäuser Verlag, 1997, pp. 60–61.

14. Eduard Sekler, "Le Corbusier's Use of a 'Pictorial Word' in His Tapestry 'La femme et le moineau'," Mary Henle (ed.), *Vision and Artifact*, New York, Springer Publishing Co., 1976. An analysis of Le Corbusier's tapestry *La femme et le moineau* (part of his *Icône* series) which shows comparisons between the tapestry and the development of the plan for the Carpenter Center for the Visual Arts at Harvard University in Cambridge, Massachusetts. See also Jamie Coll, "Structure and Play in Le Corbusier's Art Work," *AA Files*, no. 31, Summer 1996, pp. 3–15, for an analysis of Le Corbusier's paintings that proposes a connection between one of the paintings from the series entitled *Icône*, and the plan of Le Corbusier's Philips Pavilion for the EXPO 1958 in Brussels.

15. Flora Samuel, "The Representation of Mary in the Architecture of Le Corbusier's Chapel at Ronchamp," *The American Society of Church History*, vol. 68:2, June 1999.

16. Christophe Cousin, *Ronchamp. Chapel of Light*, Besançon, CRDP Franche-Comté, 2005, p. 85: "But his youth […] pushed him into studying some fundamental works: *L'art de demain* by Henry Provensal (published 1904) that details the role of artists […] destined to reveal spiritual truth to Humanity."

17. The work was published in color in numerous popular magazines such as *House & Garden, Harper's Bazaar, Life, L'Illustration* and *Paris Vogue*.

18. René Percheron, *Matisse. From Color to Architecture*, New York, Harry N. Abrams, 2003, p. 65.

19. Olivier Berggruen, *Henri Matisse. Drawing with Scissors, Masterpieces from the Late Years*, Munich, Prestel, 2003, p. 19.

20. Marie-Alain Couturier, op. cit., p. 90.

21. Alfred Barr, *Matisse. His Art and His Public*, New York, MoMA, 1959, p. 284.

22. René Percheron, op. cit., p. 238: "[…] the drawing is rough, very crude, in fact; it will dismay most people who see it. God held my hand. What could I do but obey? The others know nothing of this."

23. René Percheron, op. cit., p. 94.

24. Francis Weber, *Cathedral of Our Lady of the Angels*, Los Angeles, Saint Francis Historical Society, 2004.

25. Richard Vosko, *God's Is Our House. Re-imagining the Environment for Worship*, Collegeville, Minnesota, The Liturgical Press, 2000.

26. Jack Miles, *Robert Graham. The Great Bronze Doors for the Cathedral of Our Lady of the Angels*, Venice, California, Wave Publishing, 2002.

27. Paul Schimmel, *Robert Gober*, exhibition catalogue, Los Angeles Museum of Contemporary Art, Zurich, Scalo Publishers, 1997. The artwork is on permanent display at the Schaulager in Basel, Switzerland.

5: Power and the Place of Art

1. For a different interpretation see: Carol Duncan and Alan Wallach, "The Museum of Modern Art as Late Capitalistic Ritual: An Iconographic Analysis," *Marxist Perspectives*, Winter 1978, pp. 28–51.

2. It has been noted from meeting minutes and correspondence that the architect Harvey Wiley Corbett was the most adamant supporter of Lee Lawrie's participation, with negative comments from Nelson Rockefeller.

3. Wallace Harrison in 1926 married Ellen Milton, whose brother was then married to Abby Rockefeller, the oldest child and only daughter of John D. Rockefeller Jr.

4. Raymond Hood, "Rockefeller Center," *Society of Beaux Arts Architects Yearbook*, 1933, p. 70.

5. Simon Willmoth, "Léger and America," Nicolas Serota (ed.), *Fernand Léger. The Later Years*, Munich, Prestel, 1987, p. 45.

6. Rivera was not the only artist to have his work altered at Rockefeller Center. Frank Brangwyn's mural in the RCA lobby was revised to have the central figure appear less Christ-like (resolved by having the figure turn his back to the crowd). Also in 1937 the cast glass panel for the entrance of the Palazzo d'Italia building in Rockefeller Center, by the artist Attilio Piccirilli, was removed to eliminate the obvious reference to the Italian Fascist Party. The latest artistic censoring occurred as late as 2002 when Eric Fischl's figurative bronze sculpture *Tumbling Woman*, as a memorial to the collapse of the World Trade Towers, was removed from the Center because of negative public response.

7. Bertram Wolfe, *The Fabulous Life of Diego Rivera*, New York, Stein & Day, 1963, p. 329: "The Communist Party was caught in no man's land. It did not want to defend nor praise Rivera, nor take the side of his millionaire patron, nor did it have any 'Marxist explanation' to offer. A revolutionary painter for millionaires, a millionaire patron of revolutionary painting, and a Communist Party silent on the fight between them, constituted a triple absurdity."

8. Rivera reproduced the Rockefeller Center mural in the Teatro Nacional de México in Mexico City and included the faces of Lenin and Trotsky.

9. Leon Trotsky, *Leon Trotsky on Literature and Art*, New York, Pathfinder Press, 1970, p. 117 and 118 (source for both Trotsky quotes).

10. Johnson was one of the few architects (Robert Venturi working with the art collector Peter Brant would be another) to combine Warhol's work with his buildings: the New York State Pavilion, the IDS Center Hotel in Minneapolis, Johnson's own apartment in the MoMA Tower and a proposal for using Warhol's *Last Supper* for the Checkpoint Charlie office building in Berlin. Also in the opening for his design of the Art Museum of South Texas in Corpus Christi, Johnson advocated for the first show to be the work of Andy Warhol.

11. There were two other sculptors on the pavilion's façade: Peter Agostini and Robert Mallary both used collage-like elements, casts from balloons and overcoats to place them in an in-between area overlapping Pop Art, Minimalism, collage, expressionism and other styles. See Philip Johnson, "Young Artists at the Fair and at Lincoln Center," *Art in America*, no. 4, 1964, pp. 112–121.

12. Richard Meyer, *Outlaw Representation. Censorship and Homosexuality in Twentieth Century American Art*, Boston, Beacon Press, 2002.

13. Rainer Crone, *Andy Warhol*, New York, Praeger, 1970, p. 30.

14. Anna C. Chave, "Minimalism and the Rhetoric of Power," *Power. Its Myths and Mores in American Art*, Bloomington, Indiana University Press, 1991.

15. The tradition of decorating with tapestries was part of Nelson's childhood, for his father had

prominently displayed, in their New York City apartment, the magnificent medieval wall hangings Unicorn Tapestries.

16. Barty Phillips, *Tapestry*, London, Phaidon Press, 1994, p. 136: "In the 1930s, an enterprising French Woman, Madame Marie Cuttoli, set up a tapestry workshop in Paris. […] The results of these efforts were tapestries that were really only copies of paintings, which cost far more than the original and which had lost, rather than gained, any meaningful quality or texture through the weaving."

17. Letter from Alfred Barr to Nelson Rockefeller on Picasso tapestry, November 21, 1962.

18. Thorstein Veblen, *The Theory of the Leisure Class*, London, Macmillan, reprint 1912, p. 126.

19. At Mondrian's death in 1944, Fritz Glarner religiously documented the artist's studio at 15 East 59th Street in New York City, an environment of colored paper rectangles floating on white walls, by photography and scaled drawings.

20. The Mondrian design was built as a temporary exhibit in 1970 by the Pace Gallery in New York City and in 2001 by the Fondation Beyeler in Basel, Switzerland.

21. In 1987 the Nelson Rockefeller dining room was purchased and reassembled in the Haus Konstruktiv in Zurich, Switzerland, and is on permanent exhibit there.

22. Hilton Kramer, *New York Times*, December 10, 1978, section 2, p. 1 and 39. Robert Hughes, *Time*, December 18, 1979, pp. 93–94. Ruth Bereson, *National Review*, March 16, 1979, p. 373.

23. Interview with Christine Roussel, marketing and production consultant for Nelson Rockefeller Collections Inc., November 1, 2005.

24. Adolphe Chanaux, *Jean-Michel Frank*, Paris, Editions du Regard, 1997, p. 41.

6: Gravestones of Modernism

1. Alexander Stirling Calder, "The Relation of Sculpture to Architecture," *American Architect*, December 8, 1920, pp. 723–732: "It must here be understood that the established character of the architectural frames or spaces provided in classic design for sculpture limits the sculptor to designs that will fill these spaces and necessarily forces a general resemblance in all such designs."

2. Miwon Kwon, *One Place After Another. Site-Specific Art and Locational Identity*, Cambridge, MIT Press, 2002, pp. 60–61.

3. Carter Manny has noted that other names were suggested: *Tulip, Redskin* and *Tomahawk*.

4. Harold Haydon, "Alexander Calder. His Toys and his Swaying Sculpture," *Chicago Sunday Sun-Times*, showcase, section 1B, October 20, 1974.

5. Interview with Carter Manny at Michigan City, Indiana, July 2004.

6. Mies owned one of the *Circus* drawings produced by Calder. Phyllis Lambert (ed.), *Mies in America*, op. cit., p. 111. Also, Mies designed a Berlin private home in 1928 for Hugo Perls, the art dealer and father of Klaus Perls, who was Calder's New York City gallery dealer.

7. Robert Osborn, "Calder's International Monuments," *Art in America*, March/April 1969: "Against certain backgrounds, yes – it can help. For instance, a new one at Grand Rapids will be red because the piece is set against a black glass building." (Osborn refers to the Calder stabile *La grande vitesse*, 1969)

8. Franz Schulze, "Chicago Picasso," *Chicago Daily News*, August 23, 1969: "But of course it's a woman […] the question, however just won't go away."

9. The most elaborate analysis can be found in the Northwestern University master's thesis by Patricia Stratton, *Chicago Picasso*, 1982.

10. Picasso stated about his 1909 sculpture *Head of a Woman*: "I thought the curves you see on the surface should continue inside, I had the intention of doing that with wire […]" Quoted in: Roland Penrose, *The Sculpture of Picasso*, New York, MoMA, 1968, p. 19.

11. Dore Ashton, "Bunshaft and Noguchi: An Uneasy but Highly Productive Architect-Artist Collaboration," *AIA Journal*, October 1976, pp. 52–54. See also the correspondence between Noguchi and Bunshaft, letter of October 21, 1972, Noguchi Museum, Long Island City, New York.

12. Harriet Senie, "Urban Sculpture, Cultural Token or Ornament to Life?," *Art News*, September 1979, p. 108.

13. Bruce Altshuler and Diane Apostolos-Cappadonna (eds.), *Isamu Noguchi. Essays and Conversations*, New York, Harry N. Abrams, 1994, p. 65.

14. Isamu Noguchi, *A Sculptor's World*, New York, Harper and Row, 1968, p. II: "Things which are so far back are not like a part of myself, more like the life of somebody else, and should be written by another. To me it all seemed like chance; choice, if any, came much later. How I came to make a decision, I do not know. Perhaps choice, too, is chance, like the rolling of dice. With my double nationality and double upbringing, where was my home? Where were my affections? Where my identity? Japan or America, either, both – or the world."

15. Isamu Noguchi, "The 'Arts' called 'Primitive'," *Art News*, no. 56, March 1957, pp. 24–27, 64.

16. Isamu Noguchi, *A Sculptor's World*, op. cit., pp. 33–34.

17. For Noguchi's generation a number of new sculpture types were named. Alexander Calder's work has been divided into types titled *Mobiles, Stabiles* and *Constellations* while Jacques Lipchitz named his 1930 linear open sculpture *Transparents*. Noguchi himself named his lighting designs *Akari* to make them distinct from his sculpture using internal electrical lighting.

18. Sam Hunter, *Isamu Noguchi. 75th Birthday Exhibition*, Pace Gallery, New York, 1980. First use of the term "table landscapes."

19. The work of Noguchi and Giacometti intersected again (but missed an opportunity for dialogue) when Alberto Giacometti's sculpture for the Plaza of the Chase Manhattan Bank by Skidmore, Owings & Merrill remained unrealized – the same building that is the site of Noguchi's *Sunken Garden*, 1964.

7: Empty Spaces and Vast Horizons

1. Elisabeth Sussman (ed.), *Clark Gordon-Matta. You are the Measure*, New Haven, Yale University Press, 2007, p. 24.

2. To be added to this list would be "not-architecture," a term used to distinguish landscape work from "site-specific" art in the landscape as defined by Rosalind Krauss in "Sculpture in the Expanded Field," Hal Foster (ed.), *The Anti-Aesthetic. Post-Modern Culture*, London, Pluto Press, 1983.

3. One example of the failure of the One Percent for Art program would be the destruction in 2002 of the sculpture *This Equals That* in Ann Arbor, Michigan, by the artist Michael Heizer. This artist is a perfect example of someone whose work has retreated to an area of greater artistic control in Earth Art constructions.

4. Robert Smithson, "Aerial Art," *Studio International*, April 1969, p. 116.

5. Robert Smithson, ibid., p. 116. The term *détournement* was coined by the Situationist movement in France in the 1950s. See Guy Debord and Gil Wolman, "Mode d'emploi de détournement," *Les lèvres nues*, no. 8, May 1956. English source: Guy Debord, "The Situationists and the New Forms of Action in Politics or Art" (1963), Tom McDonough (ed.), *Guy Debord and the Situationist International, Texts and Documents*, Cambridge, MIT Press, 2004.

6. James Pagliasotti, "An Interview with Christo and Jeanne-Claude," *Eye-Level Arts Magazine*, 2002, p. 1.

7. David Bourdon and Christo, *Christo*, New York, Harry N. Abrams, 1972, p. 143.

8. S. Franke, A. Maysle, B. Eisenhart, documentary movie *Concert of Wills: Making the Getty Center*, 1997.

9. Lawrence Weschler, "When Fountainheads Collide," *New Yorker*, December 8, 1997, p. 69.

10. Richard Meier, *Building the Getty*, New York, Knopf, 1997, p. 130.

8: Sculptural Space Becomes Architectural Space

1. Greg Lynn, *Folds, Bodies & Blobs*, New York, Princeton Architectural Press, 1999.

2. Anthony Vidler, *Warped Space. Art, Architecture and Anxiety in Modern Culture*, Cambridge, MIT Press, 2000, p. 10: "The most celebrated example of this wave of warpings is, of course, Gehry's Bilbao museum, with its twisting and thrusting volumes encased in titanium scales, itself housing a sculpture by Richard Serra, whose own *Torqued Ellipses* have pushed the limits of steel fatigue and destabilized the viewing subject in extreme ways."

3. Barbara Rose, "ABC Art," *Art in America*, October 1965, p. 58.

4. Barbara Rose, ibid., p. 63.

5. The artists Sol LeWitt, Francesco Clemente and Jenny Holzer have also produced installations in gallery spaces for the museum.

6. B.J. Archer (ed.), *Follies. Architecture for the Late-Twentieth-Century Landscape*, New York, Rizzoli, 1993.

7. Karen Stein, "Project Diary. Frank Gehry's Dream Project," *Architectural Record*, no. 10, 1997, p. 86: "Gehry wants to erect two walls flanking the front of it to compress views and provide some of the tension that Serra's sculpture thrives on, but Krens vetoed the idea."

8. Tomie Ohtake, *Folds of the Soul*, Sao Paolo, Institute Tomie Ohtake, 2001.

9. John Pawson, *Minimalism*, New York, Phaidon Press, 2004.

10. Franz Schultz, "Report from St. Louis," *Art in America*, September 2002.

11. Peter Noever (ed.), *Yves Klein. Air Architecture*, Stuttgart, Hatje Cantz Verlag, 2004.

12. Dorothee Lehmann-Kopp, *Werner Ruhnau. The Space, the Game and the Arts*, Berlin, Jovis Verlag, 2007.

13. Anna C. Chave, "Minimalism and the Rhetoric of Power," *Power. Its Myths and Mores in American Art*, op. cit., p. 130.

9: Conclusion: What Shall We Do Now?

1. Sigfried Giedion, *Space, Time and Architecture: The Growth of a New Tradition*, op. cit., pp. 401–403.

2. Colin Rowe and Robert Slutzky, *Transparency*, op. cit.; and Detlef Mertins, *Transparencies Yet to Come: Sigfried Giedion and Adolf Behne, A+U*, no. 10/325, October 1997, pp. 4–15.

3. Guy Debord, *The Society of the Spectacle*, Wellington, Rebel Press, 2004, chapter I, 11.

4. Gehry has a list of six collaborative projects with Oldenburg starting with the placement of an Oldenburg sculpture in the campus of Loyola Law School, Los Angeles, in 1978.

5. Catalogue for the installation *Within Reach* at the British Pavilion for the Venice Biennale 2003. DVD titled *Chris Ofili* by Illuminations, London, 2004.

6. Benjamin Buchloh, *Gerhard Richter. Eight Gray*, Berlin, Deutsche Guggenheim, Stuttgart, Hatje Cantz Verlag, 2003.

7. Jacques Rancière, "The Emancipated Spectator," *Art Forum*, March 2007, p. 280.

8. Bettina Funcke, "Displaced Struggles. On Rancière and the Art World," *Art Forum*, March 2007, p. 285.

Quotation Sources

Page 7: Dipesh Chakrabarty
Dipesh Chakrabarty, *Provincializing Europe: Post-colonial Thought and Historical Difference*, New York, Princeton University Press, 2000, p. 109.

Page 14: John Beverley Robinson
John Beverley Robinson, *Principles of Architectural Composition*, Architectural Record Co., New York, 1899, p. 3.

Page 14: David Shapiro
David Shapiro, "Art as Collaboration: Towards a Theory of Pluralist Aesthetics 1950–1980," Cynthia McCabe, *Artistic Collaboration in the Twentieth Century*, Washington, DC, Smithsonian Institution Press, 1984, p. 45.

Page 23: Bertolt Brecht
Bertolt Brecht, "On Non-Objective Painting," Berel Long (ed.), *Marxism and Art: Writings in Aesthetics and Criticism*, New York, McKay, 1972, p. 423.

Page 37: Walter Gropius
Walter Gropius, lecture "Architects in the Making," March 30, 1936, London, manuscript at Gropius Archives, Harvard University.

Page 41: Eero Saarinen
Eero Saarinen, "Function, Structure and Beauty," *Architectural Association Journal*, July–August, 1957, p. 43.

Page 42: Albert Christ-Janer
Albert Christ-Janer, *Eliel Saarinen*, Chicago, University of Chicago Press, 1948, p. 93.

Page 49: Karl Abraham
Karl Abraham, *Selected Papers*, New York, Brunner/Mazel, 1979, p. 370.

Page 54: Eliel Saarinen
Eliel Saarinen quoted in "Furnish Home According to Principles of Architecture," *The Milwaukee Journal*, January 18, 1942.

Page 61: Georg Wilhelm Friedrich Hegel
G.W.F. Hegel, "Introduction," *Philosophy of Fine Art*, Bristol, Thoemmes Continuum, 1999, pp. 8–9.

Page 63: Marcel Billot
Marie-Alain Couturier, foreword by Marcel Billot, *Sacred Art*, Houston, University of Texas Press, 1989, p. 11.

Page 67: André Malraux
André Malraux, *Picasso's Mask*, New York, Holt Rinehart Winston, 1976, p. 157.

Page 68: Le Corbusier
Le Corbusier (preface), Maurice Jardot, *Le Corbusier–Dessins*, Paris, Editions des deux mondes, 1955. English translation in *AD–Architectural Design*, May/June 2003, p. 8.

Page 71: Le Corbusier, "In reality…"
Stamo Papadiki (ed.), *Le Corbusier: Architect, Painter, Writer*, New York, Macmillan, 1948, p. 17.

Page 71: Le Corbusier, "I am only known…"
Anon., *Le Corbusier*, Basel, Galerie Beyeler, 1971, p. 8.

Page 72: Le Corbusier
Le Corbusier (preface), Maurice Jardot, *Le Corbusier–Dessins*, Paris, Editions des deux mondes, 1955. English translation in *AD–Architectural Design*, May/June 2003, p. 8.

Page 73: Henri Matisse
Marcel Billot (ed.), Marie-Alain Couturier, Louis-Bertrand Rayssiguier, *Henri Matisse. The Vence Chapel–The Archive of a Creation*, Milan, Skira, 1999, p. 163.

Page 74: Henri Matisse
Hilary Spurling, *Matisse the Master*, New York, Knopf, 2005, p. 452.

Page 75: Brother Louis-Bertrand Rayssiguier
Marcel Billot (ed.), Marie-Alain Couturier, Louis-Bertrand Rayssiguier, *Henri Matisse. The Vence Chapel–The Archive of a Creation*, Milan, Skira, 1999, p. 42.

Page 76: Mircea Eliade
Mircea Eliade, *The Sacred and the Profane: The Nature of Religion*, New York, Harcourt, Brace, Jovanovich, 1959, p. 11.

Page 77: Henri Matisse
Pierre Schneider, *Matisse*, New York, Rizzoli, 1984, p. 675.

Page 81: Nelson Rockefeller
Rona Roob, "Rockefeller Vision and the Making of the Museum of Modern Art," *Research Reports from the Rockefeller Archive Center*, Spring 1997, p. 2.

Page 84: Vincent Scully
Vincent Scully, *American Architecture and Urbanism*, London, Thames and Hudson, 1969, p. 154.

Page 87: Rockefeller Center Publicity Statement, May 19, 1933
Rockefeller Archive Center, Sleepy Hollow, New York

Page 90: Philip Johnson
John O'Conner, Benjamin Liu, *Unseen Warhol*, New York, Rizzoli, 1986, p. 111.

Page 90: Barbara Rose
Barbara Rose, *American Painting: The 20th Century*, Geneva, Skira, 1995, p. 101.

Page 95: Nelson Rockefeller
Press Conference, New York City, January 17, 1978; Rockefeller Archive Center, Sleepy Hollow, New York

Page 99: A.M. Hammacher
A.M. Hammacher, *Modern Sculpture, Tradition and Innovation*, New York, Harry N. Abrams, 1988, p. 272.

Page 99: Tom Wolfe
Tom Wolfe, "The Worship of Art," *Harper's Magazine*, October 1984, p. 61.

Page 100: André Breton
Constance Schwartz, *Calder and Miró*, New York, Nassau County Museum of Art, 1998, p. 23.

Page 103: Robert Osborn
Robert Osborn, "Calder's International Monuments," *Art in America*, March/April, 1969, p. 32.

Page 105: Jean Clair
Jean Clair (ed.), *Picasso Erotique*, New York, Prestel, 2001, p. 10.

Page 107: Isamu Noguchi
Katharine Kuh, *The Artist's Voice. Talks with Seventeen Artists*, New York, Harper & Row, 1962, p. 175.

Page 115: Michael McDonough
Alan Sonfist (ed.), *Art in the Land: A Critical Anthology of Environmental Art*, New York, E.P. Dutton, 1983, p. 233.

Page 116: Robert Smithson
Robert Smithson, "Aerial Art," *Studio International*, April 1969, p. 180.

Page 119: Donald Judd
Gregory Battcock (ed.), *Minimal Art. A Critical Anthology*, New York, Dutton, 1968, p. 149.

Page 120: Gordon Matta-Clark
Corinne Diserens, *Gordon Matta-Clark*, New York, Phaidon, 2003, p. 188.

Page 123: Frank Stella
Maxwell L. Anderson, Whitney Museum of American Art, *American Visionaries – Selections from the Whitney Museum of American Art*, New York, Harry Abrams, 2001, p. 297.

Page 123: Carl Andre
Lucy Lippard (ed.), *Six Years. The Dematerialization of the Art Object from 1966 to 1972*, Berkeley, University of California Press, 1997, p. 40.

Page 124: Christo and Jeanne-Claude
James Pagliasotti, "An Interview with Christo and Jeanne-Claude," *Eye-Level Arts Magazine*, 2002, p. 8.

Page 125: Olafur Eliasson
Chris Gilbert, "Olafur Eliasson," *BOMB Magazine*, issue 88, Summer 2004.

Page 129: Donald Judd
Donald Judd, *Donald Judd Complete Writings 1959–1975*, New York, New York University Press, 1975, p. 138.

Page 129: Greg Lynn
Peter Noever (ed.), *Turning Point*, Vienna, Springer, 1996, p. 12.

Page 130: Richard Serra
Richard Serra, *Writings/Interviews*, Chicago, University of Chicago Press, 1994, p. 109.

Page 132: Claes Oldenburg
Claes Oldenburg, "Notes," *Store Days*, New York, Something Else Press, 1967, p. 39.

Page 133: Frank Gehry
John Tusa, *Frank Gehry Interview*, BBC Radio 3, London, 1999.

Page 134: Richard Serra
Hal Foster, *Richard Serra: The Matter of Time*, Göttingen, Steidl, 2005, p. 41.

Page 134: Gilles Deleuze
Gilles Deleuze, *The Fold: Leibniz and the Baroque*, Minneapolis, University of Minnesota Press, 1993, p. 121.

Page 135: Eduardo Galeano
Paula Goes, "Oscar Niemeyer: 100 Years of a Daring Architecture," *Global Voices Online*, December 15, 2007.

Page 135: Robert Storr
Robert Storr, "A Place in the Sun," *Frieze Magazine*, issue 99, May 2006.

Page 137: Donald Judd
Donald Judd, "Specific Objects," *Arts Yearbook*, no. 8/1965.

Page 138: Tadao Ando
Anon., "Interview with Tadao Ando," *Dialogue*, St. Louis, Pulitzer Foundation for the Arts, 2001.

Page 140: Ellsworth Kelly
James Meyer, *Ellsworth Kelly. Sculpture for a Large Wall 1957*, New York, Matthew Marks Gallery, 1998, p. 34.

Page 142: Donald Judd
Hunter Philp, "Marfa on my Mind," *Artnet Magazine*, April 19, 2006.

Page 150: Sol LeWitt
Sol LeWitt, "Sentences on Conceptual Art," *Art Language*, no. 1, May 1969, p. 11.

Page 173: Guy Debord
Guy Debord, *In girum imus nocte et consumimur igni: A Film*, London, Pelagian Press, 1991.

Page 177: Jorge Pardo
Christian Vegh, *Jorge Pardo*, Phaidon Press, London, 2008, p. 32.

Selected Bibliography

Anon, "Intégration des arts dans l'architecture," *Aujourd'hui, Art et Architecture*, January 1957, vol. 2, pp. 12–22.

Arnoldi, Per, "*Colour is Communication." Selected Projects for Foster + Partners 1996–2006*, Basel, Birkhäuser Verlag, 2007.

Barnitz, Jacqueline, "Functionalism, Integration of the Arts, and the Post-War Architectural Boom," *Twentieth-Century Art of Latin America*, Austin, University of Texas Press, 2001, pp. 166–188.

Benezra, Neal David, *The Murals and Sculpture of Josef Albers*, New York, Garland Publishing, 1983.

Berger, Ursel and Thomas Pavel (eds.), *Barcelona Pavilion–Mies van der Rohe & Kolbe. Architecture & Plastic*, Berlin, Jovis Verlag, 2006.

Bernier, Georges and Rosamond (eds.), "Architecture and the Plastic Arts," *The Best in 20th Century Architecture*, New York, Reynal & Co., 1964, pp. 180–189.

Bechtler, Cristina (ed.), *Frank O. Gehry, Kurt W. Forster. Art and Architecture– a Dialogue*, Stuttgart, Hatje Cantz Verlag, 1999.

Bitterman, Eleanor, *Art in Modern Architecture*, New York, Reinhold Publishing, 1952.

Celant, Germano (ed.), *Architecture & Arts 1900–2004. A Century of Creative Projects in Building, Design, Cinema, Painting, Sculpture*, Milan, Skira, 2005.

Celant, Germano (ed.), *Arti & Architettura*, Milan, Skira, 2004.

Chinati Foundation, *Art and Architecture*, Symposium on April 25–26, 1998, Marfa, Texas, The Chinati Foundation, 2000.

Clark, Kenneth, "Ornament in Modern Architecture," *Architectural Review*, December 1943, pp. 147–50.

Cooper, Graham, *Project Japan, Architecture and Art Media. Edo to Now*, Mulgrave, Victoria, Images Publishing, 2009.

Creighton, Thomas, "Walter Gropius and the Arts," *Four Great Makers of Modern Architecture*, New York, Columbia University Press, 1961, pp. 247–258.

Curtis, Penelope, *Patio and Pavilion. The Space of Sculpture in Modern Architecture*, London, Ridinghouse, 2007.

Damaz, Paul F., *Art in European Architecture. Synthèse des Arts*, New York, Reinhold Publishing, 1956.

Diamonstein, Barbaralee, *Collaboration. Artists and Architects*, New York, Whitney Library of Design, 1981.

Dillon, Brian (ed.), *Psycho Buildings. Artists Take on Architecture*, London, Hayward Gallery, 2008.

Eccles, Tom, Anne Wehr and Jeffrey Kastner (eds.), *Plop. Recent Projects of the Public Art Fund*, New York, Merrell Publishers, 2004.

Filler, Martin, *Art + Architecture + Landscape. The Clos Pegase Design Competition*, San Francisco, San Francisco Museum of Modern Art, 1985.

Fernie, Jes (ed.), *Two Minds. Artists and Architects in Collaboration*, London, Black Dog Publishing, 2006.

Fondation Beyeler (ed.) *ArchiSculpture. Dialogues between Architecture and Sculpture from the 18th Century to the Present Day*, Stuttgart, Hatje Cantz Verlag, 2004.

Flückiger, Urs Peter, *Donald Judd. Architecture in Marfa, Texas*, Basel, Birkhäuser Verlag, 2007.

Fuchs, R. H., "Monuments," *Claes Oldenburg. Large Scale Projects 1977– 1980*, New York, Rizzoli, 1980, pp. 97–98.

Giedion, Sigfried (ed.), "Architecture, Painter and Sculptor," *A Decade of New Architecture*, Zurich, Editions Girsberger, 1951, pp. 30–54.

Hatekayama, Naoya, Tadao Ando and Ryuiji Miyamoto, *The Chichu Art Museum. Tadao Ando Builds for Claude Monet, Walter De Maria and James Turrell*, Stuttgart, Hatje Cantz Verlag, 2005.

Hölzinger, Johannes P. and Eberhard Fiebig, *Synthèse des Arts. The Combination of Architecture and Art in the Government Buildings on the Hardthöhe in Bonn*, Stuttgart, Edition Axel Menges, 1999.

Hopkins, Henry, *The Relationship between Art and Architecture*, vols. I and II: *Summary of a Workshop Sponsored by the Frederick R. Weisman Art Foundation*, Santa Monica, Weisman Art Foundation, 1990.

Jodidio, Philip, *Architecture: Art*, Munich, Prestel, 2005.

Jorden, Sherrill (ed.), *Public Art–Public Controversy. The Tilted Arc on Trial*, New York, ACA Books, 1987.

Kampf, Avram, *Contemporary Synagogue Art*, New York, Union of American Hebrew Congregations, 1966.

Kwon, Miwon, *One Place After Another. Site Specific Art and Locational Identity*, Cambridge, MIT Press, 2004.

Margolius, Ivan (ed.), "Art + Architecture," *Architectural Design*, vol. 73, no. 3, May/ June 2003.

Mitchell, J. (ed.), *Art and the Public Sphere*, Chicago, University of Chicago Press, 1993.

Redstone, Louis G., *Art in Architecture*, New York, McGraw-Hill, 1968.

Rendell, Jane, *Art and Architecture. A Place Between*, London, I. B. Tauris, 2006.

Roussel, Christine, *The Art of Rockefeller Center*, New York, W.W. Norton & Co., 2005.

Rubin, William, *Modern Sacred Art and the Church of Assy*, New York, Columbia University Press, 1961.

Schachter, Kenny, *Art becomes Architecture becomes Art. A Conversation between Vito Acconci and Kenny Schachter*, Vienna, Springer, 2006.

Senie, Harriet, *Contemporary Public Sculpture. Tradition, Transformation, and Controversy*, New York, Oxford University Press, 1992.

Thalacker, Donald W. (ed.), *The Place of Art in the World of Architecture*, New York, Bowker, 1980.

Toy, Maggie, *Frontiers: Artists & Architects (Architectural Design)*, London, Wiley and Son, 1998.

Troy, Nancy J., *The De Stijl Environment*, Cambridge, MIT Press, 1983.

Wirz, Heinz (ed.), *Adrian Schiess – Colourspaces. Co-operation with the architects Herzog & de Meuron and Gigon/Guyer 1993–2003*, Luzern, Quart Verlag, 2004.

Rémy Zaugg/Herzog & de Meuron, *Art and Architecture. A Dialogue*, Stuttgart, Hatje Cantz Verlag, 1997.

Index

Illustration Credits

T: top of page
B: bottom of page
L: left side of page
R: right side of page
C: center of page

Cover: Florian Holzherr
Frontispiece: Getty Images

1: Introduction

6 Corcoran Gallery of Art; 7 MAK Vienna; 8T, 12T, 13T Ezra Stoller/ESTO; 8B Tom Powell Imaging/courtesy of the artist and the Public Art Fund; 10, 15, 16L, 18L, 19BL Archives of American Art, Smithsonian Institute; 9 Martha Schwartz Partners; 11T Avery Architectural and Fine Arts Library, Columbia University; 11B ARS New York; 11L courtesy of the artist Birgit Ramsauer; 12B Steven P. Harris/courtesy Jay Jopling, White Cube, London, and Sean Kelley Gallery, New York; 13C Travel Images; 13R Eduard Eckenfels, courtesy of the artist, Stephen Friedman Gallery, Fortes Vilaca, Tanya Bonakdar Gallery; 14 Erich Lessing/ARS New York; 16R Henry Moore Foundation, 17 Getty Images; 18R UNESCO Paris; 19TL Successio Miró/ARS New York/AAA; 19TR, 19BR Villanueva Foundation; 20R Berkeley Art Museum, University of California; 20L Ferenc Berko; 21L MoMA Archives/ARS New York; 21R Kurt Schwitters Archive, Sprengel Museum Hanover/ARS

2: The Red of the Sky, not the Burning House

22, 23L, 25BL, 25BC, 25BR, 26T, 26B, 27L, 30, 32B, 33, 36B, 37, 38L Busch-Reisinger Museum, Harvard University; 23R New York Public Library; 24, 27R, 34R, 36T ARS New York; 25C Stiftung Deutsches Technikmuseum; 25T Agenzia Luisa Ricciarini; 28, 29B Secretariat Schlemmer; 29T MoMA/ARS New York; 31T Josef and Anni Albers Foundation; 31B, 39T Avery Architectural and Fine Arts Library, Columbia University; 32T, 32C Herbert Bayer Collection, Denver Art Museum; 34L Richard Lippold Foundation; 35T, 35C Oldenburg van Bruggen Foundation; 35B Richard Payne; 38R courtesy of the artist Mathieu Beauséjour; 39B Musée d'Art Moderne et Contemporain de Strasbourg

3: Symmetric Identities

40, 42L, 51L, 56L, 56BL Balthazar Korab; 42R Ferenc Berko; 43TL, 44B Museum of Finnish Architecture, Helsinki; 41 Jefferson National Expansion Memorial/National Park Service; 43B Billings Library, University of Vermont; 43TR Turku Museum; 44T, 49L, 51R, 52R, 55 Yale University Archives; 45, 48, 50T, 50C, 52L, 53, 59B Ezra Stoller/ESTO; 46, 47 Hedrich Blessing Archive, Chicago Historical Society; 49R, 58T Freud Museum, London; 50B RMN/ARS New York; 54L Cranbrook Art Museum; 54R, 56BC, 57 Cranbrook Archives; 56BR National Gallery, London; 58B Millesgården, Stockholm; 59T ARS New York

4: Minotaur in the Labyrinth and Christ on the Cross

60 Tate Gallery, London/ARS New York; 61, 64T, 66, 67, 70C RMN/ARS New York; 62R, 69, 70R Getty Images; 62L, 68, 77BC Ezra Stoller/ESTO; 63, 64B, 65, 77BL Remey Tournus; 70T ARS New York; 71 Modernism Gallery, San Francisco; 72T Christian Bjone; 72B SuperStock; 73, 74, 75, 76, 77T, 77BR Succession H. Matisse/ARS New York; 78T, 78C Lara Swimmmer/ESTO; 78B, 79T Frantisek Svardo/The Cathedral of Our Lady of the Angels; 79BR Joshua White; 79BL Emanuel Hoffmann Foundation/Tom Bisig

5: Power and the Place of Art

80, 84R, 85, 86, 87 Rockefeller Center Archives, New York; 81 Andy Warhol Foundation for the Visual Arts/ARS New York; 82BR Avery Architectural and Fine Arts Library, Columbia University; 82T, 82BL, 82BC, 88BL, 93B, 94, 95, 96, 97B Rockefeller Archive Center, Sleepy Hollow, New York; 84L ARS New York; 88BR, 89R, 90R Queens Museum, New York; 88T, 89C Roy Lichtenstein Estate; 89L Eric Pollitzer; 90L Christopher Makos; 91 Richard Serra/ARS New York/Getty Images/Frank Martin; 92L Richard Serra/ARS New York/Shelton Art Gallery; 92R ARS New York; 93C courtesy of the artist Robert Yoder; 93T Fondation Beyeler, Basel; 97T Ezra Stoller/ESTO

6: Gravestones of Modernism

98, 109, 110T, 111, 113R Ezra Stoller/ESTO; 99 David Samuel Robbins/Corbis; 100L Gjon Mili/TimeLife Pictures/Getty Images; 100R Calder Foundation/ARS New York; 101, 106T Getty Images; 102 Carter Manny Archives, Art Institute of Chicago, Ryerson and Burnham Library; 104 Art Institute of Chicago, Ryerson and Burnham Library; 105 G. E. Kidder Smith/Corbis; 106C Scala/ARS New York; 106R Edward Quinn; 106L Estate of Pablo Picasso/ARS New York; 107, 112BL, 112BR Isamu Noguchi Foundation and Garden Museum, Long Island City; 108, 110B Avery Architectural and Fine Arts Library, Columbia University; 112T ARS New York/ADAGP Paris/National Gallery of Art, Washington/Philip Charles; 113L RMN/ARS New York

7: Empty Spaces and Vast Horizons

114, 125 Olafur Eliasson Studio; 115, 120 Estate of Gordon Matta-Clark; 116, 119T Robert Smithson Foundation/ARS; 117CR, 117BR courtesy of the artist Michael Heizer; 117TR Peter DaSilva; 117L Isamu Noguchi Foundation and Garden Museum, Long Island City/ARS New York; 118 Pearson International Airport Toronto; 119L Dallas/Fort Worth International Airport/ARS New York; 121, 122, 123, 124 MoMA Archives/ARS New York; 126 Rachofsky Foundation, Thomas Jenkins; 127TL, 127TR J. Paul Getty Museum; 127CR Peter Mauss/ESTO; 127B Scott Francis/ESTO

8: Sculptural Space Becomes Architectural Space

128, 133R Christian Richters/ESTO; 129 Genevieve Hanson/Pace Wildenstein Gallery, New York; 130, 134R Richard Serra/ARS New York/Dia Art Foundation; 131 Jeff Goldberg/ESTO; 132 Guggenheim Museum; 133L Gohry Partners; 134L, 141 Richard Serra/ARS New York/James Stata; 135, 136 Nelson Kon; 137, 138 Chichu Art Museum; 139, 140B Pulitzer Foundation for the Arts/Robert Petus; 140T Josef and Anni Albers Foundation/ARS New York; 142, 143L Chinati Foundation/Florian Holzherr; 143R Tate Gallery/ARS New York; 144, 145B, 145C Yves Klein Archives; 145T Kollhoff Architects/Studio Ivan Nemec

9: Conclusion: What Shall We Do Now?

146, 156R, 158, 161T, 165B Getty Images; 147 Avery Architectural and Fine Arts Library, Columbia University; 148 Estate of Pablo Picasso/ARS New York; 149 Hal Bromm Gallery; 150R Renzo Piano Building Workshop; 150L courtesy of the artist Matej Andraz Vogrinčič; 151B courtesy of the artist AP@ Jeff Koons; 151T LACMA; 152 Oldenburg van Bruggen Foundation; 153 Corbis, 154, 155B Jörg Rüger, BMF, Berlin; 155T Susan Barr/View/ESTO; 156L courtesy of the artist Rachel Whiteread and Luhring Augustine Gallery, New York; 157 courtesy of the artist Antony Gormley; 159C, 159B MoMA Archives/ARS New York; 159T ARS New York; 160B Richard Serra/ARS New York; 160T Gordon Linoff and Giuseppe Scalia; 161B courtesy of the artist Barbara Trautmann; 162 Museum of Fine Arts Houston; 163 Archphoto; 164 Public Art Fund/photograph Seong Kwon; 165T Isamu Noguchi Foundation and Garden Museum, Long Island City/ARS New York; 165C Albright-Knox Museum of Art; 166, 167, 168T, 169 National Opera House, Oslo; 168B courtesy of the artist Andrea Blum; 170 photograph Margherita Spiluttini; 171 Andy Warhol Foundation for the Visual Arts/ARS New York; 172L Ábalos & Herreros, photograph Dietmar Tolerian; 172R Thomas Mayer; 173 Riepl Riepl Architects; 174, 175T Victoria Miro Gallery, London; 175B Städtische Galerie, Munich; 175C AMO

Further Architect and Artist Collaborations

176 courtesy of the artist Olafur Eliasson; 178L Getty Images; 178R courtesy of the artist Hans Haacke; 179 Thomas Mayer; 180 Herzog & de Meuron; 181 LACMA

All floor plans drawn by Christian Bjone.

We are especially grateful to these image providers. Every reasonable attempt has been made to identify owners of copyright. Should unintentional mistakes or omissions have occurred, we sincerely apologise and ask for notice. Such mistakes will be corrected in the next edition of this publication.

Acknowledgements This publication would not have been possible without the cooperation of architects, artists and photographers. In addition, assistance in locating archival images was very valuable to me. As well as those credited for illustrations, thanks are due to many individuals who helped along the way; their support is much appreciated.

Brenda Danilowitz, The Josef and Anni Albers Foundation, Bethany, Connecticut

Michael Slade, Art Resource, New York

Val Bertoia, Bertoia Studio, Bally, Pennsylvania

Lin Bjone, Sonoma, California

Peggy Brooks, New York

Joshua Burdick, SBLM, New York

Gwen Chanzit, Denver Art Museum, Herbert Bayer Collection, Denver

Joseph Cho and Stefanie Lew, binocular, New York

Stuart Cohen, Cohen & Hacker Architects, Evanston, Illinois

Mark Coir and Leslie Edwards, Cranbrook Archives, Bloomfield Hills, Michigan

Amy Fitch, Rockefeller Archive Center, Sleepy Hollow, New York

Amy Hau and Bonnie Rychlak, Isamu Noguchi Foundation and Garden Museum, Long Island City, New York

Wendy Hurley, Archives of American Art, Smithsonian Institution, Washington, DC

Joseph Katanik, New York

Martina Kupiak, Olafur Eliasson Studio, Berlin

Mary McClean, New York

Ingrid Mecklenburg, Sprengel Museum, Hanover, Germany

Carter Manny, Chicago

Augusto Morselli, Richard Lippold Foundation, Locust Valley, New York

Tom Nimen, T. R. Nimen Inc., New York

Janet Parks and Julie Tozer, Avery Library, Columbia University, New York

Christine Roussel, Rockefeller Center Archives, New York

C. Raman Schlemmer, The Oskar Schlemmer Secretariat and Archives, Oggebbio, Italy

Terry Simerly, New York

Ria Stein, Birkhäuser, Berlin

Laura Stella, Gehry Partners, Los Angeles

Erica Stoller, ESTO Inc., Mamaroneck, New York

Walburga Krupp-Stiftung, Hans Arp and Sophie Taeuber-Arp e. V., Rolandswerth, Germany

David Weiner, David Weiner Architects, New York

Ivan Zaknic, Lehigh University, Bethlehem, Pennsylvania

About the Author The author is a practising architect who graduated from Princeton University. Previously employed at the office of Johnson/Burgee and Pei Partnership, he now works for SBLM Architects, New York. He contributed to various architectural journals and is author of the publication *First House: The Grid, the Figure and the Void*, London, Academy Editions, 2002.